LIVE
TO
WIN

By the same author

GOING FOR IT!

LIVE
TO
WIN

Achieving Success in Life and Business

Victor Kiam

HARPER & ROW, PUBLISHERS, New York
Grand Rapids, Philadelphia, St. Louis, San Francisco
1817 London, Singapore, Sydney, Tokyo, Toronto

A previous edition of this book was published in Great Britain by William Collins & Co. Ltd. under the title KEEP GOING FOR IT! *Living the Life of an Entrepreneur.*

Library of Congress Catalog Card Number: 89-45677

ISBN: 0-06-016261-9

89 90 91 92 93 CC/HC 10 9 8 7 6 5 4 3 2 1

I want to thank my loved ones who have
been so involved and so supportive, and all
those who have helped me "Go for it"
. . . especially my partners, the
employees of Remington who
have contributed so much.

I would like to thank Dick Lally, whose
ability to organize my thoughts and
assistance in getting them down on paper
were an invaluable aid in the
writing of this book.

Contents

Contents

1

Leveraging Your Assets:
You Have to Keep Going For It

Hello. I'm Victor Kiam. A couple of years ago I wrote a book chronicling the entrepreneurial experience. *Going For It!* was the first book I had ever written. I enjoyed it so much, I tried to buy the publishing house. It wasn't for sale. Being an entrepreneur, I settled for the next best thing. I wrote another book.

The entrepreneurial adventures in *Going For It!* ended with my successful acquisition and turnaround of the Remington Company. In an era that has seen a rash of leveraged buy-outs, takeovers, and attempted turnarounds, I thought it would be worthwhile to lead off by reviewing what has happened since that purchase.

First, some quick history. Many of you are probably already familiar with the Remington story. I bought Remington from Sperry-Rand in 1978. At the time, the once-popular Remington electric shaver had lost most of its consumer appeal. Sperry couldn't wait to get the virtually comatose company off its hands. Using the leveraged buy-out, I was able to purchase Remington and begin taking the steps for its revivification.

You might recall the ads we've run. I spoofed one at the top of this chapter. They feature an unknown actor named Kiam who tells how he loved the Remington shaver so much he bought the company. It's funny. Many people believe that our subsequent success was due to the unusual approach of our TV ads. Untrue. Sir Carol Reed could have directed Sir Alec Guinness in the greatest commercials of all time and they still wouldn't have accounted for the 180-degree turn made by Remington.

That turnaround began with the Remington employees. We came in and removed all the perks and privileges that had served as walls between management and the rest of the company. The employees learned that Remington no longer had blue-collar or white-collar positions. There was only one collar: the Remington collar. Incentive programs, benefiting everybody, were introduced. Lines of communication were opened. We created an esprit de corps that had been lacking in a failing company. We also painted a vista vivid with the promise of success and then got our employees excited about sharing that triumph.

With a solid team in place, our attention was turned to the shaver. We had recognized some of its problems at the outset. Sperry was a successful high-tech company that didn't understand the marketing demands of the shaver business. They changed shaver styles too often, leaving the public confused and retailers exasperated. Store owners and buyers were leery of stocking a heavy Remington inventory; they didn't want to get stuck when the company made its latest stylistic innovation. This hurt the shaver immeasurably. Norelco, changing its styles only rarely, was outselling Remington four to one. Stores were stocking ten times as many Norelcos as Remingtons. You couldn't blame them. They were going with the more stable product.

Remington had also gotten into the habit of raising its prices to keep pace with the competition. Norelco would raise its prices; Remington would follow suit. This was more than just unsound fiscal policy. It was a public relations disaster. Remington was made to look like a follower, not a leader, in its field.

Once inside, we reversed these trends. We took away the chrome and fancy trimmings that had inflated our shaver prices but had done nothing to improve the product. For example, the shavers came packed in a metal case that cost us two and a half dollars and was heavy enough to inflict a slight hernia on Arnold Schwarzenegger. Unfortunately, it contributed nothing toward a great shave. An expensive, unwieldy item that was difficult for the consumer to carry, it was consigned to our scrap heap.

We also let our retailers know that our lines would be stable and that all orders would be filled promptly. One new addition was made to the line, however, but it was a positive one. We introduced the Triple Head Shaver (now known as the Triple Action Shaver), a no-frills Remington that retailed for $19.95. At the time of its debut, the lowest-priced Remington was selling for $34.95. The new shaver was a hit. The company sold more than half a million Triple Heads in the first year. That represented over four million dollars in gross profit. Its success played a large role in the Remington comeback. Combined with cost-cutting measures, improved distribution, the hard work of our employees, and new advertising and marketing strategies, it helped push Remington to the top of the shaver business. In a few short years, we have quadrupled employment and increased sales five-fold.

So What Have You Done for Us Lately, Kiam?

That's the pleasant, recent past. What have Victor Kiam and Remington been up to lately? I'll be happy to tell you. *We've done what any entrepreneurial company must do: refused to become complacent with our success.* An entrepreneur cannot stand still. If he does, those laurels he chooses to sit on will attach themselves to his backside, wend their way up and over his body, and transform him into nothing more than an inactive piece of vegetation.

We had no intention of letting Remington become part of the flora and fauna. During my first three and a half years of ownership we concentrated on the shaver business. We didn't even think about introducing any new products. Once we re-established the shaver as the best on the market, then we looked to expand our operation. A solid cash flow had been established, our market share was jumping, and the company base was strong. We were still a one-product enterprise, but what a product! Now, in order to ensure our continued growth, we felt it was time to move into new territories.

That was a choice any entrepreneur would make. But how do you implement the decision? What are the obstacles to your expansion?

At Remington there was one element that would hamper our growth and it was really a toughy. As a leveraged buy-out company, you are undercapitalized. This means all inventory-intensive businesses are out of bounds for you unless they gross a sufficient profit. Why? Simply stated, if a product generates only a marginal gross profit it won't pay for you to borrow the money needed to launch the enterprise. Let me give you an example. One of the first opportunities brought to Remington was a hair dryer business. As a grooming product it was related to our shavers. Unfortunately, those dryers could only generate a profit margin of about 18 percent. After settling the interest on the seed-money loan, the company would be left with less than 8 percent gross profit. Obviously you could do a lot of volume in dryers, but show very little on the bottom line. Your capital would be consumed too rapidly. Entrepreneurs also must avoid getting involved with "me-too" items, products that are unabashed copies of whatever is currently hot with consumers. You have to ask yourself, What is this product's Unique Selling Proposition (USP)? What makes it stand out among its competitors? Does it have a better motor or does it offer comparable quality at a better price? I was not convinced that our hair dryers could make these claims or that they would be decidedly different from any of those already on the market.

Leveraging Your Assets

Given the situation, what is an entrepreneur to do? The only possible option is to leverage off your assets. I don't want to confuse you. In the normal, financial sense, leveraging off your assets pertains to using your tangible assets—say, the land your store sits on or your inventory—as collateral when securing capital. I didn't have that luxury. In buying Remington I had leveraged myself to the brink.

I had to make the most of Remington's intangible assets. In

Going For It!, I talked about the Personal Balance Sheet (PBS). Drawing a line down the center of a sheet of paper, I would list my positives (willingness to work hard, sound education, some marketing flair, fluency in several languages, etc.) on one side and my negatives (procrastinator, hatred of paperwork, lack of punctuality, etc.) on the other. The main thrust of the exercise was to enable me to turn those weaknesses into strengths. There was, however, an equally important philosophy behind this self-examination, one that I think should have been given more emphasis: knowing your strengths, you can see where they will lead you. My assets led me to Lever Brothers, an international conglomerate where it seemed my marketing skills and fluency in languages would put me in good stead.

The PBS can be just as easily applied to a company as an individual. Here it takes the form of an Intangible Balance Sheet (IBS). This balance sheet has little to do with the dollar value of a company. Instead, it measures the worth of such things as location, the skill of your work force, and consumer goodwill. Your enterprise is a living, breathing entity. It is your baby, and the IBS can serve as its Dr. Spock. Do you want to know in which direction this growing child should be going? Ask the IBS.

For example, a fellow has a newspaper stand not far from my home. He has always done good business, but some time ago he decided that he wanted to do still more. He was located near a subway that served hundreds of commuters dashing off to work in the morning and coming back home at night. Up the block was a large university, many of whose students also used that train. The stand's biggest negative was its size. There was nothing he could do about that; zoning laws and the high price of New York real estate prevented the owner from physically expanding. The stand's greatest positive was its location and the unused, albeit limited, space in the inner back portion of his booth.

Aware of these factors, the stand owner made several choices. First he brought in a line of cigarettes. He correctly reckoned that many of his customers would run out of cigarettes overnight and that he would be the morning's first opportunity to quell a nicotine fit. Size restrictions dictated that he stock only the most popular brands. Cartons were stored in a box on the floor of the booth. Samples of these wares were kept prominently displayed. Catering to the students who bought his newspapers, the owner installed wire shelves in his stand's inner rear wall. These were lined with inexpensive items such as ballpoint pens, erasers, and pencils. To call attention to these he put brightly colored signs on the stand's awning. Business grew dramatically. With his increased profits, this entrepreneur had larger, plastic windows installed in the stand, enabling his customers to get a better look at his full line of merchandise. The owner is now dickering to buy another stand across town, to be run by a cousin. All this was the result of the IBS he drew up for his enterprise. Using its strengths and recognizing its weaknesses, he has turned the newspaper stand into a personal and financial triumph.

The biggest plus on the Remington PBS was obvious: the Remington name. Remember, we weren't concerned with the inventory or the value of our factory. I was focusing on our intangible assets. We were spending an awful lot of money advertising our shavers. Each commercial or ad was also celebrating Remington. That name and the quality it now stood for had a real value. This meant that any venture launched under the Remington umbrella was automatically enhanced by the association.

To take advantage of our name, I wanted to launch a product that could be closely tied in with the shavers. We developed a combination beard, mustache, and hair clipper. This was a product with a built-in USP: it was the only grooming product on the market featuring three separate clipping functions. All the other clippers on the market came with numerous attachments. It took an instruction book, two guides, and a translator to figure out which attachment performed which task. Our product wasn't such a puzzle. It took up less space on the consumer's grooming shelf and performed all three functions without fuss. Retailers loved it because it was three products combined to form one stockkeeping unit. It didn't wreak havoc with their inventory. It also commanded less space for storage. Retailers were also thrilled with the way it jumped off the shelves and into the hands of consumers. Being our first grooming product other than the shaver to carry the Remington name, we were especially pleased with its reception.

One segment of the business already bearing the Remington brand was our service centers. I decided to do an Intangible Balance Sheet on them and this was the result:

INTANGIBLE BALANCE SHEET
Subject: Nineteen Remington Service Centers

Liabilities
1. Money losers.
2. Require a parts inventory, bleeding our cash flow.
3. Tied to long-term leases in now rundown neighborhoods; customers afraid to visit.
4. In-house staff not trained in sales.

Assets
1. Goodwill engendered by service centers.
2. Tied to long-term leases at what was now a low rent.
3. An in-house staff of expert servicepeople.

I was working under many of the same conditions as that newsstand vendor I mentioned. Short of closing the shops down—which I couldn't do because the centers were a necessary part of our business and the buy-out of our leases would have cost us a bundle—I had to deal with the limitations of a physical space. Looking at our list, we attacked our problems. The long-term lease liability canceled itself with a low rent. I solved the inventory question by carrying the stock for all nineteen stores in our Bridgeport plant. This created more room in the centers and allowed our staff to concentrate on shaver repair, rather than the shipping of spare parts to dealers.

Next we needed to improve customer traffic. At the time, Remington had 19 percent of the shaver business in the U.S. Service center customers were being drawn from that slice of the consumer universe. Yet we had the technology and could get the spare parts to service our competitors' products as well as our own. This was a great convenience for the consumer; many of our competitors would do servicing only through the mail. Enabling customers to simply drop items off at our shops doubled our service center business.

With the numbers moving up, we decided to train the service center staff as salespeople. Now whenever someone brought in a Norelco to be fixed, the salesperson would try to get him to try the Remington option. These employees became so confident we felt we could introduce a line of products to be sold exclusively in these stores. We were transforming the service centers into retail outlets.

Choose the Right Product

In picking the product line to be launched in these outlets, I followed the example set by my friend the newsstand owner. I looked at the service center's clientele. It was 90 percent male. We were already offering shaver accessories such as replacement foil heads. We were about to introduce a cleaning lubricant for the shavers and a powder stick, designed to keep the beard dry and stiff for an even closer shave. But we wanted to offer a line that represented a small but significant break from the shavers.

We tried several items including cigarette lighters and key chains. None of them took hold. Finally, I found just the thing we were looking for in Canada. The discovery was something of a fluke. I had walked into a cutlery store in Toronto. The shop was nothing but wall-to-wall knives. I had not come in hunting for a business venture. To be honest, I wasn't looking for anything more than a good nail clipper. *But when opportunity knocks, the entrepreneur is always home.* I was so fascinated by the focus of this specialty shop that I started quizzing the manager. He said that knives were an interesting business. Generally a customer didn't buy one knife, he bought five or six. Most importantly, the bulk of his customers were males.

There was no way of telling how the shops would fare in the

United States. For whatever reason, hardly any stores here carried cutlery exclusively. Stores that sold knives kept a limited variety of stock. They carried the incomplete lines of only two or three major brands. You could buy a company's steak knife, but they might not carry that same manufacturer's utility blade. This was uncharted territory. The entrepreneur, a modern pioneer, can think of nothing more attractive. We decided to do a market test of the cutlery line in three of our service centers. They went through the roof. We expanded the operation to include all our shops. Our salespeople were tutored until they became cutlery connoisseurs. We augmented the knives by offering knife-honing and key-making services. Certain stores were told to place greater emphasis on particular types of knives. For instance, in coastal regions we did a large business in maritime, fishing, and scuba knives. In the landlocked Midwest, our displays featured utility knives. We were leveraging our assets. In this case, the location was the asset. We tailored the stock to meet the demands of the area.

The response of these changes was such that those nineteen shops have grown to eighty-five. This proved something I had always believed. Just by building on your strengths—using them to offset your liabilities—and paying attention to your market, you can turn a big loser into a winner.

Experts Don't Always Know

We exported that cutlery business to the U.K. Remington had four service centers in England; they became six retail centers. The English experiment was not without its risks. We were told that the British did not, as a rule, spend a lot of money on knives. European marketing experts claimed that the British would rather use a two-dollar kitchen knife to cut a magnificent piece of beef than spend an extra dime on a more elegant blade. One Englishman told me, "Victor, you have to understand. We don't care how quickly the blade works, how it looks, or even if it cuts particularly well. All we want to know is, 'Will it cut the meat?' "

Manufacturers told us the same thing. Everyone we spoke with told us to forget the English market.

There comes a time when an entrepreneur has to follow his own instincts. You have to ignore the experts. I did a bit of research on my own and came away convinced that upmarket knives hadn't found a niche in the English market for one very good reason: no one had bothered to try to establish one. The English consumer had been fitted to a stereotype that had been accepted by an entire industry. I wanted to challenge that idea. We started offering our cutlery line in one store in Bristol. Guess what? The experts were wrong. The English loved our knives. Not only are we now selling our knives there, but we have negotiated to get full distribution rights from all the great knife distributors around the world. We will be the knife distributors for the U.K., selling not only in our own stores but in other shops as well.

As an entrepreneur, you're going to run into more than your share of pessimists. By his nature, the entrepreneur is often cutting against the grain of popular opinion. You can't reject experienced advice outright. You can give it a certain amount of weight before coming to a decision. However, you also can't allow it to overwhelm your gut feelings. Investigate. Take the time to find out the cause or source of contrary opinions. That negative feedback can be a plus. It should force you to look deeply into the heart of your venture and to take that view with a clear and critical eye. If your investigation convinces you the experts are in error, damn their torpedoes and full speed ahead. If we had listened to the experts, we would never have launched in England. A valuable business would never have gotten off the ground.

Entrepreneurial Synergy

The best ideas don't just materialize out of the ozone. They can come as the result of synergy. One idea spawns another or is merged to a second concept to create a third entity. Remington now had outlets possessing an inventory of attractive male items. We had an impressive mailing list built on the warranty cards from our shavers. We also needed to make our cutlery available to those millions of consumers who didn't live near a Remington store. The list, the inventory, and our need combined to become the Remington mail-order catalog. In turn, having a catalog forced us to look for an even wider range of products.

The first catalog featured specialty shavers, accessories, and cutlery. We've increased our selection to include beer steins, pens, leather goods, jewelry, and—a product line with as strong a USP as I've ever seen—Samurai ceremonial swords. If a Ninja's favorite weapon isn't a unique gift item, I don't know what is. These catalogs have grown into a formidable business. Four years ago, the revenues of the shops and catalogs was roughly three million dollars. The revenues for the last fiscal year were over thirty-two million. They're still climbing.

The Hidden USP

In choosing a new product or venture, its USP isn't always obvious. You can have a wonderful snow tire, but unless it outperforms all of its competition, it is still just a wonderful snow tire. In cases like this, *your marketing concept can be a product's most powerful USP.*

We found this to be true when the success of the cutlery and catalogs persuaded us to launch a second product line. Again, we wanted it to be male oriented. Someone suggested we jump into travel products. I found a supplier, but I was leery. I wasn't sure the items were substantially better than anything already being sold, though I knew they were at least as good. This USP had to represent something other than superior quality. We went out and did some research. We found that while these products—alarm clocks, voltage converters, steamers, and travel irons—were available, consumers couldn't find them under one roof. They had to mill through six or seven departments or stores to put together a decent travel kit. Boy, did the lightbulb go on. We brought the products together in a self-contained display unit in a single location. They were labeled Remington Travel Plus. The ease of purchase was the USP and it made the products especially attractive. Since introducing that line, Remington has acquired a company whose travel products are rated number one throughout the world. We are now the largest company in the travel appliance business.

Building this business has not been easy. One problem we're still wrestling with is that created by multiple buyers in larger stores. Some of these stores will have a clock buyer who deals with nothing but clocks, and an iron buyer who works exclusively with irons. There wouldn't be any one buyer authorized to buy a travel kit embracing these and other items. The clock buyer also resented having someone else offering travel clocks in another department. The iron buyer would raise the same squawk. Some stores try to solve the problem by separating the kit and offering the items in different departments. That violates our USP. Remington has been adamant about keeping the kits whole and in one section. As retailers see how well the approach works, we're bringing them around to our point of view. Nothing sells better than success.

Entrepreneurial Teamwork

In *Going For It!* I described a practice we instituted at Remington to improve employee communications. We held Friday morning coffee meetings. About a dozen employees, representing all levels including management, would meet for coffee and Danish pastries and discuss a topic pertinent to the company. Over a period of time, each one of our employees has an opportunity to participate at least once. We want our employees to share in our entrepreneurial adventure. These coffee meetings are their forum. They can ask questions, air criticisms, and make suggestions. These meetings are designed to give everyone a sense of participation. But they also do much more than that.

Management does not have the corner on great ideas. *As a*

business leader you want entrepreneurs working for you on every level.
You can encourage this by giving your employees a forum, allowing their ideas to be heard and given serious consideration.
The best feedback they can possibly get occurs when one of
their concepts grows into something tangible. For example, one
of these brainstorming sessions was attended by a young woman
from our assembly line. She said very little during the first three-
quarters of the meeting. Then a fellow employee made a product suggestion. He did a lot of painting and often had to paint
around glass. No matter what he did, some paint would always
run down and harden on the pane. It was a holy terror to remove. You had to scrape it off with a razor blade or some similar
instrument, all the while hoping you didn't damage the glass.
The process was time consuming and exhausting. They started
to kick around the idea of an electric scraper. It would run on
the same principle as our shavers.

While they were focusing on this subject, that young
woman, unaccustomed to speaking in front of groups, found
herself inspired. She timidly raised her hand and said, "You
know, three months ago, I was in the hospital for an operation.
As part of the pre-op procedure, the nurse had to shave me. I
got nicked. The wound wasn't particularly large, but it was
enough to get them to postpone my surgery. They couldn't risk
the possibility of infection. This company's business is shavers.
Isn't there anything Remington can do about that?"

Everyone in the room got excited. A pre-operative shaver!
What a marvelous avenue to explore. We researched the hospi-
tal-hygiene market and discovered it was still in the dark ages.
No one was being shaved electrically; patients still had to submit
to the horrors of blade and cream. Soon after this meeting, the
company started developing a medical shaver. It would be used
in hospitals and doctor's offices. Having heard of our plans, 3M
offered to join us in the venture. Remington would manufacture
and 3M, already a giant in the medical field, would distribute.
We came up with a project and put it through FDA clinical
testing. The result was a shaver that virtually eliminates any
possibility of nicking. Its head is disposable for sanitary reasons.
Surgeons use it on a patient once and then throw it away. The

doctors love the implement. Cutting the hair at a perfect length, it prevents the growth of ingrown hairs. These hairs can be a major annoyance if located near an open wound.

The hospitals only have to buy each shaver once. The repeat business is in the disposable heads. One major hospital in the U.S. is using 20,000 heads a month and this year we expect to do over three million heads worldwide. That little product has given us a foothold in the medical field. We are actively looking to acquire a small medical company. Remington is also busy developing new mechanical and electrical products specifically for hospital use. One is an offshoot of the disposable shaver head: a throwaway electric shaver. It will be run by a battery. The battery charge will last for six weeks, much longer than the average hospital stay. When the power runs out, the shaver is thrown out. We are also working on a *Star Wars* version of a shaver. This will be a shaver for the handicapped. Set on a track and using laser beams, it will allow quadriplegics or anyone who has lost the use of their hands to shave themselves.

All of these ideas are spin-offs of the hospital shaver. They might not have happened if Remington hadn't created an environment where a young assembly-line worker could feel comfortable sharing her ideas with upper management. By the way, that idea for a paint scraper did not get lost in our enthusiasm for the hospital shaver. The concept was researched. It wasn't viable. The small size of the market and the cost of the blade made it an unpromising product. A follow-up was done with the idea's originator. We wanted him to know we had tried to turn his concept into reality, but that it wasn't for us. Knowing the consideration we gave his idea can only encourage him. It was a heck of an idea and I want to keep him thinking. Who knows? He just might come up with the next great Remington product.

Entrepreneurial Teamwork, Part Two

As an entrepreneur, you want your executives to share your approach to business. You don't want them seeing life as a long cafeteria line leading to a mundane menu. Have them think of it as a grand buffet, glimmering with golden trays overladen with opportunity. You want these people to do more than just feast on the delicacies; you want them to bring something to the party. A case in point is the story of the pool alarm.

The Canadian government had awarded a grant to two engineers. It called for the development of a device that would cut down on the number of drownings. Canada had suffered an unusually high number of such deaths. Tragically, most of the victims are children. The grant represented an entrepreneurial answer to the problem on the part of the Canadian government. The two engineers were up to the task. They created an alarm that emitted an easily heard warning whenever an object weighing eight pounds or more fell into the water.

It was easy to see this product's USP. Nothing like it was being sold anywhere. By a happy coincidence, one of the inventors was a neighbor of our Canadian company's president. He was shown a prototype of the gizmo. Immediately recognizing the pool alarm's potential, he started the process of acquiring the rights to it for Remington. We are currently selling it throughout the world. The president might have had a harder time netting the product in other companies. He could have been caught up in the bureaucratic red tape and political backbiting. Before it could be straightened out, a more entrepreneurial company—one supporting its executive's initiative—would have made off with the goods.

Seeing the Tree for the Forest

Sometimes the next great product or idea can be right under the entrepreneur's nose, only he doesn't see it. He needs an outside influence to place it in a proper perspective. Not too long ago, I was in Washington, D.C., to take part in a discussion with other businessmen and politicians. The main topics centered around the trade deficits and the fluctuating dollar. During one of my exchanges on the telephone, a U.S. senator changed the subject, saying, "Victor, I use your shaver. I like it a lot but I have one problem with it. I have an annoying amount of excess hair in my nose and ears. I can't shave inside either of those two places; shavers are too big. Have you got anything that can help me?''

I knew we had some small item that was being offered in our retail stores, but I wasn't sure it met the senator's needs. Returning to our Bridgeport factory, I called in Lee Feist, the man in charge of our retail department. I asked him what we had that would meet the senator's needs. He showed me a Rube Goldberg device featuring a small crank on the side of a cylinder with cutters at the top. I looked at it and asked, "Do we sell many of these?" Lee said, "You bet. We have them in forty stores and we're going to sell about 10,000 of them this year." My God, that was 250 a store, almost one a day! It was quite a number.

I sent one down to the senator. He replied with a gracious thank-you note and a check for the product. He had it wrong. It was I who should have been sending a letter of thanks to him. I hadn't realized how well this little item was doing or how much people really needed them.

I couldn't get the clipper out of my head. Calling in our engineers, I showed them a model and said, "Look, we're selling these things like they're the latest hit by Bruce Springsteen. Is there any way we can make an electrical version?" I wasn't making this suggestion merely for the sake of modern technology. I wasn't satisfied with the way the current model performed. It took a lot of elbow grease to crank the apparatus. The manual turning also made the user susceptible to cutting. You couldn't stop the thing in mid-crank, so if it grabbed hold of your skin, you could suffer a pretty good nick.

The engineers worked on it. The result was an electrical version that trims you without exertion. A safety device automatically cuts off the motor at the cutter's first touch of skin. We've introduced this model in our catalogs. The nose clipper is already the catalog's second biggest seller. It's just hitting the retail market. We don't have any conclusive numbers yet, but we have large hopes. It's funny. If not for the senator, it might have been months before I knew what a hot item the clipper was. It was such a tiny part of our business. That one conversation led me to a real revelation and gave this company another potential blockbuster.

Is the Door Closed? Open Another!

One of the other products we tried to introduce was an air purifier. It would rid your room of dust, pollen, smoke, and other impurities. I thought it was pretty spiffy. I couldn't wait to show it off at the annual housewares show in Chicago. Couldn't imagine anyone offering anything quite like it. Talk about having your enthusiasm dampened. When I got to the show, I found no less than twenty-five different manufacturers hawking their version of the air purifier. I thought, "My God, I'm going to be lost in the crowd here. There's too much competition." I wanted to pack my tail and my air purifier between my legs and go home.

I know I've often preached that when an entrepreneur finds the door closed, he's got to find a way to bang it open. This, however, was an unusual situation. If I rammed the door ajar, I might not like what I found on the other side. It could be like opening up Dracula's crypt. The market was going to be so overcrowded there wasn't going to be any way to make a decent profit. Realizing this, I thought, "Hold on. This entrance is locked, and now I doubt I want to waste time trying to find its key. I still believe in the product. Why not try another door? The air purifier hasn't been introduced in Europe. We would have heard about it. All the manufacturers are at this show. I bet they're so busy trying to sell the U.S. and Canada that they're not paying any attention to the other side of the Atlantic." What's an entrepreneur to do? Leave the housewares show and return to his hotel. I spent the rest of the afternoon calling all the major Remington accounts in England. My calendar became glutted with appointments.

The next day, I drove out to the airport, hopped on a plane, and took my sample across the Atlantic. My competitors were cutting each other's throats in Chicago; I was working my buns off in the U.K. By the end of the week, it had been placed in all the major stores. Today, Remington is number one in the air purification business in England. I think we tried the right door.

Drawing the Line

There were a large number of products that we chose not to pursue. Some of them were tempting. We rejected them because research showed their market was too narrow. Others were downright wacky.

I remember one in particular. Its inventor had been referred to me by a mutual friend. This friend had said, "Victor, you must talk to Robert. He's always coming up with ideas and he has one now that he thinks is a world-beater." Okay. You're an entrepreneur. You're supposed to be in the world-beating business. I agreed to see the man.

About two weeks later, the inventor meets with me and my engineers. He tells us a little something about himself and then says, "Let's get down to business. I have a product here that is going to revolutionize the industry. I just know you won't believe it when you see it." With that, he opens up a container and takes out what looked to be a watering can with a flashlight taped to the side of its nozzle. The reason it looked like that is because that is exactly what it was.

He was right. None of us could believe it. My engineers just sat there trying to hide their quizzical expressions. Finally, after a few moments of throat clearing, I looked at the beaming inventor and asked, "What's it for? Watering the garden at night?" He replied, "Oh, no. That's to see where the water is pouring. You can't always tell if you're actually covering the intended area of a garden or flower bed." I can be dense at times but I just had to ask, "Well, can't you just feel the ground with your hands?" That silenced him for a moment. Then he said, "Sure you could do that, but then you'd get your hands dirty." I didn't need to do any market research on this baby. I already knew that most people who garden like to get their hands dirty. It's part of the experience. When I told him this he looked at me as if I had grown an extra head. He couldn't believe that I couldn't see the genius of his invention. The inventor said, "You just wait and see. This is going to be the biggest product on the marketplace. I'm taking it to your competitor." He may have been

bluffing. We'll never know. The last time we checked, the il-
luminated watering can hadn't replaced the Hula Hoop or
Rubik's cube in the hearts of worldwide consumers.

Right around that time, we rejected a product that did have
merit. A fellow brought us a food vacuum. This was a glass bell
fitted over a glass plate sided with rubber grooves. Having
placed food on the plate, you covered it with the bell and used
a suction pump to pull out all the air. The bell was then locked.
The food retained no moisture in this vacuum. You could keep
it fresh indefinitely. We research the product. In America, we
came up against a spendthrift mentality. They'd rather not go
through the trouble of vacuum-packing food, even if it saved
them money. They would just throw the leftovers out.

We didn't give up on this idea. We decided to research the
European market. Generally, Europeans tend to be less wasteful
than Americans. The overseas test killed it. The average European kitchen is smaller than its American cousin. This product
was about eighteen inches tall and twelve inches wide. It took
up too much counter space. We found the best market for it
would be in less developed countries where food storage was a
problem. They, however, couldn't afford it. We rejected the
food freshener. It proves that sometimes a Unique Selling Proposition isn't enough. This product had a fabulous USP. It just
wasn't strong enough to overcome American profligacy or
European space limitations.

You sometimes have to ask yourself how long a product's
USP will last. One man brought us his variation of a hot plate.
This was a smaller version. It would automatically shut off once
the food or beverage placed upon it had reached a desired
temperature. When that temperature dropped a few degrees,
the power returned. This seemed like a great product, particularly for offices. A person could heat up a cup of coffee and then
maintain its temperature throughout the day. Wow! Here was a
product that would enhance coffee drinking, one of the great
rituals of Western life. It was also economical. You would no
longer have to throw out and replace cold half-cups of coffee.

As we took a closer look at this creation, our enthusiasm
waned. This was really little more than a hot plate with a heat-

responsive timer. It was the result of already known technology. Therefore, we would be unable to protect it with a U.S. patent. We felt the heater's market outlook was glowing. But only in the short term. Within months, there would be fifty knock-offs of ours, all at lower prices. Remington is an advertising-intensive company. If we took the product out, the company was going to back it to the hilt. We didn't want to spend the time and effort building up a business for someone else. There are entrepreneurs who love to grab the short-term success. Nothing wrong with that. They introduce a new product at a maximum margin, make their money, and then bow out as soon as the market is glutted with imitators. Remington likes to look at the long haul. Our kicks come from building businesses. This heater was a great idea. We still had to pass.

Remington had to make a similar decision on another interesting idea. A fellow brought me a leather saddlebag. At first, I thought he had mistaken me for Roy Rogers, but then he explained that the saddlebag wasn't supposed to be thrown over a horse. It was designed to fit over a briefcase. Serving as an overnight case, it meant the user only had to carry one item when off on a short trip. The saddlebag would hold pajamas, a couple of shirts, a few ties, and toiletries. The inventor offered us an exclusive on what I thought was a neat item. Unfortunately, the exclusive was worthless. Even though it was a fine concept, at base it was nothing more than a saddlebag adapted to a new use. Remington didn't have any way of protecting the idea from copiers. We tried to create an additional ingredient that would bring it under the sanction of the patent laws, but we came a cropper.

I'm looking at a product now that has a chance. An automated jar-opener. Have you ever bought a jar of spaghetti sauce or pickles and found yourself in traction after trying to open the darn thing? They are so well sealed by mechanization they would give Houdini fits. This is especially true in the States. The rash of product poisonings has engendered an understandable caution in the food and drug industry. No one wants to be the next Tylenol.

Women find the jars especially trying. Women also form the

bulk of the kitchenware market. This device is going to make their day. It has a gripper that electrically twists off the jar top. Nothing to it. That gripper adjusts to various jar sizes. The technology behind its adaptability is something that can be protected. A patent search is already in progress. We already know there is a market for it. The tool is a natural fit with the can opener. If our investigation works out you might be seeing the Remington jar opener by the time this book is out.

Sometimes a product is victimized by having too much technology. I was acquainted with two entrepreneurs, Rick O'Malley and Don Hamer. Their corporation sold premium products. They would sell things like drinking glasses bearing pictures of rock stars. Companies would buy them and then give them away in promotions. They did a nice business.

One day, a supplier called them with a proposition. He had acquired the rights to a garbage bag clip gun. Shaped like a weapon used by Rambo, it discharged a metal clip. You could fire it at the twisted neck of a plastic garbage bag and seal it for disposal. O'Malley and Hamer are both entrepreneurs. When an opportunity comes into their sights, they react as heat-seeking missiles. They asked the supplier to send over a sample.

They both liked the look of the thing. O'Malley, being the wackier member of a zany duo, decided a test was in order. First, he took an ordinary, full to bursting, plastic garbage bag. He sealed the neck with the gun and then swung the bag around the office. Vigorously. When he was finished, he was so dizzy he couldn't walk for ten minutes. The bag had held fast.

As soon as he recovered from vertigo, he put the clip gun through another drill. O'Malley has often proclaimed that he likes to get close to a product. He proved it in this instance. Going down to his building's cellar, he came back with an industrial-size garbage bag. He placed it on the floor. Then he crawled into the bag and assumed a fetal position. Hamer clipped the bag shut. O'Malley spent the next five minutes trying to push the clip off from the inside. It was quite a sight. A secretary came into the office and found Hamer sitting at his desk, calmly reading an inventory, apparently oblivious to the large black bag rolling back and forth across the office floor. The only sound heard was emitted from the bag. It was O'Malley yelling, "Wow, what a great product!"

The boys fell in love with the contraption. They negotiated a deal with the supplier, giving them an equal share in the rights. This covenant contained one important stipulation. The two had to sell 10,000 units in ninety days or the full rights would revert to the supplier. Neither of them saw this as a problem. They thought the clip gun was such a winner, vendors would be knocking down their doors with orders.

No such luck. Sixty days into the agreement, they hadn't sold a unit. Rick and I happened to be meeting over an unrelated matter right around this time. He told me about the clip gun and asked, "Do you have any idea who might be interested in this thing?" I suggested that Remington take a look at it. It seemed as if it might fit in our catalog.

Rick and Don sent over a sample. It turned out to be everything they promised. Unfortunately, it also carried a high price tag. Too high. With import duties and two markups, the gadget couldn't have been sold for less than $10.95. Extra clips would cost $3.95 a bag. In America, we have a variety of manually operated garbage bag seals. Some are plastic; others composed of thin wire. All are free with the purchase of the bags. Using them is fairly easy. We didn't think that consumers were willing to pay the price to bring the process into the mechanized age. We had to turn the guys down. The final thirty days went by in a blur. No sales. Apparently, other possible distributors shared our sentiments. They ended up surrendering the rights back to the supplier.

Climbing Pike's Peak, or Entrepreneurial Kismet

Sometimes the marriage of an entrepreneur and a venture is little more than fate. A product that has received a good deal of attention was brought to me by its creators. As you've seen, that wasn't unusual. How I ended up with the worldwide rights to it, on the other hand, is quite a story.

A little over two years ago, I received a call from a British chap. He said, "Mr. Kiam. My name is Jeffrey Pike. I am an entrepreneur and, like yourself, have acquired a company through a leveraged buy-out. I have a product that is simply sensational. We think you're the man to sell it and we would like to show it to you as quickly as possible." The call came on a Thursday. I was heading to Europe on Sunday.

Explaining this to Mr. Pike, I said we could get together on my return. He wouldn't settle for that. He said, "Look, surely you can give me an hour or two on Saturday?" As it happened, I did have two hours open that day, but I didn't intend to devote them to business. Mr. Pike, though, was insistent. He said, "Look, just give me two hours. You won't regret it. If after that time you don't think this is the greatest thing in the world, I'll not bother you again. You'll love what I have to show you. There's nothing like it." Whoa, baby, now there was a brightly painted vista. His unrestrained enthusiasm won me over. I also liked the sense of urgency he brought to his pitch. He made it seem as if Remington would be missing the product of the century if we didn't meet that weekend. I made an appointment to meet this ball of fire and two associates. One would be his chief engineer, the other his company's president.

The three of them arrived promptly. Mr. Pike had his product in a canvas bag. Before they had a chance to say very much, I presented them with a Remington disclosure agreement. Pike refused to sign. He responded with a confidentiality form of his own. I wouldn't sign his.

Such an odd stalemate. For a moment, it looked as though we would spend the whole two hours haggling over these protective covenants and might never get to see the darn thing they were protecting. Finally, I suggested a compromise. I would agree to sign his confidentiality form provided it excluded everything Remington was either already in or planning to enter. To my surprise, he agreed.

I checked off the categories—personal care, grooming, cologne, and apparel among them. I went through every business I could think of, and Pike still said they bore no relation to his product. This exchange accomplished two things. It made me sanguine about signing his form and it made me maddeningly curious to see what the heck they were trying to sell.

I couldn't wait to get a look at this miracle machine. Mr. Pike had other plans. Without so much as glancing at the canvas bag in his possession, he asked if he could have a cup of coffee. His engineer asked for a glass of grape juice. The president opted for a Coke.

I served them and sat down, certain Mr. Pike would unveil his creation. Wrong again. Mr. Pike stood up, casually sipping his coffee, and then suddenly spilled the majority of it onto a patch of carpet. The engineer stood up and said, "You know, I really don't like grape juice. I think I'll just dump it on the rug." With that, he emptied his glass on top of the spreading coffee stain. The chairman followed his friends' example with his Coke.

What was I to make of this? I found myself trying to humor these fellows until the boys with the butterfly nets appeared. The carpet was a Technicolor mess. None of this seemed to perturb Mr. Pike. He took his contraption from its canvas home and plugged it into the wall socket. The machine had a suction nozzle on one end with a clear plastic front. Mr. Pike set the nozzle on top of the stain. Within seconds, I'm watching this goop being sucked out of the carpet. The excess moisture was soon gone. Only a colorful blotch remained.

Mr. Pike attacked that problem with the other side of his machine. It squirted some detergent on the spot. An attached brush sloshed the liquid cleaner into a nice froth. The suction device was then reapplied and bingo! No more stain. I was impressed, but Mr. Pike wasn't finished. He asked me if we had a particularly stubborn spot anywhere in the apartment. We sure did. It resided on our living room rug. For ten years, we had kept its presence hidden with a strategically placed chair. Professional cleaners had taken regular turns with it. No amount of scrubbing could persuade it to vacate the premises. Not too many Ahabs wanted to tangle with this Moby Dick of stains, but Mr. Pike was an entrepreneur. He loved this sort of challenge. He got to working on the spot and had it all scooped up within minutes. I couldn't believe it. This stain had been with us for so long, I almost wanted to hold a memorial service for it.

Flabbergasted by the results, I told the three men I was interested in acquiring the rights for Remington. Remington agreed to put up the capital for development and to perfect the design. We would test the product and, if the results were satisfactory, sell it around the world. Mr. Pike agreed to a deal. It had only one hitch. Remington could distribute the cleaner only in the United States, Australia, New Zealand, and the Far East. Jeffrey was going to keep the Canadian rights and Electrolux, the vacuum cleaner company, was apparently about to be named as European distributor.

I was disappointed. We were increasing Remington visibility in the European market. This seemed the perfect product for our continued expansion. Still, I was more than willing to make do with what I had.

The machine was christened the VicVac. We brought it to retailers in April 1986 with the promise of a September–October launching. I took it out on the first round of sales calls. Though I am busy running Remington, I often like to participate in the selling of our products, especially the new ones. I was particularly excited to take the VicVac on its rounds. I wanted a firsthand look at how clients responded to it. The first account we called on gobbled it up at $37 wholesale. That was a nice start. At that price, however, the margins wouldn't allow us much advertising. So I turned to my salesman and said, "Gee, it sold pretty easily here. Let's raise the price to $40." Another quick sale. We kept raising the price with each succeeding customer. By the end of the day, we found we could sell it for $52. Accounts still thought that was a great buy and it gave us a tremendous amount of money for advertising.

Shortly after the VicVac's U.S. launch, I attended a meeting of major European retailers in England. I brought along a tape that chronicled what Remington stood for and what we were up to around the world. The VicVac was featured on the tape. The European retailers flipped. They rushed me asking when they could order their VicVacs. That was frustrating. I told them,

"You should be talking to Electrolux. They have a representative here. We've only got it for the United States." With that, I left for my hotel room and a good solid hour of banging my head against the wall.

Instead of that indulgence, I decided to accompany the president of our English company to his office. I was being overwhelmed by a good case of entrepreneurial persistence. I turned to the president and said, "My God, I just know we could sell the heck out of this thing if we had it in Europe. I've got to give it at least one last shot. Let's get Pike's number at your office. I'll call him from my hotel."

We got back to my room at about 7 P.M. My wife Ellen and I chatted. I looked over some mail. We made arrangements for dinner. Finally, I said to my president, "Let's make the call." I grabbed the number from my wallet. Before I could put my hand to the receiver, the phone rang.

It was the switchboard operator. Someone was calling from CBS for an interview. I told her to put the caller through. Seconds later, I was being greeted by a familiar voice. It was Jeffrey Pike! He had used the CBS ruse to ensure that the hotel would put the call through. I was in shock. I thought I had just walked into a Steven Spielberg fantasy—Business Encounters of the Third Kind.

I said, "Jeff, you won't believe this, but I was just about to call you. This very minute! I have something to discuss with you." Pike replied, "Don't talk. Let me say something first. It can't wait. How would you like to have the VicVac for England and all of Europe?" A sudden chill tap-danced up my spine. This was getting scary. He proceeded to explain that Electrolux had been sitting on the product for too long without coming to any decision on it. Jeffrey Pike was a mover. He was through waiting. He liked the aggressive way Remington had handled the product in the U.S. and wanted to throw in with us. All the way.

I wasted no time coming to an agreement. When it was concluded, Jeffrey said, "Great. Now that that is out of the way, what did you want to talk about?" What could I say? I didn't think anyone would believe this. I replied, "Oh, nothing important, Jeffrey. Just thought I'd call to see how you were doing."

When I hung up, I sat down in a trance. My English president and I just stared at each other. I was awed. Remington and the VicVac. I guess it was fate.

Over the past six years, Remington has come to mean more than just shavers. Besides the ventures mentioned we have entered into the machine-washable necktie business, and we've introduced a designer cologne. A new shaver, the Ultimate, was brought out in 1987. Shavers, VicVacs, pool alarms, colognes, and neckties. What's it all mean? Simply this: the entrepreneur works hard to build a company into a success. He's pleased by his good fortune, but never lulled by it. Remington's willingness to expand proves that we approach new business with the same entrepreneurial zest that led to the original purchase and turnaround of the company. This is essential for any company hoping to survive in today's market.

 We'll pursue any avenue in trying to improve the company. Nothing is sacrosanct. Not even our advertising. Remington has had continued success with our commercials. Over the years you may have noticed some subtle changes in them. Despite this, the commercial is basically the same one we've been running since I took over the company.

 I read and answer every letter addressed to me. Some correspondence concerns my ads. Many of the writers seem to think the commercials would be better if they were to star in them instead of me. They're probably right, but since no one has given a compelling reason to take my place—a USP—I've resisted their suggestions.

 Recently, however, I received some advice from a celebrated source. During a sojourn to California I was introduced to world-champion wrestler Hulk Hogan. The Hulk is apparently a Remington fan. I asked if it was because it gave his face such a close shave. He said that was one reason, but that he was especially enamored of how easily it could shave the hair off his entire body! Hulk liked the sleek look. The lack of body hair made it especially difficult for opponents to get a firm grip on him.

 Hulk admired the shaver so much, he offered to join me in

a commercial. Mr. Hogan is about 6 foot 7 and weighs over 300 pounds. If there is an ounce of fat on his sculptured frame, it is hiding in his wrestling boots. I've seen him throw 300-pounders around as if they were Frisbees. I gave his suggestion serious consideration. I haven't come to a decision yet: I'm not sure a shaver's ability to whisk off all of your body hair is a USP with a broad-based appeal. Also, using a wrestler in my ads would be a radical departure. It would certainly be entrepreneurial. Hulk and I could take turns reading the commercial copy and then we could finish in unison proclaiming, ". . . shaves you close as a blade or your money back!" Of course, we might just have Mr. Hogan drop by your house to pick up any returning shavers!

2

Failures? Everybody Has Them!

It was nice reviewing some recent successes. Sounds as if life for the entrepreneur is filled with nothing but triumph. Don't kid yourself. History shows that Thomas Edison went through over 5000 different filaments before discovering the one that made his lightbulb a shining reality. He didn't let those first several thousand mistakes dissuade him from his task. You must have the same fortitude. You are a pioneer. Failing will be part of your adventure. *Show me the person who has never failed, and I'll show you someone who has never taken a risk. I'll show you someone who is not an entrepreneur.*

You Can't Be Half-Pregnant

On the other hand, show me someone who learns from his mistakes and keeps persevering, and I'll show you an entrepreneur. Everyone experiences failure. I've certainly had my share of turkeys. I am, after all, the fellow who failed to see the full commercial potential of a product called Velcro. That adhesive fabric now serves as the base for a multi-billion-dollar industry. I had a chance to be a partner in it when Velcro was little more than an idea. It was something I really wanted to do. I let friends and colleagues talk me out of it. They all thought I would be crazy to leave Playtex, a company where I was doing so well, and tie my fortune to this untested product. I learned from that mistake. *When your guts tell you to move forward with a project, don't be swayed by the doomsayers.* Those same people warned me off Remington twenty years later. Who knows? I might have listened to them if I hadn't remembered the advice they gave me on Velcro.

Time for a little trivia quiz. Have you ever heard of the Catholic Record Club of America? No? You mean you haven't heard of the company that launched "We're Going to Have a Cookout at Your Cremation"? Don't worry. You won't be ostracized by the "in crowd." They haven't heard of it either. That record club was a Victor Kiam rocket that never got airborne.

It was about 1955. I was fascinated by the sudden proliferation of record societies. A music lover, I had joined the RCA club. It sent out a monthly catalog, inviting members to choose discs from its vast library. Every conceivable musical style was represented: classical, pop, jazz, folk, and early rock. It even included records produced by labels other than RCA.

After months of receiving their catalog, I realized something. This club and its competitors were broad-based. Each offered the same general music mix. I thought there might be room for a club that would go after a niche market. This was a generally sound idea, but exactly what kind of club could it be? It couldn't contain any of the elements already offered by existing associations. That would detract from its USP. No, it had to be something that no one else was offering. This was a tall order. It takes a variety of skills to be an entrepreneur, but creating a new form of music out of thin air is not, thank heavens, one of them.

As it turned out, I didn't have to be quite that inventive. Record clubs were not the only thing catching the American public's fancy in the mid-fifties. Religion had come to television. A leader of this phenomenon was Bishop Fulton J. Sheen, a Catholic prelate. His hourly show was watched by millions across the nation. I felt this new religious fervour could be translated into a business. A friend—someone already in the music business—and I put together a proposal for the Catholic Record Club of America. The organization would be aiming at a very specific group: religious music fans. In addition, it would offer albums featuring lectures by the leading Catholic orators of the day. Actors, appearing on other records, would read famous religious works. This was going to be my first entrepreneurial effort outside corporate confines and I thought it looked like a zinger.

Jumping right in, we put together a mock catalog. Many of the records were obscure, but some of them were well-known works such as Bing Crosby's "Ave Maria." The company obtained a mailing list comprised of people who regularly bought religious items and took pains to bring together a high-powered board of directors. Everything seemed to be falling into place. Even the Catholic Church played a role. After hearing our plan, they agreed to give the club its—if you'll pardon the expression—blessing. This official sanctioning did not come free. The Church was to receive a cut of the profits on every record sold. I liked that. The priests and their representatives were fair, tough businessmen. They taught me that you could find entrepreneurs anywhere and that they didn't necessarily have to come clothed in Brooks Brothers suits.

An informal board meeting was convened before our launching. First topic on the agenda: Who would run the actual ongoing business? Minutes after airing the question, I thought, "Whoa, not so fast, now. Don't everybody volunteer at once!" I mean no one stepped forward. It didn't take very long to realize I had made a terrible mistake. This board of directors was high-powered all right, too high-powered. Not one member— including my recording expert friend or I—had any time to run our new enterprise! We were all too occupied with our full-time careers.

The company had to make a decision. It either had to find someone to take the club's helm or dissolve. The quest began immediately. Unfortunately, it was doomed by two factors. First, none of us had time to conduct a thorough search. Second, the few candidates we did unearth were unwilling to chance involvement with what they perceived to be a risky idea.

We were about to abort. Then RCA, having heard of our concept, came forward and offered to buy it. We sold. I probably should have been elated at making money on my first sizable venture. I wasn't. RCA had bought little more than an idea, an unfinished catalog, a mailing list, and Church approval. The club itself was still an untried, unproven commodity. Having been forced to sell too early, none of us realized a meaningful profit. We did, however, pick up a valuable lesson: you can't be half-pregnant. An entrepreneur must be able to give his enterprise a full commitment. If I really believed in the club's viability, I should have at least taken a leave of absence from my job at Lever Brothers, and given the thing my best shot. It's a lesson I've never forgotten.

Best Laid Plans . . .

There are going to be times when your best idea is going to be a victim of circumstances. A friend of mine, a fellow in the marketing business, had heard that a major American tobacco company wanted to do a sports promotion. Sports have always been an attractive advertising opportunity. In America, despite our free market and freedom of speech, there are certain products that active athletes cannot pitch. These athletes are considered role models for American youth and are discouraged from setting anything resembling a "bad example." Cigarettes and other tobacco products are further restrained by a ban preventing their being advertised on TV or radio. Not only are tobacco companies unable to use players as spokespersons, they are also banned from buying commercial time during events featuring these athletes.

There is a slim loophole around this limitation. A company can sponsor a televised event. It is still unable to advertise during its broadcast. It cannot use the event's participants in its advertising. It *can* have its name tied to a sport by financial support. Witness horse racing's Marlboro Cup, or the Virginia Slims Tournament in women's tennis.

Having heard of the tobacco company's search for a sports promotion, my friend approached it with an idea: a tennis yearbook. This manual would be a review of the past year's major tournaments and a preview of the upcoming tennis season. It would feature statistics, records, full-color photos, and, most importantly, interviews with star players.

The company loved the idea. By featuring pictures of the athletes on the cover and highlighting the interviews, they could form a legal, indirect relationship with the players. After review by the promotions department, the concept moved forward. It grew bigger at each step of the corporate ladder and the company was soon considering an order of six million copies. My friend was already counting his profits. You can imagine his disappointment when the idea collapsed.

Apparently, the company felt the best way to distribute the book was as an on-pack. The paperback would be attached to a carton of cigarettes. Everybody thought this was brilliant. Everyone, that is, except for one of the company's marketing executives. He came to a meeting armed with a ruler. Measuring the book's thickness, he pointed out that every four copies meant one less carton of cigarettes shipped to the vendors. One less carton shipped. One less carton displayed. One less carton sold. With an order of six million books, the vendors would be stocking over a million and a half fewer cigarette cartons. This was not the sort of mathematics companies like to hear.

Suddenly the concept lost its luster. It met a firm rejection. The idea was still solid, but it was done in by its own logistics. Shortly after the turndown, my friend told me, "I really made a mistake there. I was so caught up looking at the advantages of the program, particularly the advantages to me, that I didn't really pay close attention to the disadvantages. If I had taken a better look, I would have recognized the problem before making the proposal. Then, I would either have suggested an alternative route of distribution or come up with an entirely different idea. I just didn't consider the needs of the sponsor or his market."

In any negotiation, you have to know what the other side wants. Sure, it may be a super idea for you. But what makes it sizzle for the fellow across the table? Do a balance sheet on your concept. List its weaknesses and strengths from the other side's point of view. Build your proposal around the pluses and then do everything you can to eradicate or soften the negatives. Had my friend done this, he might have anticipated the shipping problem up front. He could then have offered either a new plan of distribution or a different version of his idea.

Coincidentally, I had once found myself in a similar situation with a tobacco product. A man by the name of Bill Stengel had brought an item to me that seemed best suited for a magic act. A self-lighting cigarette. It was normal in every aspect, except for a small bit of sulfur residing in its tip. When struck against a rough surface, it lit without matches. This was terrific. You could light it in almost any weather. Gusty winds had no influence on it. You wouldn't have to worry about running out of matches or lighter fluid. I thought the cigarette would be particularly useful for hunters, sailors, and outdoorsmen. Invented by a man named Decapitano, it had been christened the Deca. Stengel had an opportunity to pick up the rights for it and he asked if I would like to get involved as part of a joint venture. I agreed.

Bill and I took the creation to two large tobacco companies. One did an enormous business in snuff and chewing tobacco, but had only a small percentage of the cigarette trade. It was excited by our idea. The Deca seemed to be a unique vehicle that could sizably increase the company's cigarette market share.

The second company was one of the tobacco business's leaders. It was similarly intrigued, but for different reasons. Aware of its position, it wanted to be first with any item that might have a major impact on its industry.

Both companies researched the product thoroughly. Both gave it the thumbs down. The reasons for the rejections were simple. Their research showed that smoking a cigarette was ritualistic. The lighting of that smoke was an integral part of the process. Smokers, creatures of habit that we are, are loath to abandon or change this initial step to nicotine pleasure. The research also found that when a man reached over to light a woman's cigarette, the act was fraught with sexual overtones. The striking of the match or flicking of the lighter was often the opening note to the mating dance. Heavy stuff. Our reaction was, "Fine. Then market the Deca as a cigarette for outdoorsmen!" Not a bad comeback. Unfortunately, we discovered that these findings had only had a minimal impact on the decisions of both companies. The biggest reason for their rejection was fear. The two corporations were scared to death of the Swedish match cartel. They were certain that the introduction of any self-lighting brand would put their other cigarette lines in bad odor with the cartel. All those free match packs accompanying the cigarettes bought in vending machines would suddenly disappear. Add in the research results and you can understand the company's reluctance to buck the cartel.

We took the rejections in stride and tried to sell the product to several other companies. No dice. Everyone liked the Deca, but the feature that gave it a USP was the thing that made it anathema to an industry that wouldn't risk the wrath of the matchmakers. An entrepreneur has to have the courage of his convictions. We were convinced that the Deca was a hell of a product. You also have to know when you're licked. We now knew that no company would agree to distribute it. Bill and I dropped the Deca.

Okay, your big idea has met an untimely death. You're grieving. You're depressed. How long do you stay down? About two and a half minutes. There is no better therapy for the pain accompanying rejection than to throw yourself back into your work. I started by examining the presentation we made for the Deca. Where did we go wrong? Was there any way to salvage the enterprise? If such an examination discloses a chink in your proposal, perhaps some tinkering will improve it. If it illustrates that you've done all you can, then it's time to turn the page and move on to something else.

Satisfied that the Deca's turndown was unavoidable, I sought the balm of a new idea. It could have been months before another attractive opportunity came along. However, in this case I was lucky. Another venture presented itself just as the Deca was put to rest. It came in tropical wrappings.

I had visited Bermuda on several occasions. During these trips, I had become quite friendly with the island's inhabitants. Bermuda had a racially mixed population, about two-thirds black and one-third white. A prosperous island, it probably had the best social relationship of mixed races found anywhere in the region. Despite this, there was no university of any kind for anyone, regardless of race. Most of the white families sent their children to universities in either the United States or England. The majority of blacks and low-income whites could not afford this luxury.

I became fascinated with the idea of founding a University of Bermuda. The island already had a number of leverageable assets. Its people were an industrious group who, given the opportunity, would probably place a premium on higher education. An old navy base featuring buildings that were ideal candidates for classrooms and dorms could be bought for a song. Its locale, alive with crystal-clear calm seas and balmy breezes, would attract young people from other countries. I thought American students would find our offering particularly compelling. The timing certainly seemed right. Four-year colleges in the U.S. were grossly overcrowded and junior colleges had sprouted like dandelions. These were two-year schools that offered students the hope of eventual transfer to a regular college. Ours would also be a two-year school, featuring a solid education and all the amenities this stunning island had to offer.

I found several Bermuda-based businessmen who were willing to invest in the venture. They thought it was a worthwhile idea. They also believed it would create an atmosphere conducive to their doing business on the island. With their backing, I contacted a man who came highly recommended, the president of a medium-sized junior college in the United States. This fellow had won high marks for running an outstanding learning center at a considerable profit. His academic credentials were impeccable. With his portfolio, the money, and a sound business plan in tow, I was ready to seek government approval.

Bermuda's Superintendent of Schools relished the idea. He arranged to have us present our plan in a session of the Bermuda Parliament. I actually had to wax poetic over the idea on the country's legislative floor. I think I do a pretty mean sales presentation, but no one has ever mistaken me for Sir Winston Churchill. Somehow, I managed to stumble through without embarrassing myself before this august body. The net result was a charter endorsed by Bermuda's Governor General.

We were pumped and ready to go. Then I became victim of a good news/bad news story. The good news was that I had suddenly been given an opportunity to buy the Benrus Watch Company. The bad news was that this would prevent my giving a full effort on the school's behalf. None of my investors had the time to take over the reins either. Remembering the Catholic Record Club of America, my options were clear. I immediately resigned as head of the group and named the college president as my replacement. That was a mistake. The president was an educator, not a businessman. He didn't know how to move the project off square one. That wasn't his fault, it was mine. Eventually, the charter lapsed and the idea died. It was later done by some other group. Another lesson learned. It's not enough to delegate. You have to put your enterprise into the hands of the right people. If I had made a better effort to find someone who really knew his way around a profit-and-loss sheet, we probably would have opened the school.

Ahead of Your Time

By his very nature the entrepreneur is an innovator. He doesn't follow fashions, he sets them. Unfortunately, you will have times when you are too innovative. You think you're bringing the word to the faithful, but the faithful's ears are filled with cotton.

When I was with Playtex we introduced the world's first machine-washable bra. Revolutionized the industry. Before its debut, bras had to be washed by hand. Our new version was so successful—we sold ten million in the first year—we decided to take a look at our girdles. We found that women rarely washed their girdles. The girdles were hard to clean and just couldn't stand up to repeated washings. As a result, the used girdles quickly became soiled and odorous. These wrecks had to be liberally doused with colognes and perfumes before they were made suitable for wearing. Knowing this gave me an idea for what was later known as "The Dirty Girdle Promotion." It became part of the Playtex legend because it was the only marketing idea in the company's history that nearly caused its creator's arrest.

The concept was simple enough. We chose the Stone and Thomas department store in Charleston, West Virginia, as our first test-market outlet. The public was offered a girdle trade-in. You brought in your tired, dirty, old girdle and we gave you a four-dollar discount on the purchase of a brand-new Playtex model. Vic Kiam, innovator at large, was sent down to conduct the test.

We erected a large container in the Stone and Thomas corset department. On the first day, the women came as a swarm. Girdles were flying through the air, most of them landing in the container, but a few probably struck some hapless buyers. We did terrific business. In fact, business was too good.

I had planned every aspect of the promotion with the same meticulous eye for detail as the fellows who set up D-Day. The only difference being, once my troops hit the beach, I didn't have the means to move them inland. I hadn't made arrangements to have the dirty girdles picked up during the day. It never occurred to me that we would get such a large turnout.

On the second day, a noxious air settled over the corset area. Somebody maintained consciousness long enough to call the sanitation bureau. Within the hour, three burly representatives of that department made their way across the floor. They were accompanied by a large police officer. Eyeing the delinquent container, one of the men asked, "Who's in charge here?" I replied meekly, "I guess I am, sir." He shook his head in disgust, turned to the officer, and said, "Book him." Book him! Oh Lord, welcome to my nightmare. There was a storeful of customers, newspapermen were waiting outside, and I was about to be a martyr for Playtex. I thought, "Hey, I know I'm an entrepreneur. I'm supposed to stand out. But there's got to be a better way of getting attention than this!"

Fortunately for Mr. and Mrs. Kiam's little boy, the officer was a touch more laid-back than this hard-eyed civil servant. He talked with the three gentlemen. They decided to let me off with a summons for creating unhealthy conditions in the city. I was given a $100 fine. They also made it clear they wanted me and the girdles out of town by sundown.

All right, I had a lemon. The promotion started well, but ended in disaster. What kind of lemonade could you squeeze from this? An image kept coming to me. It was that container of used girdles. I thought, "This is obviously a problem for women. Maybe we can do something about it?" You're an entrepreneur. You recognize a need, you try to come up with a product or service answering that need.

I went down to a store in Miami to conduct further investigations. I had deliberately picked a city with a tropical climate. This locale's heat and humidity translated into heavy perspiration. The resulting problem of feminine odor was so pronounced that once a woman tried on a girdle, she had to buy it. The store wouldn't take it back. This was embarrassing for the store and the customer. I was also positive that it was hampering girdle sales.

I got together with the Playtex ad agency, Young and Rubicam. They hired a psychologist to interview women on their hygienic needs and his report convinced us that a new business had been discovered. We developed a group of cosmetics to be named "Body Magic." The line included an after-bath tingler, a powder, a body lotion, and a feminine deodorant. All were applied with an aerosol spray. The feminine deodorant was the line's primary USP. It was the first product of its kind.

Playtex ran limited tests on the products and the results were overwhelmingly positive. We couldn't wait to launch. Then the monkey wrench came flying into the works. It was tossed by Mr. A. N. Spanel, Playtex's chairman of the board. He insisted that we place the new line in either our accounts' "notion" departments, where small items for women such as sewing materials, hangers, potpourri, etc., were sold, or in the corset sections. At the time, these represented the traditional Playtex outlets. We were barred from selling Body Magic anywhere else in the store.

This was a mistake. Body Magic was a cosmetic line and we wanted to sell it in cosmetic departments. We did everything we could to change Spanel's mind. I pleaded with him to let us do a broad test of the market, allowing it to determine where the line should be sold. If I did this once, I did it twenty times. Spanel was sent daily memos and was beaten over the head with the idea at every opportunity. We weren't being obstinate merely out of a love for our own concept. The entrepreneur, especially in the corporate environment, has to check his ego at the door. You have to ask yourself, "Is this good for the company?" We felt it was. Body Magic would have brought Playtex into a whole new market, one that no other corset company had explored.

Mr. Spanel could not be persuaded. He was one of the great entrepreneurs. As founder of Playtex, Spanel had introduced marketing concepts, products, and ad campaigns that had innovated the industry. This was a risk-taker. But he did have some blind spots. Though he loved to implement new ideas, Spanel felt that Playtex already had a basic, strong distribution base. He didn't want to tamper with it. He saw the introduction of a Playtex product in the cosmetics department as a risk. It could mean weakening our relationships with the buyers in either the corset or notions departments. Spanel wasn't about to do that.

Playtex brought Body Magic out over my protests and with Spanel's restrictions. It posted tremendous sales for about six months. Then every major cosmetic company jumped into the market. They, of course, sold their lines in the cosmetic departments. We got wiped out. My associates and I had created a new market, but the company had been unwilling to capitalize on it. This was quite depressing. It stands as a defeat that can still rankle me. With good reason. Every now and again, I run into some executive from Revlon or Alberto Culver. Invariably, they pat me on the back and say, "By the way, Kiam, thank you so much for building one hell of a business for us." Through gritted teeth I tell them, "You're so very welcome."

If you're an entrepreneur in a corporation, you are likely to run up against your own Spanels time and time again. You can't let it discourage you. Go back, salve your wounds, and get ready to assault their petrified attitudes with your next great idea. It's been my experience that eventually you will be given the opportunity, even if it's just to shut you up. Playtex gave many of my more entrepreneurial ideas a chance to fly. Fortunately, the concepts did just that. If you are an entrepreneur and your company doesn't give you any chances to explore risks, you'd better consider finding another situation.

A Common Error

Bill Constanza is in the dilemma described above right now. He was a full partner in a small, successful advertising agency in New England. The company—alias the CC Agency, for the purposes of this story—was formed in 1984 and did $1 million in billing during that first year. By late 1986, business had quadrupled.

A large conglomerate—we'll call it Diehard Associates—was the firm's major client. It, and its affiliated companies, represented almost 40 percent of CC's business. CC handled all of Diehard's big campaigns. This gave Bill an opportunity to hobnob with the company's president, board chairman, and leading executives.

Constanza is an impressive fellow. Whenever a campaign seemed in trouble, Constanza would solve the problem. For example, Diehard wanted to set up a national ad campaign built around toll-free telephone numbers. These numbers would be advertised in national periodicals and on TV. Consumers would be asked a question requiring a yes or no vote and the poll would be tied in with the company's latest product.

From the very beginning, the campaign provided nothing but headaches. There was the expense of the national phone line, the high costs of national TV advertising and nationwide print ads. The price tag was becoming more than the budget could absorb. A fundamentally solid idea was about to be nickeled and dimed to death.

Constanza went to work. Doing some fast research, he discovered that it would be more cost effective to get national coverage on a region-by-region basis. Bill could arrange deals with each of the regional phone companies and buy local print ads. This not only lowered the bills, it also allowed Diehard to maintain tighter control on the campaign's demographics. The phone promotion went through without a hitch.

One week later, CC tackled another Diehard emergency. This time, the company needed a print ad. For reasons too complex to chronicle, they had to have it done immediately—as in yesterday. Constanza and his partner, Ray Calo, wrote the copy in less than two hours. They hired a photographer and models, and scouted a shooting location. Constanza even acted as prop man for the shoot. Within forty-eight hours the photos were finished and the ads were being processed. It was a first-rate job. Had it been bungled, a national promotion would have been postponed, and possibly shelved. Constanza had saved Diehard's bacon.

These were entrepreneurial solutions and they bowled Diehard over. It decided to make the CC Agency part of its big happy family. An offer was made to Bill and Ray. They would join Diehard as vice-presidents in charge of advertising and promotion. As they learned Diehard's business, they would be dealt a hand in marketing and public relations. In return, they would each receive base salaries of $100,000. This would be augmented by bonuses and profit-sharing incentives. A sweet deal, especially for a company that had only been in existence for just under three years.

Calo, a bachelor, turned the offer down. He walked off with a nice buy-out for his share of the agency. Constanza, married with twin sons and a third child on the way, grabbed the security the offer represented.

Bill has now been with the company for a year. In addition to his base, he picked up a $15,000 bonus and is due for an equal sum from his profit-sharing plan. The company loves his work. It is thriving, and its success makes his position that much more secure. Bill is miserable.

When he got hooked up with Diehard, Bill figured they were as entrepreneurial as he was. Once in, he found he had been operating under an illusion. Since Diehard had always appreciated his troubleshooting, he thought they would allow his freewheeling approach to influence their ad campaigns. No way. Diehard had a preconceived notion of how their ads worked. Constanza was allowed to deviate only when obstacles arose. Whenever he asked why the company had to follow a certain line, he was told, "Because that is how we've always done it and that is what has always worked."

Bill also found the corporate structure unpalatable. He was used to informal brainstorming sessions with Ray at all hours of the day. At Diehard, he was chained to a system of boring meetings and dueling memos. One afternoon, he tried to drop by the office of the guy in charge of marketing. He wanted to have a quick chat about the direction of the company. Since Bill didn't have an appointment, his sudden appearance nearly caused cardiac arrest in both the marketing director and his secretary.

Being an entrepreneur, Bill was turned off by corporate politics. It seemed as if most of the executives spent an inordinate amount of time avoiding failure rather than risking success. They cared little about the company's growth. As long as their paychecks cleared and no one was able to accuse them of making even the tiniest mistake, they were happy. There is no way an entrepreneur can survive in this environment. Bill now realizes that all the security in the world can't replace that entrepreneurial sizzle. He is looking to make a move. His family has adopted a strict budget. A large part of Bill's earnings is accumulating in a savings account, and he is already in discussion with Ray and his former cronies. Despite the salary and the perks, I think a vice-president's slot will open up at Diehard before the year is out.

Bill made a mistake getting involved with Diehard. That's understandable. It's easy to be dazzled by monetary rewards and the seeming safety of a position with a prosperous organization. But before signing on, you have to be sure you're not entering into an agreement with the Devil. Take a look at the company's public face. Is it an enterprise that always seems to be forging new ground? Talk to the company's personnel and clients. Find out how the corporation reacts to innovation. Make sure you can fit. An investigation of a few hours can save you a lot of grief.

Riklis 1: Kiam 0

I've always advised fledgling entrepreneurs to join companies in a "line" position. This means you want a job that produces results that can be measured on the bottom line, such as salesman. You need to have a measurable impact on the company. Don't worry about salary. The financial rewards will come. Whatever route you're on should lead to the top of the company.

You want to be president of every enterprise that employs you. That's the ultimate. If you miss—and there can be, after all, only one president—you should still reach a pretty high level. I wanted to be president of Lever Brothers. Had I stayed, I like to believe I would have made it. I also wanted to be president of Playtex. I came close. I was on a fast track until outside forces derailed me. Losing the opportunity to reach my goal was one of my biggest disappointments.

In 1967, I was president of Playtex's Sarong division. Sarong had been a rival girdle manufacturer. I had helped Playtex acquire the company and had been installed as its head. The Playtex president—and my immediate superior—was the dynamic Harry Stokes. Playtex itself was a subsidiary of the Stanley Warner corporation, a movie theater company owned by Si Fabian and his brother-in-law, Sam Rosen. Rosen and Fabian had acquired the company in 1953 as part of a diversification program. Now that they were getting on in years, I thought they might consider selling the company.

Al Peterson, the head of our U.S. company, joined Mr. Stokes and me in making a proposal to Rosen and Fabian. This had to be delicately handled. I mean you couldn't exactly barge in on Si and Sam and say, "Look guys, neither one of you are long for this world, so we think it might be a good time for you to sell the company." Instead, as in any good negotiation, we concentrated on what was in it for them. I said, "Gentlemen, you're both past seventy. We're sure you might want to consolidate your estate at some point. If you ever do, we have a plan for the selling of Playtex that should maximize your benefits. It will also present the best opportunity for your employees."

Contrary to what you might think, neither man was offended. They were pragmatic businessmen. In fact, they thanked us for showing so much concern for the company. They also promised to read our plan.

We had proposed selling the company to Avon Cosmetics. Avon was the number one cosmetics company with massive door-to-door distribution. Playtex was number one in girdles and bras. We could give Avon a vital entry into the retail world through department stores, notion shops, and discounters. Avon would also have been able to augment Playtex by marketing some of our products door-to-door. It seemed a good synergy. Al Peterson—a crackerjack executive not given to superlatives or patting his own back—thought the proposal was brilliant.

Unfortunately, I don't think either Si or Sam gave it much consideration. They did come to a decision to sell shortly after our meeting. They did not come to us or Avon. Instead, they turned the transaction over to the Boston banker who had arranged their original purchase of Playtex.

That gentleman arranged to sell the company to one Meshulam Riklis. This prospect didn't please me. I felt Mr. Riklis was more of a financial operator than a business builder. His history seemed to indicate that he bought companies only to sell them for a quick profit. Nothing wrong with that. However, entrepreneurs are interested in more than just a fast dollar. If all you want to do is increase your capital, do the world a favor. Play the horses. Take a gamble on the stock exchange. Don't pass yourself off as an entrepreneur. Entrepreneurs want to build businesses, to take them beyond their perceived potential.

Playtex's continued growth was my number one priority. I doubted it would rate as high under a Riklis stewardship. The welfare of the employees was another strong concern. If Playtex underwent a radical change in direction, there could be a destabilizing effect on everyone in the company.

As a corporate stockholder, I was also unhappy with the price Riklis was offering: about fifty-five dollars a share. Playtex was as successful as any company you could name. Almost every one of our divisions stood at the top of its market. I felt the company was worth much more than Riklis was offering.

I called Harry Stokes. We found we shared the same feelings. At thirty-seven years old, I was a novice in high finance. Naivete breeds confidence. I was positive we could come up with the money to beat the Riklis offer. Harry suggested we convene a meeting of like-minded executives.

We invited Al Peterson. A good choice. He had joined us in our proposal to Fabian and Rosen. I also judged his business philosophy to be diametrically opposed to this particular takeover. My last call went to an executive vice-president named Stan Youmans. Wrong move. In *Rumpole of the Bailey* you are taught never to ask a witness a question if you're not sure of the answer. The results can be disastrous. In attempting this sort of clandestine operation, never ask anyone to join unless you're certain of where they stand. Youmans's response to my invitation was a curt, "No, I don't think I can make that meeting." I didn't have to be a breaker of codes to decipher that line. It meant trouble.

We proceeded with the meeting anyway. I told Harry and Al that I was certain Youmans was about to throw in with Riklis if he hadn't done so already. After thinking about it none of us was surprised, making my mistake seem all the more glaring.

The meeting opened with an outline detailing my opposition to the Riklis bid. To my amazement, Peterson disagreed with my assessment. He felt we had no way of knowing what Riklis would do with the company after the purchase. More importantly, he doubted we could attract a better offer. Al didn't think our risk-reward ratio looked very promising. He decided to sit this one out.

Stokes and I were on our own. We decided we couldn't afford to approach the usual financial markets for capital. There was no way of going down to Wall Street without our actions becoming public knowledge. Instead, our proposal was taken to Avon, our original choice. They shot us down. We then called on some friends possessing contacts in the corporate investment world.

One of them, a fellow named Ed Williams, was the executive

vice-president of the Schlitz Brewing Company. Owned by the Uhlein family, it was the number two brewery in the U.S. and it was looking to diversify into other consumer products. Williams thought Playtex offered some intriguing possibilities. After speaking to me, he put together a meeting with the Uhleins.

Harry and I were brought to the estate of Bob Uhlein—the Schlitz chief executive officer (CEO)—by a company helicopter on a rainy Sunday evening. A meeting of the family was convened two hours after our arrival. The most respected family member was Uncle Irwin. Owner of 15 percent of the company, he had been Bob Uhlein's corporate predecessor. At first, I directed a good deal of our presentation toward him, since I thought his voice could help sway the others.

This was probably my second mistake. Uncle Irwin was eighty-seven years old. He really didn't have much enthusiasm for this sort of affair. I'm bombarding him and the others with charts, graphs, facts, and figures. Uncle Irwin responds by dozing off during most of our dog and pony show. He seemed intent on punctuating my talk with the worst snoring you've ever heard. That wouldn't have been so awful if he had stayed asleep. He didn't. Every five minutes or so, he would wake up and announce: "When you lay down with dogs, you get up with fleas." Then he'd nod off again. It was awfully encouraging. Making it worse, he made this withering pronouncement with the timing of Perle Mesta, America's legendary society hostess. It always seemed to cut through the room right as I was making a particularly telling point. For example, I would say, "And Playtex has gone through twenty-five years of sustained growth, proving . . ." ". . . when you lay down with dogs, you get up with fleas." Arf!

Somehow, we got through the presentation without my strangling Uncle Irwin. The family voted to take up the matter at a full board meeting one week from the following Monday. Harry and I were encouraged. We felt we had made a pretty good pitch, despite Irwin and his dogs. From words spoken after our meeting, we felt we already had Bob Uhlein in our corner.

The presentation before the board of directors went smoothly. Uncle Irwin was on good behavior. When it was over, we were asked to wait outside while the matter was put to a vote. There were only twelve people being polled so I figured we'd have a decision in about fifteen minutes. Boy, did I have a lot to learn. Four hours later, we were called back into the room.

The result had been a tie. I've often heard athletes say that playing to a tie is like kissing your sister. It doesn't quite make it. I've got news for them. Their assessment is generous. The feeling you're left with is that of an ill-used rope after a tug-of-war. You're pulled by elation because of the closeness of your dream, you're wrenched by depression over the proximity of disappointment.

Bob Uhlein told us he would push for us. He also explained that the person with the tie-breaking vote was on a trip to Europe and would return for a second vote on the following Monday. Bob told us we needn't bother to come back. He would call us with the result. I thanked Bob for his support and thanked God the tie-breaking vote wouldn't be cast by Uncle Irwin.

Perhaps it should have been. The board turned us down a week later. Harry and I scrambled to find other investors. We pitched Scott Paper. No interest. We went to Darrel Ruttenberg of Studebaker. He had recently merged his company with Worthington Pump. Darrell just couldn't see acquiring a corset company after having just bought a pump manufacturer. He felt the businesses were too diverse. On Thanksgiving Day, we brought the idea to Nate Cummings of Consolidated Foods. The decision to meet with him on a holiday was entrepreneurial. We wanted to stand out. On a normal business day, we might have been one of ten companies on his agenda. An early Thanksgiving meeting guaranteed we'd be his only business meeting of the morning. Our enterprise didn't sway him. He rejected our proposal.

Looking back, I can now say we took the wrong route in this attempted acquisition. There was a group of companies that could have been approached that would never hear about the opportunity because we didn't call on them. We had felt limited in our choices by our decision to conduct this as a clandestine operation. Major error. Within twenty-four hours of our initial proposal to Schlitz, Riklis and his associates knew exactly what we were doing. He didn't need Mr. Youmans to tell him. Though we didn't know it at the time, you couldn't keep something like this a secret.

Right after we had left Schlitz, its financial officers were phoning investment bankers, asking them for information on us and Playtex. It didn't take long for word to hit the street. Apparently, the only two people who were unaware of the attention our actions were receiving were Harry and I. Two babes in the woods. In the financial world, if one more person than you knows your secret, it is no longer a secret.

I now realize that we should have made our intentions public from the outset. We should have gone to the institutions that had invested in Playtex and had seen a healthy return on their money. We were the people who had built the business; they would have backed us. That might sound like conjecture. It's not. Months later, I was in the process of buying the Benrus Company. One of the investment firms involved had held a financial stake in Playtex. I told him how we had fought to hold on to the company. He said, "Yes? Well, why didn't you come to us? Hell, we would have backed you to the hilt."

I wish we had been wise enough to have known that then. Riklis took over the company. A week after the acquisition, Stan Youmans—Playtex's new CEO—called me into his office and simply said, "Too bad, old boy." I knew what that meant. One, it was too bad that you picked the wrong side and two, I am the new head man and you, Mr. Kiam, will be working under me. If, of course, you're working here at all.

In early Roman history, when a coup against the emperor failed, the plotters lost their heads. Fate was only slightly kinder to our Gang of Two. It was strongly suggested that I seek employment elsewhere. I left Playtex in mid-January 1968. Sixty-five-year-old Harry Stokes was forced into early retirement. Al Peterson, having kept himself above the fray, was moved to the corporate staff of Riklis's other entities. Stan Youmans was rewarded with the company's top spot.

It was a bitter ending. On the surface, I took my departure with my usual equanimity. In reality, I was shattered. I felt as if malignant elves were prancing about my stomach, shredding my innards with razor blades. My career with Playtex had lasted thirteen years. In the marrow of my bones I had never doubted that I would one day be company president. Everything I had accomplished there seemed to affirm that opinion. When I was forced to leave, it seemed as if my world had come to an end. I had to start all over.

I must admit it gave me very little satisfaction to see my predictions about Playtex come true. Once Riklis took over, Playtex's growth just about came to a halt. Youmans was a cost-cutter. Under his regime, the company reduced their investments in advertising, marketing, and development. Everything that had made Playtex the giant that it was had been truncated. The company tried to coast on its past reputation. Not good enough. Market share and profits dropped off dramatically. Riklis began dismantling the company. He sold divisions, merged Playtex with another outfit, then disposed of some more pieces. Finally, he sold the whole company to the Swift Packing Company. That gave us a chuckle. Throughout my tenure with Playtex, we had had an indelicate nickname, the "Meatpackers." Now the company had been sold to one of the largest meatpacking firms in the world.

I have to admit something. Despite my failure to pull Playtex out of the Riklis grasp, I'm glad I made the attempt. Yes, my approach was haphazard. I should have modified it. But I'm glad Harry and I took a stand. The entrepreneur has to have values. These values can only be defined by how strongly you're willing to fight for them. The most important thing to us was the company's continued growth and the happiness of the employees. When we felt these were threatened, we couldn't turn our backs. Playtex meant too much to us. As it turned out, my failed attempt to take over the company was one of the greatest experiences of my life. It was the start of an education. Our shortcomings forced me to be better prepared for participation in the world of finance. It also made me look for new opportunities. Without this temporary failure, I might never have become "The Man Who Bought the Company."

A Haunting Failure of the Soul

I've often said that the entrepreneur can't measure his success with mere dollars and cents. He also can't always find his losses in the red ink of a bottom line. Believe me. The greatest failure I've ever had didn't cost me a dime. It just took a huge chunk out of my soul.

It began while I was still with Playtex as head of Sarong. I was calling on the buyer for a large department store in Brooklyn, New York. On the way up to her office, I noticed a sizable crowd had gathered on one of the selling floors. They had been drawn together by a baby-faced young salesman hawking a manually operated kitchen utensil that did everything. It sliced, diced, mashed, and juiced meat, fruit, or vegetables. The salesman demonstrated it with all the nimbleness of a top-flight surgeon. His hands were flying in twelve different directions at once. This guy really put on quite a show.

His implement was made out of tin. It couldn't have cost more than $1.25 wholesale. This fellow was selling them for ten dollars each and with the way the crowd was reacting you would have thought he was giving away gold. He sold out his entire stock in less than ten minutes.

When he was finished, I approached him. I found out his name was Bobby Dugan. We exchanged small talk for a few minutes and then I said, "Boy, you are a sensational salesman. If you can get people to buy this gizmo, you can sell anything. Take my card. If you ever want to change your job, give me a call."

He came to work for me about six months later. His first territory included Brooklyn and the Bronx. These were not prime locales. The stores were small, a large number of them had bad credit, and few of them carried our complete line. He did a superb job. Within six months the area had gone from a perennial loser to a prosperous territory. Less than a year after that, Bobby was named district sales manager for New York State.

By the time I left Playtex, Bobby was a regional manager in charge of half the country. He had married a beautiful model and they had an adorable little boy. He eventually moved over to Puritan Fashions as executive vice-president in charge of sales for one of its larger divisions. From all appearances, you had to conclude that Bobby Dugan was living the American dream.

Bobby called me one day. Since last hearing from him, I had taken over the Benrus Watch Company. He congratulated me and said, "Vic, I'm going to go into business for myself, too. I want to run some thoughts by you and get an opinion." He was going to go into the direct-mail clothing business. The idea was to pick an area, invite housewives to a fashion show in a local hotel, and provide them with food, drink, and entertainment. He would later take orders and money for the clothes modeled in the show. The concept had jumped past the planning stage. Bobby had contracts with several suppliers and had already chosen two cities as test markets. Those first shows were scheduled for Syracuse, New York, and Columbus, Ohio, in February.

I thought it might be a worthwhile venture, but I warned Bobby that he had better make darn sure that his test was run properly. Syracuse and Columbus were not ideal places to test anything in February. Both cities were prone to heavy snows. Bobby's financing was small; the majority of it was his own capital. The tests would eat up most of that money. It was easy to see that it would only take a slight glitch to halt this enterprise before it really got started.

Bobby didn't share my view. He said, "No, I think this is the right way to go about it. I don't want to wait. Vic, I've been working for companies for fifteen years and it's time to be my own boss again. I'm so sure this is going to work that I'm going to resign from Puritan next week."

I felt this was an error. Bobby had a family to support and there was no reason why he couldn't run these tests while staying with his company. Most of the preparation could have been done over the phone at night. Working at it only part-time, he still could have given the run-through a full shot. If the tests proved positive, then he could disconnect the umbilical cord. Should they fail, he could keep collecting a salary until he could afford another test or find a different venture.

I hated to put any dents in his enthusiasm, but I was trying to be realistic. Bobby responded by promising to think over my recommendations. He said he'd get back to me with his final plans.

I didn't hear from him for five months. I subsequently learned that he had followed his original strategy. Bobby left Puritan and ran his February tests in Syracuse and Columbus. On the day of his exhibition, an unforgiving snowstorm blanketed Syracuse. No one came to the event. Bobby lost every nickel he had in the venture. On top of that, he had accepted money from the people who had given him orders at the Columbus test. Their cash was used to cover some of the expenses for the aborted Syracuse run. Now he didn't have the capital to fulfill his customers' orders or to give them a refund.

Bobby's life became unhinged. Lawsuits for non-delivery of goods were being processed. He had fallen behind on the payments for his estate in Connecticut. He and his wife had separated and Bobby was desperate for a reconciliation. The guy needed help. He called me and asked for a job.

Benrus had a jewelry division, the Wells Company. We hired him to sell women's jewelry to accounts on Long Island. It was Playtex all over again. Bobby just set the region on fire. Within three months he was the best salesman we had. He had gone through a rough time, but he still had the magic and I was positive things were going to turn out fine.

Then one morning, while driving to the barbershop, I was listening to a news broadcast. It was the usual potpourri of mundane events until the announcer said, "Connecticut police are investigating the murder of Alicia Dugan and her maid in Mrs. Dugan's palatial Greenwich home. Mrs. Dugan's young son was found crying but unharmed in his playroom. Both women were killed by gunshots in the back of the head. Police are trying to locate Mrs. Dugan's estranged husband Robert. They are not yet calling him a suspect in the crime." I nearly drove off the road.

As soon as I reached the barbershop, I called the president of Wells, told him what had happened, and pleaded with him to track Bobby down. He found him calling on a customer. I met with Bobby. Still in shock, he assured me he had nothing to do with the crime. He continued to protest his innocence to the police, but he was unable to supply them with a coherent alibi.

The police grilled him for hours. When they were finished, he was booked on suspicion of homicide.

Bobby spent a month in jail. This portion of his ordeal ended when he was released for lack of evidence. He was still a prime suspect in the killing. The police restricted his movements to three states—New York, New Jersey, and Connecticut. He could visit his son, who had been staying with Bobby's parents in Florida since the arrest, but such a trip would require police permission.

We had to fill Bobby's job during his absence. When he returned, we gave him a new position representing Christian Dior—our line of jewelry and leather goods for men—in New York City. Talk about admirable performances. Here was a man under suspicion for homicide. He was separated from his only child who was living with his parents. The region he returned to had recently lost all of its key accounts. Didn't matter. He built the business back up from nothing. I don't believe I've ever seen a better natural salesman.

During all this, I had taken an interest in a trading company in Kuwait. I needed someone to go overseas to run it. This was a sales-oriented company. The job demanded the talents of someone who was skilled in opening up untried territories. I thought to myself, "Holy Christmas, of all the people we have on the payroll, the one guy who can run this thing is Bobby Dugan."

I asked Bobby if he'd be interested in the position. He wanted it badly. However, he doubted the police would allow him to travel to Kuwait. I said, "Look, why don't I call the chief of police. I'll explain the conditions of the job and we'll even look into posting bond for your return. We'll let him decide." I should explain that I was willing to take a certain amount of responsibility for Bobby, because I was certain of his innocence. He had already given me his word that he had had nothing to do with the crime. My instincts told me he wasn't lying.

I made my case to the chief a few days later. The first thing he wanted to know was Bobby's present whereabouts. I told him he was working out of New York while awaiting this decision. That information turned out to be wrong. Bobby *was* working out of New York, but not that day. Without telling the police, he had gone off to Florida the previous afternoon—violating the conditions of his release—to visit his son. He had mentioned to me that he might possibly go to Florida. However, when the chief asked me where he was, I assumed Bobby had changed his plans. It didn't occur to me that he would have left without telling the police.

The chief said he wanted to think the idea over and that he would get back to me on the following day. About an hour later, I got a call from the manager of our New York office. Twelve cops had come barging in looking for Bobby Dugan. They had a warrant for his immediate arrest. I was frantic. Now assuming he had indeed gone AWOL, we tried to reach Bobby at his parents'. No luck. We left word with anyone who might see him to make sure he got in touch with us immediately. We didn't hear a peep. That night I was driving home. Once again the radio brought sad tidings. Bobby Dugan had been arrested in Miami. The police had already arranged his extradition back to Connecticut.

Have you ever been smacked between the eyes by a sledge-hammer? That's how I felt when I heard the news. My first thoughts were, "This is my fault. My phone call triggered all of this. If I'd just kept my mouth shut and not thought about Kuwait, none of this would have happened." I hadn't foreseen the tempest my request would cause. As soon as the chief heard the word Kuwait, he probably had visions of Bobby disappearing overseas, never to be seen again. Bobby's turning up in off-limits Florida only confirmed his suspicions.

Bobby's bail was set at $1 million. We couldn't raise it. He was placed in a Bridgeport, Connecticut, jail. When I finally got to see him, he had been in prison for three weeks. It had been harrowing. Bobby was not a big man. He was baby-faced, slim, and almost pretty. The prisoners welcomed him as easy prey. He had been beaten and raped. Two of his front teeth had been knocked out of his head.

We put up money for the defense. The lawyer won his release, again on the grounds of insufficient evidence. It had taken nine months. Though out of jail, Bobby's freedom of movement was again restricted. The state had held the case open and Bobby was still the number one suspect.

The Saturday he got out of jail, I picked him up at the prison. Bobby was beside himself. Claiming to need the protection, he said he was going to buy a gun. He was frightened that some of his fellow inmates, since released, would come looking for him. It was as tragic a thing as you would ever want to see. His eyes no longer glowed with confidence. The effervescent salesman, a guy who could sell flying lessons to eagles, was gone. In his place was this beaten shell whose furtive gaze saw menace in every shadow. I didn't know what I could do for him. I took the afternoon off and spent the entire day with him. We went to see my son in a tennis tournament. I thought that would be good therapy. His parents and son were down in Florida. Bobby was all alone and I wanted to create a family atmosphere for him.

We spoke for hours. By dinnertime, his mood was unchanged. He described the horrors of prison in graphic detail. When I told him that was behind him he said, "Yes, it is. And I'll never go back there again." There was nothing vehement in the declaration. It was just a simple truth laid bare.

We gave him his old position with Dior. He threw himself into his work. Meanwhile, the investigation of the Connecticut police failed to furnish any further evidence against him. In fact, stories were now circulating that it had been the maid, not Mrs. Dugan, who had been the target of the hit. The maid had apparently worked for figures in the drug trade. She had allegedly stolen something from them, either drugs or money, and the killing was their retribution. Poor Alicia Dugan had merely been in the wrong place at the wrong time. It looked like Bobby was in the clear. Six months after his release, the direct-mail clothing venture came back to haunt him. He had never settled with his customers. We had offered to cover those obligations, but it didn't make a difference. The case was coming to trial.

The results of the hearing were disastrous. Bobby told me that the judge had promised to throw the book at him. I tried to calm him. I couldn't believe that he would get too harsh a sentence for what was a relatively small mistake. After about an hour of commiseration, I said, "Trust me, Bobby, everything will work out. You have to hang in there." He cried, "Vic, it's got to be all right. I just can't face jail again. I can't."

I had to go down to the Virgin Islands the following afternoon. I was testifying before the Islands' legislature on the question of watch tariffs. Midway through the testimony, the bailiff tapped me on the shoulder. There was an urgent call for me from the U.S. I asked if he could take a message. He shook his head and said I had better answer the phone immediately. It was the New York police department. Bobby Dugan had committed suicide. He left a note proclaiming his innocence but declaring he couldn't spend another day in prison.

When you're an entrepreneur, business demands such a large portion of your life. Always remember that any business you're involved with revolves around human beings. Try not to forget that life has the unseemly habit of taking the most vibrant souls and stripping them down to their most naked frailty. When that happens, you have to put the contracts, the appointment books, and the ledgers aside, and give of yourself. Completely.

I honestly believe I did that with Bobby. When he needed advice, money, a job, or just a shoulder to lean on, I had made myself available. But a nagging voice in me charges that I let him down in the end. I'm the guy who has always said business is where you are. My business should have been with Bobby that weekend. I should have listened better when I saw him that last time. I should have recognized the desperate patter that was the final moments of his tap dance toward the abyss. Maybe I could have found the right words to soothe him. Maybe I should have brought him with me to the Virgin Islands. Maybe I should have cancelled the trip and helped him make it through that hellish final weekend.

Maybe.

There is no greater failure than maybe.

3

Selling, More Selling

The entrepreneur is always selling something: an idea, a service, or a product. Business is a game, a lifelong Olympics. Selling is the easiest event to score. At the end of the day all you have to do is ask yourself, "Did I get the order?" More times than not, the winners answer "Yes!"

Every sale is a point in your favor. Those of you who have, or are trying to obtain, the entrepreneurial spirit have a distinct advantage over your competitors. The entrepreneur is a risk-taker, daring to be creative. So many people approach selling as just another job. They do everything by rote and their paltry paychecks and inability to rise on the corporate ladder are direct results of their ho-hum approach.

Don't be afraid of bringing some pizzazz to your work. Sometimes this can take the form of humor. Twenty years ago, when I was with Benrus, I was trying to convince the buyer for K Mart, the world's largest seller of timepieces, to place more of our watches in his stores. He was already carrying some of our products, but we were his smallest selling line.

I had just taken over the company and wanted to improve our standing with this important client. It had the potential to be a prized account. An appointment was arranged with the buyer. He was a medium-sized, wiry fellow named Bruce Weill. This guy was one ball of fire. Having been with K Mart for over thirty years, he worked fourteen-hour days as a matter of habit. He loved what he did. Companies place a high value on executives of his stamp. They know if they ever lose them it will take three or four people to fill the vacuum. They also treasure his opinion. I knew if I could get Bruce behind Benrus, he'd be a powerful ally.

I liked dealing with Bruce. He could be abrupt and quick with his judgments, but his position demanded decisiveness. I enjoyed that because Bruce never wasted your time. He also wasn't a buyer who placed a strong emphasis on personal relationships. Often a buyer depends on a clique of salesmen: having done business with these men for years, he feels comfortable with them and is loath to entertain any new faces. Bruce didn't care if you'd been dealing with his company since the time of the Big Bang or were the newest kid on the block. If you represented an item that could earn profits for his company, he would see you.

I was confident that the right approach could sell Bruce on our watch lines. Upon meeting him in his office, I started to go into my presentation. I must say I thought I was scintillating. I trotted out samples and painted a vista of future business that was blinding in its promised magnificence.

Bruce sat through my performance without uttering a word. As soon as I was finished he said, "You're a newcomer to the watch business, aren't you?" I admitted I was. He continued, "I thought so. You see, you don't really understand our customers. Let me look at your shoes." This was not the usual request I encountered at the end of a presentation. In fact, it seemed more than just a bit strange. I thought, "My God, I'm a president of a company. How can he ask to see my shoes? What does he want to do, see if they are polished to a spit shine?" I was tempted not only to show him my shoes, but also to tell him where he could put them. Then I thought of the large number of outlets this man represented. Without saying a word, I lifted my feet for his inspection.

Glancing at them, Bruce said, "How surprising. They're just plain leather." Puzzled, I asked what was so astonishing about that. He explained, "I expected them to be made out of alligator or some other exotic hide. You see, your watches are priced for the alligator-shoe customer. Most of our customers wear tennis sneakers. I like your watches. The styles are attractive and I know they keep good time. But if you want to sell us, you have to price them for the tennis-shoe consumer. Until that happens, I can't buy them from you because our clientele won't buy them from us."

That was discouraging, but for the entrepreneur, every rejection is only temporary. If you keep your ears open, today's turndown can bring the opportunity to score more points tomorrow. Bruce had done me a favor. When an account is that clear in his objections, he has given you something tangible to overcome.

I left Bruce's office and headed back to Benrus. The next few days were spent in brainstorming sessions. We needed to create a lower-priced watch that retained our product's style and timekeeping ability. This was not an easy problem to solve. It wasn't as if we could merely lower our prices for this one privileged customer. Had we done that, our other accounts would have had our heads for paperweights. No, if the cost was going to drop for this large chain, it was going to drop for everyone. After running through the numbers in every possible combination, we finally hit on a solution.

We had been preparing to launch a national TV campaign and had figured the cost of this advertising into our markup. Common sense said that the TV ads would be useless if we didn't have enough outlets carrying our lines. We decided to reduce the amount to be spent on those commercials. We also made some minor changes in the watch construction. For instance, we went from a five-micron gold plating to a three-micron version. The switch did nothing to alter the product's attractiveness or performance, but it did save us some money. Combined with the major adjustment in our TV marketing mix, we were able to trim our gross profit margin from 33 to 20 percent.

Three weeks after the price drop, I called on Bruce Weill. Knowing his love of brevity, I had created a way to get my message across while using as few words as possible. I entered his office, pulled up a chair, and plopped my feet up on his desk.

Bruce seemed stunned. He was probably about to ask what the hell I was doing, but my shoes caught his attention. They were tennis sneakers. He broke out laughing and I said, "Bruce, since I was last here, I've been wearing these and thinking about nothing else but your customers. I think I understand their needs. Let me show you our tennis-shoe watches at their tennis-shoe prices." Bruce liked my presentation. More importantly, he liked our new price tags. He gave me a large order and his company became our largest account.

This presentation was a good ice-breaker. A few laughs go a long way toward making a potential client comfortable. In this case, the joke served a more important role. It immediately told Bruce we had heard his message and had given it our attention. It told him we hadn't given up. This was the key. If we had passively accepted his initial rejection without attempting to solve the pricing puzzle, we would never have opened the account.

Throughout the years, I don't know how often I've heard salespeople complain about accounts that were particularly hard to crack. You'd ask them why they can't make the sale, and they'd say, "I don't know. I guess he doesn't like our product." That may be, but it's also possible you're not listening to the buyer. If all you hear is the rejection, you're probably missing valuable clues. *Don't be afraid to ask why you're not getting the order.* Have the buyer be as specific as possible and write down every comment he makes. Then approach that list the way you would approach the Intangible Balance Sheet we mentioned earlier. Turn those negatives into positives! You still won't be able to satisfy everyone. Nobody can. But you will see a dramatic change in the number of nos that turn into yes.

It's not always going to be easy. You have a product, service, or a program. You know that it is the greatest thing since peanut butter. You run up against a buyer or customer who just doesn't share your enthusiasm. His reasons are vague and he's unresponsive to any suggestions you make. In your heart you know that his store is the perfect outlet for your merchandise. If this is the case, it might very well be necessary to go over the buyer's head. My friend, this is one of the most critical situations in selling. It must be delicately handled.

I was up against these circumstances very early in my career as a salesman for Lever Brothers. We had just come out with a wrinkle remover called Ayer Magic. Every buyer I called on thought it was a great product. Every buyer, that is, except an elderly man—call him Moe Kates—who represented Gray Drugs. When I asked Kates why he wouldn't order Ayer Magic, he replied, "No reason. I just don't think it's much of a product."

That was all he would say. Now, I know I told you to examine any clues you get during a rejection, but I think you'll admit even Miss Marple would have a hard time with this one. I went back to Kates several times, and always left with the same response. I did write down, "Doesn't think it's much of a product," but what could I do with that? Have Kates lobotomized until he docilely accepted anything I stuck in his hand? I didn't think that solution sounded very promising.

I had to come up with something. Gray's was potentially my biggest account and a failure there would have been damaging. I took a hard look at Ayer Magic. Was it everything I thought it was? Every other buyer I had sold it to seemed to agree with my assessment. Thumbing through their purchase orders I thought, "This is ridiculous. These results prove I have one hell of a cosmetic here." Certain I was right, I called Gray's merchandise manager Robert Meachum. I said, "Mr. Meachum, I have a product called Ayer Magic. It's going great guns throughout the region. This cosmetic has been presented to your buyer three times and he doesn't see any merit in it. I think he's wrong. Gray's is missing out on a tremendous opportunity here and I would like you to review this decision." I requested a meeting with Meachum for the next afternoon and insisted that Kates be invited.

Once in Meachum's office I said, "Bob, I admire and respect Moe. I've worked with him for eight months and think he is a real pro. But what we have here is a simple difference of opinion. I want to present my program, let Moe air his objections, and then let you be the arbiter." Then I made my pitch. I showed him what Ayer Magic could do, pointed out how there was nothing like it on the market, and showed him how other accounts had enthusiastically greeted the product. In selling, this is known as "painting the vista." I was enticing the customer with a picture of the product in all of its potential glory.

When I was finished, Meachum turned to Kates and asked him why he was against Ayer Magic. For the first time in my presence, Kates explained that he was introducing a new cosmetic with Revlon and that he doubted the store could get behind two big promotions simultaneously. Meachum asked if they were similar products. They weren't. Meachum replied, "Well, Moe, normally I would agree with you about supporting two promotions at once. But this Ayer Magic is something brand new and different. It could really be exciting. I think we ought to try it. You and Vic should get together and see if you can't work out a program."

That's exactly what we did and it was such a big success that after a while Moe forgot that he had ever had any objections to carrying Ayer Magic. Let's look at what happened here. First, I examined the product to make sure I wasn't fooling myself on its viability. Then, I went to the buyer's boss but insisted Kates be brought into the meeting. You don't want anyone to get the impression you're sneaking around behind the buyer's back. No matter what the outcome, you will probably have to be dealing with that buyer in the future. You don't want this person as an enemy.

At the start of the presentation, I tried to smooth things over by complimenting Kates. That bit of ego massage and my calling the matter nothing more than a difference of opinion took some of the edge off our dispute. Finally, when I made the presentation, I was ready for anything. Every piece of information I needed to make my case was at my fingertips. This was so important. If you jump over a buyer's head, you want his boss to believe you had just cause. A dazzling, well-informed presentation will go a long way toward accomplishing this.

Of course, your best evidence will be the product itself. You have to believe in it with all your heart. If you have any doubts about it at all, don't try to trump the buyer. Understand the risks. A failure will see you hit over the head with "I told you so's" for as long as you call on the account. You'll never be able to go over his head again and you'll be hard-pressed to sell the buyer on any other new ideas. If, however, you know you have a winner, go get them. A success will heal any wounds suffered by the buyer's pride, and it will make him more receptive to any programs you bring him in the future.

I've always maintained that the entrepreneur has to stand out from the mob. Tennis shoes and jumping over a buyer's head when the situation calls for it were, in a sense, offshoots of that philosophy. You can't be afraid to put yourself on the line. However, don't get the idea that the entrepreneurial salesman is given carte blanche to exercise his creativity. Be as wild and wacky as you want in the planning stages of any concept. Stretch your imagination to the limit. But when it comes to the actual fulfillment of a program, you have to ask yourself, "Does this help sell the product? Will it be cost and time effective?" Importing twenty hula dancers from Hawaii to accompany you while calling on an account might set you apart from your competitors, but will the expense lead to a loss? Will the hoopla get you the order or is it just gossamer hype?

Wells, the jewelry division of Benrus, had a salesman named Dick Dotson. A bright, personable fellow, he was a crack operator. He did have one problem. No matter what an account asked him to do, no matter how extravagant, Dick would do it. He would hire fashion models to walk through the stores wearing our jewelry. Another time, he gave away a free bottle of perfume with the purchase of any Benrus item. These small promotions were costly and they did nothing to increase his bottom line.

Once a large account told him they didn't want to carry the same jewelry as their competitors. They asked if all the pieces we sent them could have at least a subtle difference from those sent to other stores. For instance, if an ornamental gold leaf on a bracelet went from left to right, they wanted the leaves on their bracelets to go from right to left. Dick should have told them it was impossible. He had some leverage. Our jewelry line was a best-seller for this retail chain and they were as interested in making profits as we were. Instead, he said, "No problem. We'll custom-design stuff specifically for your store." That was just great. Our factory was going to be suddenly discombobulated by the new, separate line. This would wreak havoc on our inventory. Because these items would be for one customer, the volume would be very low and our margins were going to get shot to pieces. Even if we sold every piece, we couldn't make money.

Dick and I had quite an argument over this one. I listened to his reasoning, took a look at his plan, and overruled him. Then, I took the time to explain my thinking. This was a creative guy. You can't have him racing off with every promotional zephyr that blew his way, but you also do not want to suppress that terrific mind of his. A fellow like this has the makings of a master marketeer, he just needs direction.

I told him that there had been one thing essentially wrong with all of his recent promotions. It wasn't the expense. You can justify a short-term decrease on your bottom line, if the long-term results are sufficiently beneficial. I wasn't all that upset that the programs had been duds. Minor failures like the perfume give-away should not discourage the entrepreneur. They should, though, make him examine his methods.

Hiring the models wasn't a bad idea. It was a common practice in our industry. Bedecked in our latest pieces, they would parade throughout the store and entice customers into the jewelry department. But since everyone else was doing it, without Dotson coming up with a creative new wrinkle—which he hadn't done—the promotion lacked a USP. In addition, Wells jewelry was not ultra-chic. It really shouldn't have been showcased in such a high-fashion promotion. Dotson made another mistake by hiring the models to work from store opening to closing, six days a week. There just wasn't enough customer traffic to justify this expense. On certain late nights, he could very well end up with more models on the floor than shoppers. If you were going to launch this program, it should have been targeted for a day when it could reach its maximum audience. Saturday and certain weekday afternoons would have been better choices. You could have reached more customers in a concentrated time period and maximized the return on your marketing dollar. As it was, the pithy increase in business could not offset the expense incurred by the promotion. Again, it wasn't an awful premise. But even the best concept is worthless if it lacks proper execution.

The perfume give-away was a bomb. I believe in give-aways when they are used to introduce products to the public, act as a market test, or lead directly to an additional sale. For instance, we once gave away charm bracelets. With each one, we also gave the customer two free charms. Do you know how naked a charm bracelet looks with only two trinkets dangling from it? This give-away was almost guaranteed to compel the customer to buy our full set of charms. In another example, Remington recently brought out a powder shaving stick. It is made to stiffen whiskers for an even closer shave. We introduced and in a sense market-tested the item by including a sample with every Remington shaver. The consumer could try it and, if he liked it, purchase additional sticks for future use. Dotson's free scent promotion did not have this advantage. We were not in the perfume business. The program did not introduce a new product. Had it increased our volume, which it hadn't, most of the additional profits would have been wiped out by the cost of the perfume. It was just a bad idea.

After our meeting, Dotson took a different track. Every program he proposed was created with the idea of bringing the public to the product. Sometimes this involved nothing more than physically enhancing the display of our merchandise. Other programs featured special prices for jewelry sets. Pieces bought as part of a group would cost less than pieces bought individually. The profits were affected only marginally and this was outweighed by the increase in volume. That's the sort of promotion you have to love.

I mentioned earlier how going over a buyer's head was one of the most critical situations you would ever face. Here's another toughy: taking over a territory from a popular salesman. Some people have such dynamic personalities that they become as important as the product. To many of their customers, they *are* the product. There is no telling what can happen when these buyers are confronted by a new face. It's very hard to transfer personal loyalty.

When I took over Sarong girdles for Playtex, I met with our district manager in Boston. His name was Joe Rafter and he was seventy-three years old. His sales force was made up of three other guys: Eddie Kramer, who had been with the company for forty-six years, Howard Hunt, a thirty-seven-year man, and Freddie Gibbons, who had twenty-four years of service. The others referred to Freddie as the new man. If you included Joe, the four of them had been with the company for over one hundred and sixty years!

You can imagine the relationships these fellows had built up with their accounts. Howard Hunt was especially well loved. Whenever he went into a store he gave every salesperson and buyer a stick of chewing gum. It was his calling card. People would come up to him and say, "Howard, don't you like me anymore? You haven't given me any gum yet!" Howard would hand them a stick, chat about the weather, and then make a sale. I knew these boys could not go on forever. When it came time for their retirement, the company had a chance to be in a hell of a fix. How on earth do you replace a lifetime of goodwill?

We formulated a plan. I asked each of the four to inform us of their retirement four to six months prior to the fact. As soon as they did, I would give them a hand-picked replacement. The new salesman would travel around with the veteran and get to know his accounts. Eddie Kramer would go up to a buyer and say, "This young boy is going to be taking over for me when I retire in a few months. He's a good man and I've taught him everything I know. See that you take care of him or I'll come back to haunt you." Howard Hunt had his replacement handing out chewing gum. It made for a nice, smooth transition.

When I was with Lever Brothers, I took over a territory from a living legend. Harold Paine had been with the company for over thirty years. He was forced out of action one day when he fell in his bathtub and injured his back. I was moved into the breach. Harold had the same strong ties to his buyers as the four sunshine boys in Boston. Unfortunately, his injury kept him from introducing me to his long-time friends. Realizing this, Harold called each one of his accounts and explained why I was taking over the territory. He told them to be nice to me. Believe me, they were, and it made my first selling experience a lot easier than it might otherwise have been.

One of the things I learned in that early time was to keep parts of my predecessor's system intact. We drew up a list of every account's foibles. If Harold had coffee with a particular buyer on Wednesday, I continued the practice. Eventually I would exert my own personality, but only after establishing myself with the accounts.

Of course, if you're taking over from a popular salesman who has been fired, your task becomes that much harder. Like the loss of a loved one, accounts can take the dismissal of a friendly salesman very badly. All you can tell a disgruntled buyer is, "Look, I know you loved Barry. I loved Barry, too. But for reasons not known to you or me, he's no longer with the company. I had no part in that decision, but I promise I will do as good a job as Barry did, if not better." Then work your buns off to deliver and hope time really does heal all wounds.

It's going to take a while. I learned that the hard way. We had a salesman at Benrus—Bill Whitson—who was practically the king of Lower Manhattan. He made over $100,000 a year and would call on accounts in a chauffeur-driven limo. Talk about calling cards, this one was several steps ahead of a stick of chewing gum.

I went into Benrus with Al Peterson. He was very conscious of our bottom line and when he got a gander at Whitson's earnings he nearly had apoplexy. Al figured we could hire three salesmen for what we were paying Bill. I said, "Yes, but this guy has been with the company for over forty years. He knows the buyers and their families. We have to protect those friendships." Al wouldn't hear it. All he thought about was how three salesmen could cover three times the territory of one. The sales force was my domain, but I respected Peterson's greater experience. I acquiesced to his decision.

What a catastrophe! The first thing Whitson did was sign on with a competitor. We lost every large account in Manhattan. They figured that they had lived with Whitson for forty years. He was family. If our company was going to treat him so shab-

bily, they weren't going to do business with us. The three salesmen who replaced Bill couldn't even earn their keep. We ended
up with one man for the entire territory and he did less than 20
percent of the business Whitson had delivered.

I learned two things from this. First, in selling, treat relationships as if they were precious gems. Second, never think you
can save corporate funds by merely cutting loose a large salary.
Don't worry about what an employee is making. What is that
person's value to the company? You will often find the person
was worth every single penny he earned and more. As an entrepreneur, I want to see everybody on our payroll making as much
money as possible. If they are enjoying an enormous success, so
is the company.

Taking over from a popular salesman is hard enough, but
taking over from someone who has been ripping off his accounts
brings a whole new set of problems. When I was a regional sales
manager with Playtex, we employed a man named Ralph Carney. He had to have been the hardest working salesman I'd ever
seen. On the few occasions when we called on accounts together, he would pick me up at 6:45 A.M. We'd be on the
customer's doorstep before the store was opened. I always recommend that salespeople make the most of their day—don't
even stop for lunch. Eat on the run and use that valuable time
to call on accounts. Carney took this philosophy one step further. He wouldn't eat at all. His entire waking day was consumed
by his drive to get the orders.

Every week, he led all the other salesmen in our region in
volume. He didn't seem to sell any large orders to any single
customer, but he had a remarkable consistency. Every store he
called on would buy one of everything. In the trade, this was
known as "selling ones" and it was not an uncommon practice.
Stretched out over a fourteen-hour day the sales mounted up.
When I asked him why he used this method, he explained, "I
have a daily goal. I want to sell one of every item we have to
every account I call on. That way they have a complete range of
our merchandise. The stuff moves very quickly, so I get immediate reorders on my next trip back. I think it's a good way to
gradually build up the business. The total volume is impressive,

but none of my individual customers feels that he's been squeezed by a hard sell."

This made sense, but I later found out that there was another reason why Mr. Carney was so bent on selling ones. We had a big promotion earmarked for late September. During his last few trips prior to the campaign, he accumulated more orders than ever. I mean his volume went through the roof. He wanted all these orders tied in with the autumn promotion. This meant they would be processed and delivered after September 25. On October 25, we gave Carney his monthly commission check. Naturally it included all those sales we had processed for him in September. It was over $12,000. In 1958, the average American worker was earning slightly more than half that amount as a yearly salary. The day after cashing this check, Carney shocked everybody by resigning. He offered personal reasons as his excuse.

Personal reasons, my foot. Less than a week after his resignation, we started to receive an unusually heavy number of returns. It went on for days. Almost all of the merchandise came from Carney's territory. I called on the accounts to find out what the problem was. I was afraid that there might have been a product defect that our quality control people hadn't caught before shipping.

It was nothing like that. Instead, each of the accounts claimed they had received more bras and girdles than they had ordered. Checking the paperwork against our shipping files, I couldn't see a discrepancy. Each purchase order showed four of each item had been bought and signed for by the account.

I called on several buyers with this proof of purchase. When they took out their own records of the transaction, we found they matched ours. In every store, I received the same reaction. The buyer would scratch his head and say, "I don't care what I signed or what these say. I did not order four of everything. I always buy ones. Why would I suddenly change?" After hearing this same story two or three times, I started to sniff a noxious smell. It was emanating from Carney's documents.

I thought back to the last time I had gone out with him. He was very meticulous. Whenever he got through with a sale, he would go over the order with the customer and verify exactly what had been bought. As he checked off each number he would put a check mark next to it. Then he would have the buyer sign his slip. Examining these purchase orders carefully, I soon realized what Carney had done. He had followed his usual procedure. Only this time he used a tiny L-shaped check mark and he had slashed it through all of the ones. This transformed the ones into fours! He did this with every damned order. No wonder his sales had quadrupled. No wonder he had been so quick to resign.

All his accounts were overloaded and we now had to contend with one angry group of accounts. I called in Fred Talbot, the fellow who had replaced Carney. I told him what had happened. There is only one thing you can do in a situation like this. Your company's reputation is at stake and you know how much value is to be placed on that. You have to be honest with your accounts. Then pray that they understand.

We called on each of the injured buyers. Before anyone had an opportunity to throw something at us, we explained we weren't looking for new orders. We had come to pick up their returns. Then we showed them the signed forms and explained how they had been fleeced. Realizing the mistake was partially their own made them that much more forgiving. Taking back the extra stock ensured we were restored to their good graces.

Funny thing. During this minor tempest, one fellow in St. Joseph, Missouri, got as overstocked as anyone, but he didn't seem to mind. He paid his bill without complaint. From all appearances, he must have been doing some business. Fred and I called on him one afternoon.

We were looking over our merchandise when he joined us on the storeroom floor. We told him we were his Playtex representatives. He said, "Ah, Playtex. You boys make this item here." He pointed to one of our more well-known models. I proudly replied, "Yes, sir, we do. That's our Living Bra!" He answered, "Well, for you it may be living, but for me it's a dead duck." I broke up. It turned out he was just as overladen with undergarments as his competitors but had been too timid to say anything. He explained, "Well, the temperature can get up there in August when I made this order. After it arrived, my records confirmed I had signed for the purchase. I figured the heat must have gotten to me, so it was my headache." Poor guy. He had a small shop and was stuck with enough inventory to last him for a decade. We took back all of his overload too. If your customer thinks he's been had, you have to make him happy. He is your lifeline to growth and profitability. We could have looked at the matching records, seen all those bogus fours, and said, "Tough. If they didn't want them, they shouldn't have signed for them." We could also have slit our wrists. It would have had the same result.

As a salesperson, keeping the customer satisfied is your chief responsibility. Getting the order is your goal, but you're not going to reach it without that customer's or buyer's help. It's a basic fact of business. Yet I've seen salespeople violate this ancient bromide time and time again. Then they wonder why they aren't enjoying success.

Teddy Barnes is a copywriter I've worked with on occasion. Let me share a story he recently told me. Teddy's staff is always expanding. As his operation becomes more computerized, he is constantly investing in new software. One day he needed a program that allowed him to place the information stored in his computer in orderly files. Without it, the computer's access time would be markedly slowed. He was told about a piece of software that not only maintained a streamlined system, it would also retrieve any material that had been accidentally deleted.

He picked this little marvel up at a newly opened computer shop, we'll name it Blotto Computers, around the corner from his office. It cost $35.00. He brought it back to work, slipped the disk into his PC, pressed his keyboard, and . . . nothing. The program didn't work.

On his way home that evening, he took the software back to Blotto. The salesman put it up on his computer and got the same result. A blank screen. The salesman checked and found there weren't any replacements in stock. Then he turned to Ted and sniffed, "Here is the phone number of the manufacturer. The best thing to do is to call them and tell them what happened." Teddy couldn't believe his ears. He said, "I bought the software here and I am bringing it back to you. You see it doesn't work. I want my money back!" I should mention that Teddy is the sort of guy who believes you can get more with a left hook and a kind word than just a kind word. The cavalier attitude of this salesman was pushing him toward his usually low boiling point.

Recognizing this, the salesman called over his store owner. The boss was a fat little guy who looked like the Michelin man dressed in a Hawaiian shirt and Jack Nicholson sunglasses. He told Teddy, "I'm sorry. But store policy is that we don't give refunds." When angered, Teddy has eyes that would put the fear of God into Clint Eastwood. He turned these lasers on the boss and said, "I don't give a damn about your store policy. You are the owner. You are the store policy. Give me back my money or I'll stuff you into your cash register." As negotiations go, this was one hell of an opening gambit. The owner reached over, took Teddy's software, and again placed it in the store's PC. Another blank screen. Noticing Teddy's ham-like fists, the owner said, "Well, I guess we should give you a refund."

Teddy shook the owner's hand and left with his money. When he told me the story he said, "You know, I was really pleased that this store had opened so close to the office. Its prices were excellent and I was going to be needing a lot of software. It's really too bad because I will never walk into that store again. Not too long ago I bought a program at a different shop, a member of a large chain. Their stuff is more expensive than Blotto Computers. I had a problem with it. It required a color monitor and I have a monochrome. My fault. I didn't read the packaging thoroughly. I brought it back and started to tell the salesman about the mistake I had made. He would have been perfectly within his rights to say tough luck. Instead, the salesman stopped me in mid-explanation. He said, 'Mr. Barnes, it's no problem. This happens all the time. Would you like a credit, an exchange for another product, or your money back?' I took an exchange. I was so impressed with the way I was treated that I've been a regular customer of this store ever since. It doesn't make any difference that their software is often slightly more expensive than their competitors'. I'm willing to pay a few extra

dollars because I know they stand behind their merchandise."
Teddy then told me that he had already spent over $6000 in that
store. Blotto lost that business over a $35 piece of software. A
little bit of courtesy and caring. It goes such a long way.

Making the customer happy has to be your first priority. I
was recently visiting London and stopped into a local store to
buy some magazines. The person behind the counter didn't
smile, offer any help, or seem to know very much about their
stock. I came away without making a purchase. A few days later,
I stopped into a different shop. The salesperson greeted me with
a warm hello, helped me with my selection, and—without being
asked—offered me some idea of when certain American publications were delivered. When I'm in London again, which shop do
you suppose will get my business? The answer is obvious.

The old saying "Any job worth doing is worth doing well"
had to have been conceived by an entrepreneur. Too often, we
see people who think of themselves as trapped in mundane jobs.
How absurd! They are not trapped by the job, they are trapped
in their own attitudes. There isn't any reason why you can't put
color into the drabbest of jobs and turn it into an entrepreneurial springboard.

A young woman started out as a clerk at Macy's. She was
one of over 2000 clerks working at this department store.
Along with her usual duties, she made it a point to learn the
whereabouts of every department in the building and what merchandise it featured. When a lost customer turned to her for
assistance, they weren't sent to the nearest directory. They were
given clear instructions to aid them in their search.

Two months into the job she was assigned to the quilt
department. This woman spent as much time as possible talking
to the buyers and soaking up their experience. Any salesperson
calling on her department represented another opportunity for
improvement. She would ask him a series of prepared questions
in an attempt to learn everything she could about the product
she was representing. During her lunch break she read books
and trade magazines on quilts, fabrics, and weaving. This was a
remarkable display of enterprise for a young clerk. Did these

exercises make her a better salesperson? Did it get her noticed by her superiors? You bet it did. She rose rapidly, becoming first an assistant buyer and then a full-fledged buyer. At her rate of progress, it wouldn't surprise me if she were running the entire store someday.

Doing the best job you can might often have unexpected benefits. One day my wife Ellen went out shopping for shoes at one of her favorite stores. For whatever reason, she just couldn't find anything that struck her fancy. The salesman lugged out enough pairs to shoe Imelda Marcos for a lifetime. Ellen felt awful. The poor guy worked so hard and put so much time in with her, yet he didn't make a sale. You know it had to beat the heck out of his commission for the day, but he seemed unperturbed. This fellow was as gracious when Ellen left as when she had first entered the store. When she said how sorry she was for not buying anything, he said, "Please, don't worry about it. I'm only sorry we didn't have a shoe for you. Come back again soon and give us another try."

When Ellen got home she couldn't stop raving about this salesman. She was so impressed with his enthusiasm, energy, and utter professionalism. Not to mention his patience. At the time, we had just opened an Italian jewelry business. We were desperate to find a top-notch salesperson to help launch our line in the United States. After hearing Ellen sing this man's praises, I said, "Look, if he's really that good let's go back to the store and try to hire him for our business."

We did exactly that. This fellow accepted our offer and then did a sensational job. Built the business right up. Within a year and a half, he left our company for another position that could pay him more than double what he was making with us. We were sorry to have him go, but we were happy for him. He's gone on to a number of tremendous successes. It just goes to prove that an entrepreneurial approach to your job can yield surprising rewards.

That salesman is a rarity. I believe one of the big problems in retail stores today is the lack of customer attention. Too often I see salespeople standing behind their counters as if they had taken root. They are all waiting to be asked for help. The customer doesn't bite. One or two might growl on occasion, but that shouldn't prevent you from approaching them.

If I were working in a shop, I wouldn't let a customer leave without going up and letting them know I was there to assist them. Don't come on like a hurricane. You don't want to intimidate them out of the store. But give them something more than the cursory "Can I help you?": How often have you been asked that by a salesperson? If you tell him "I'm just looking," what's the usual reaction? Most salespeople I've said that to disappear quicker than Jumping Jack Flash. It's almost as if they're glad they don't have to deal with you.

Instead of using this mundane line, go up to the customer and say something like, "Hi, my name is Victor and I'm here to help you. I think you'll find we have a lot of nice things here today. Take your time to look everything over. If you have any questions at all, please feel free to ask me." Now you've given the customer a human presence to deal with. You've shown an enthusiasm for them and your merchandise without being pushy. Try this the next time out and see how it works. I think you'll be amazed at the results. I don't know how many times I've heard people complain, "I went into the store to buy something, but nobody seemed to want to bother with me so I left." Every time an order walks out the door, you're losing points that are going to be hard to win back.

Talking with your customers will also give you an insight into their needs. Since an entrepreneur is often a trail-blazer, this can be especially vital when he's attempting to introduce a new idea or concept. The greatest product in the world has no value if you can't find someone to buy it. You have to know your market.

That point was driven home for me when I was president of Sarong. Our girdles featured a patented criss-cross that gave it an extra-firm hold. Another company made a knockoff of the girdle and was underselling us by offering its version in discount basements across the United States. We sued it for patent violations. The dispute slowly crawled through the courts while the copycat continued to slash into our sales.

I wanted to best this company in its own neighborhood. Neither Sarong nor Playtex, its parent company, had ever bothered with the bargain-basement business. I decided we would launch a new lower-priced girdle called the Tahiti. We put together a marketing program for the product and chose Litt's, a department store in Philadelphia, for its introduction. Litt's had one of the largest bargain basements in the country and it was one of our most valued accounts.

Its merchandise manager was a fellow named Al Ritchie. He was a real no-nonsense type who was quick to let you know where you stood. I called on him, showed him our samples, and then started painting a vista. I told him we weren't going to run the usual basement ads. We were going to shoot splashy, four-color, full-page ads featuring Polynesian models wearing our girdles. Very upscale. These ads were going to run in *Harper's Bazaar.* When I finished what I thought was a grand presentation, Al looked at me and said, "*Harper's Bazaar?* You're going to advertise a basement girdle there? Fellah, you must be cracked." After assuring Al I was quite sane, I explained that I was an entrepreneur and that I wanted to do things differently. He said, "That may be true, but this is as ridiculous an idea as I have ever heard. My customers have never even heard of *Harper's Bazaar!*" I thought that was an exaggeration. I figured even if you didn't read the magazine, a person had to have at least heard of it. When I told Ritchie this he replied, "You think so? OK, let's go to the basement and find out."

We go out to the floor and Al stops the first woman he sees. She was five feet tall and five feet wide and dressed like Rosie the Riveter. "Madam," Al says, "this gentleman and I are conducting a survey. We'd like to ask you a few questions." He then asked her how long she'd been shopping in Litt's basement (about ten years) and why she was such a regular customer (she liked the prices). Then it was my turn to ask the big one: "Miss, have you ever heard of *Harper's Bazaar?*" This haughty look came over her face and she peered at me as if I was some new kind of insect. She said, "Of course I've heard of it! It's a deadly disease!" I looked over at Al. He could scarcely suppress his laughter.

We made the same inquiries of several other customers. They weren't any better at identifying the magazine than Rosie. In fact, her guess probably came the closest. Case closed. We did launch the Tahiti, but as a basement-priced line without the highfalutin fashion image. It did very well and put a real dent in that other company. If I hadn't taken the time to listen to my account and ask a few questions of his customers you would have probably read about the Tahiti in an earlier chapter. The one on failures.

Talking to your customers is an ideal method of building a strong business relationship. I used to call on one buyer who was a football fanatic. Before dropping in on him I would bone up on all the latest football statistics and standings. We'd start off by chatting about the fortunes of his favorite team, then we'd get down to doing some business. Another account was represented by a fellow who was quite an outdoorsman. A quick reading of *Field and Stream* let me shoot the breeze with him. These little chats created a pleasant atmosphere for selling. They also made me something more than just an impersonal tradesman hungry for an order. I was a compadre with similar interests.

Knowing what to talk about is easy. Just listen attentively to the other person, ask a few questions, and you'll find out what his interests are. Knowing what not to say can be tricky. Generally the traditional conversational taboos of polite social gatherings—sex, religion, and politics—apply to business. Let me tell you the story of a salesman who forgot this. He talked himself out of one sweet deal.

He represented an office-supply dealer and had been working for months on a potentially large sale to an international conglomerate. In his final meeting with the company's buyer, he struck the mother lode. He was given every indication that he would leave with a whopping order.

During a lunch break, he and the buyer passed the time with some chitchat. Nothing earthshaking. Just the usual gab about weather and business. Suddenly, out of nowhere, the salesman starts talking about the Iran-Contra hearings. He goes into a blazing diatribe about how the Congress was abusing Colonel

Oliver North, and how the colonel was a great patriot. He went on for a good ten minutes.

The salesman had been accompanied to the meeting by an assistant. This perceptive man kept trying to shush him. Failing that, he looked for a table to hide under. When the bombast subsided the meeting reconvened in a suddenly arctic atmosphere. The poor boob did not get his order. It seemed the buyer was not an Ollie North fan. To the contrary, he thought what North had done was immoral and he was leery of doing business with anyone who could so heartily endorse the colonel's actions. He also didn't want to have an account handled by someone who could exhibit such inappropriate behavior. The salesman learned a hard lesson. In business, keep all small-talk small. Stay away from controversial subjects. They have no place in business. You never want to be in a situation where you win a debate but lose the order.

I once said a few things I shouldn't have to an account. It cost me dearly. I had been trying for quite a while to sell a certain large retail chain on Remington. The account carried only Philips shavers and, for some reason, wouldn't let us in the door. Occasionally, the buyer would order a smattering of our products just to prove they wouldn't sell. Well, of course they didn't sell. You can't expect any item to move if you don't back it with a full commitment. If you had walked into the shaver department of this store, you would have seen a wall devoted to Philips. The few Remington shavers would be buried in some drab little corner. This didn't strike me as a very fair test.

This was an important account. Establishing a strong Remington presence in its stores would have been quite a plum. Finding the buyer's attitude frustrating as hell, I finally decided to take the bold step we discussed some pages back: I was going over his head.

I thought I might have a bit of an advantage with this risky move. Some time before, as president of Benrus, I had done business with the company's chairman, an older man who now took only a semi-active role in the company. We had gotten along just fine. His son was the company's CEO. Hoping to trade off on some old family ties, I called the young man to plead the Remington case. I introduced myself as someone who had dealt with his father and said, "I've been trying to sell our product to your buyer for over a year. I believe I have the best shaver on the market. We are backing that claim with a major advertising investment. I'd like an opportunity to come in, show you our product, and lay out our strategy. I think we could be very good for each other."

The first thing he asked me when I finished was, "I think I might be interested in seeing you. But, first, tell me who you've been dealing with?"

I said, "George Frazier, and he's my biggest problem!"

"He is? Why?"

"Because he is one of the stupidest, most opinionated buyers I've ever run into. I keep bringing him product and programs and he won't even discuss them. He keeps saying no, but offers no explanations."

The CEO cleared his throat and said, "Well, you also don't understand something else."

"What's that?"

"That stupid, opinionated buyer is my brother-in-law!"

Oh.

It took quite a crowbar to dislodge my foot from between my lips. I think I lost three toes during the process. I still don't know what took hold of me. I guess I had been swallowing a lot of bile while trying to deal with the buyer and it had to be purged. No matter, I should have used the perfect scenario drawn up when I dealt with the head of Gray's drugstores. If I had kept the scathing, personal remarks to myself, praised the buyer to the skies, and then presented our dispute as a simple difference of opinion, I think I would have had a decent hearing. We might have had a sale. Instead, we were banned by the buyer for more than three years. As long as he retained his position, we couldn't even get an appointment. It taught me something I've never forgotten: never, ever blast an employee or a co-worker when you're dealing with an account, no matter what the provocation. Once you do, you've jumped into a mined harbor. It's only a matter of time until something explodes.

Throughout much of this chapter, I've said or implied that

you have to keep the customer satisfied. You do. However, you should never let anyone use you as a doormat. My wife runs a company called the Friendship Collection. It is the largest importer of jewelry from the People's Republic of China in the U.S. About three years ago, it was approached by a department store chain—call it Bigstore's—to put together a mammoth promotion. It required our flooding the chain's over forty stores with a huge selection of Friendship jewelry.

The company asked to be billed on consignment. Every thirty days they would settle up with us on whatever they had sold. I'm usually against consignment. I've always believed that you should make an account pay for its merchandise as soon as possible. Let them share in the risk of moving the item. It increases their incentive to make the merchandise a success.

Despite this, it seemed like a good idea to make an exception in this case. Bigstore's was a prestigious account, a trendsetter. If we made a big splash there it would receive widespread publicity throughout the industry. This would have to impact favorably on our business with other stores. They would be clamoring for our lines. We decided to go along with their request.

We developed a marketing and advertising program with Bigstore's. At the end of the first month, we send them a bill for what they had sold. Six weeks go by without payment. We send them another invoice. This time it reflects their current balance plus the amount past due. We don't hear a thing. When we call the company's accounts payable department, we receive the eighties version of that old standby, "Your check is in the mail." The manager tells us, "Oh, I'm sure we've approved that payment. Your check must be in the computer." He assures us it will be forthcoming.

We accepted this and went right on shipping merchandise. The stuff was selling like crazy, and we became so caught up in its success that we no longer pressed to collect the balance due. The Friendship Collection was doing so well, we assumed it was in Bigstore's interest to keep us happy. We also thought of Bigstore's as an established, trusted name in the business. You can expect your bigger clients to fall behind in paying. Their sheer size often ensures this will happen and you make allow-ances for a prized customer. You do want everyone to pay on time. If you offer terms of net thirty and you get paid in ninety, you are undoubtedly going to suffer a bit. However, it's not a tragedy as long as you do get paid. We knew we'd get our money and, after a while, we did.

Sort of.

Nine months into the relationship, I was going over Friend-ship's accounts receivable. We had sent Bigstore's goods worth a total of $400,000. They had, as promised by that manager, sent us a check.

One check.

For $322.87.

Of course the first thing I wanted to know was where did the eighty-seven cents come from? The next thing I wanted to know was the whereabouts of our $399,677.13!

I called Bigstore's jewelry buyer and asked him the same question. He said, "I can't believe that hasn't been paid yet. Let me check with our merchandise manager and one of us will get back to you." Between the two of them I got the royal runaround for the next three months. When I called to ask why we still hadn't been paid, the buyer explained that they were trying to pull together the sales records of each individual store to make sure our billing was accurate. I knew I was in trouble then. That sort of undertaking could take forever, and that's if they were doing the job quickly. Of course, I didn't think they were doing the job at all.

As an alternative, we offered to wait till the end of the year, when the figures would be easily lifted from Bigstore's annual chain-wide inventory. Those numbers would arrive in less than two months.

When they came in, Bigstore's claimed they showed a wide disparity between what they owed and what we billed. They alleged we had failed to deliver some of our goods. The mer-chandise manager refused to pay us a cent until we produced proof of delivery for every single shipment to each of the chain's forty stores.

That took six months. We'd now been dancing with these

fellows for more than a year and a half. The promotion was going great guns but it was tearing our insides out. We produced the evidence substantiating our claims and presented Bigstore's with a bill for the full amount. You'll never guess what they did. Looking at the invoice, a Bigstore's executive said, "If you're going to give us a statement for this kind of money, we don't want to do business with you. Our records don't agree with yours." I had presented them with documentation supporting every figure on our invoices. These forms were signed by his employees, but this bozo was acting as if the numbers and signatures didn't exist.

Now what do you do in a case like this? As a salesman, your cardinal rule is to bend over backwards to satisfy a customer. Never do anything to destroy a relationship with a valued account. Well, we had bent over backwards. All that did was allow Bigstore's an opportunity to twist the stiletto in a bit deeper. If a customer is going to do that, don't worry about the relationship. You haven't got one.

We sued to recoup the debt. The threat of that action forced them to settle with us for a figure close to our original claims. We haven't done business with them since and don't expect to do any in the future. It was quite an account to lose. That's all right. Our company made the right decision. We got our money and our decisiveness won us a lot of respect throughout the industry. Shortly after we split with Bigstore's, a rival chain gave us a better deal on an even bigger program. And this time we got paid on schedule.

I'm often asked what makes a successful salesperson. Energy, self-confidence, confidence in whatever you are selling, an enthusiasm for your current job and its potential for growth, an ability to get along with people, and a thick skin to handle rejection, these are the primary ingredients; you combine them with good old-fashioned hard work. Since you want to get to know as much about your customers as possible, it also pays to be observant. It is often the unspoken things that can tell you the most about a person. I'd like to close this chapter with an example of what I mean.

Every year, when certain forecasts weren't met, Benrus had

to unload its excess watch inventory. Some styles would be discontinued and we would have a number of odd lots that were unattractive to retailers. The cost of storing these unwanted pieces was punitive. There were few places that would buy the extra stock. One man who operated in New York's Bowery became the watch dump site for the entire industry. His name was Tiny Grossman.

Tiny was six foot three and must have weighed a good 350 pounds. He would sit in his ramshackle office at a battered, old desk and drive the toughest bargains in the business. An ancient sign written in Yiddish hung on the wall directly behind him. The first year or two, I tried to make a few dollars in our negotiations. I'd think, "The watches cost us fourteen dollars. I'll ask for twenty dollars a watch and settle for eighteen." I quickly learned I was dreaming.

Tiny would look over the pieces. Blowing cigar smoke in your face, he'd ooh and ah over their fine craftsmanship. He'd tell you they were the most magnificent watches he'd seen all year. Then he'd offer you ten dollars apiece.

We're talking about 100,000 watches at a clip. That worked out to a $400,000 bath for Benrus. I'd do everything I could to persuade Tiny to up his offer. My pleadings did the trick every time. Tiny would move his price all the way up to $10.25. That was his final deal. What could I do? Tiny was the court of last resort. I'd take his check and use it to dry my tears on the way home.

This went on for four years. Finally, after once again being drubbed, I asked Tiny if he didn't have any pity for us. He pointed to the sign in back of him and said, "Can't you read?" I couldn't read or understand a word of Yiddish, so I asked him to translate. He said, "That's my philosophy. It says 'Your hernia is my blessing!'" Great! All this time that placard had been staring me in the face. If I had just bothered to have it translated earlier, if I had paid more attention to Tiny's environment, I'd have had an insight into the man. It might have helped with the negotiations. You just can't tell what a difference this might have made.

Why, I might have even got him up as high as $10.50!

4

Business Is a Game, But Not Everyone Plays by the Rules

I've often told novice entrepreneurs, "Business is a game. Play it to win." That advice is not, however, license to pursue victory at all costs. The player who will double-deal to win has no place in my game. He is not an entrepreneur. An entrepreneur loves challenges and risks. What sort of thrill can you possibly get from winning a contest you've rigged?

In playing by the rules, however, you mustn't ever forget that you will sometimes run into businesspeople who lack your integrity. Be alert! A well-fanged viper can take a healthy chunk out of your entrepreneurial dream. That reptile can cost you money, ruin an enterprise, or, worst of all, destroy a reputation. I know. I've been bitten. Fortunately, I've come out of these skirmishes relatively unscarred. I'd like to tell you about four of them.

The Opera Ain't Over Till the Fat Lady Sings

One of my first encounters with this brand of snake occurred during my early days at Remington. We were expanding our overseas operations. Under Sperry, the distribution for our shavers in Italy was handled by a Mr. Belmudo. He had won this right by making a very questionable deal with Remington's Italian representative, Mr. Crassi. Mr. Belmudo was slipping under-the-table payments to Crassi. These gratuities often came as cash, but would occasionally take the form of a trinket, like a Mercedes Benz. You ever try to slip a Mercedes Benz underneath a table? That must have been one large piece of furniture.

Sperry, of course, was unaware of the arrangement. Nothing in Crassi's past suggested he was capable of this sort of skullduggery. When he told Sperry that Belmudo was the man to distribute the shavers in Italy, the company took him at his word. It assumed Belmudo was a first-class distributor. Sperry had no way of knowing that Belmudo didn't know a thing about the appliance business. He had run other, unrelated companies with little success and saw the Remington deal as a chance to finally make good.

To manage the business, Belmudo wanted to hire a mysterious Italian beauty named Madame Destazia. During her initial meetings with Belmudo and Crassi, she represented herself as having contacts at the highest levels in the Italian government. Her credentials were impeccable. So impeccable, in fact, that no one could verify them. Among other things, she claimed she had been an administrator under the Italian Secretary of State and had been a paid government consultant for the last ten years. She also claimed her job involved the handling of sensitive information, requiring her to work under deep cover. Therefore, if anyone asked the government anything about her, they would deny she ever worked for them. Well, it's not every day you get to hire one of John le Carré's characters to run your operation. Crassi agreed to Destazia's coming on board.

Belmudo named her as his company's managing director. She took over the distributorship just as I took title to Remington. Our first days on the job were somewhat dissimilar. I arrived in Bridgeport in my faithful old car, dressed in what I hoped was a tasteful but unextraordinary business suit. The only piece of glitter on me was my watch. Madame Destazia showed up for work in Italy in a block-long Rolls-Royce, bedecked in mink from head to toe and dripping with enough precious stones to make the Liz Taylor collection look paltry. If this woman was playing a part, she was certainly playing it to the hilt.

Remington's Italian operation came under the jurisdiction

of our English managers. In a first meeting with them, Madame Destazia overwhelmed these guys. She laid out a plan that utilized all her connections. It vowed to make Remington Italy's number one shaver in a short time. That was quite a promise. When it was made, Remington commanded less than 10 percent of that country's shaver market.

She worked out a deal with the English representatives that required our shipping an enormous amount of product. As a rule, Remington gives its distributors terms of net ninety days. You have to pay for the shavers within three months of their delivery. Madame Destazia wanted net 180 days. My English managing director cabled her request to me. I refused. He called me and said, "I'm convinced this woman can triple or even quadruple our business. However, she'd be building the business from almost nothing and feels she needs these terms to make a go of it. I've seen her plan; I think she's worth the risk." I still wasn't convinced, but he kept the pressure on until I finally gave him the go-ahead.

We shipped her order. The first results were miraculous. She claimed business had immediately shot up to almost six times over what it had been the previous year. Every cable from Italy brought news of even greater sales by them and orders from us. After the four months, our market share had zoomed. My managing director was more than just a little pleased with himself. His monthly reports from England would often carry five pages on Italy and only a few paragraphs covering the rest of Europe.

We had shipped Destazia's order in early July. By the end of the year the invoices, now totaling almost $400,000, were coming due. We didn't receive a penny. Letters were sent to Destazia and Belmudo demanding payment. Their response was a purchase order for an additional $100,000. They hadn't paid for a single shaver and they were trying to order several thousand more!

By now, the managing director of our English company was feeling a bit uneasy. He sent a representative down to Italy to demand either immediate payment or the return of the shavers. The rep was picked up at the airport and whisked off to Mr.

Belmudo's warehouse. Once there, he was brought to the Remington holding area by Madame Destazia. There wasn't a shaver in sight. Madame Destazia gushed, "You see, we have sold them all. That is why we need another order and we need to have it soon." Though the sight of the bejeweled Madame Destazia reveling in her triumph was dazzling, our rep was able to maintain his senses long enough to ask a simple question, "If you sold all the shavers, where is the money?" Destazia giggled and said, "I've been naughty. I gave our customers longer terms than I should have. Their payments are only just starting to trickle in, but there is no need to worry." With that, she produced a small mountain of invoices indicating payments due. They seemed to back up everything she was claiming. To put our man even further at ease, Destazia wrote out a check to Remington for $10,000. She said, "Here, take this as a sign of good faith. It is not a company check. I have so much trust in my clients and this enterprise that I have drawn it on my personal account. But please, ship me that order. We have a growing business here, but it is a fragile one. We must keep it moving or our momentum will die."

What could the rep do? He didn't want the company to be ripped off, but at the same time he couldn't risk destroying everything Remington had accomplished in Italy. Torn by doubts, he called our managing director in England and explained the situation. He was told to deposit the check in the Remington account. If it cleared, the company would ship Madame Destazia's order.

The check did not bounce. The order was sent and we drew up a schedule of payments for the rest of the monies owed. The first deadline came. The first deadline passed. No cash. This time, we sent a private detective and a lawyer to Italy for a surprise visit. Finding Madame Destazia at the warehouse, they asked to see her books. Madame Destazia couldn't have been more gracious. She brought them to her office, gave them espresso and pastries, and allowed them access to all of her records. She then explained that she was about to have lunch with her accountant and that she would return with him as soon as they had finished. That meal has to be in *The Guinness Book of*

Records as the longest lunch in history. It must still be going on because Madame Destazia was never heard from again. She just vanished.

Sifting through her records, we discovered that she had indeed sold all those shavers and had received payment. However, the corporate account showed almost none of the money due. It looked as though Madame Destazia had apparently given herself one whopping commission. We later found out that she had kept very little of the swag for herself. She had donated the bulk of the proceeds—over $200,000—to the La Scala opera house. We also found out how she had been able to turn the business around so dramatically. She had been selling the shavers for less than she was paying for them! Destazia, traveling about in her limo, would deliver them personally to the retailers and accept payment in cash. Talk about bizarre twists, this one absolutely boggled my mind.

With her gone, we sued Belmudo for getting us into this mess. He immediately declared bankruptcy. We couldn't pierce his corporate veil and the court held he had no responsibility as an individual. It was just as well. Despite his shady dealings, Belmudo was an innocent in this case. He had been taken for a ride by Destazia and found himself ruined.

We went after Crassi for his under-the-table dealings with Belmudo. He claimed he was an American citizen and could not be sued in Italy. We pursued the case in the U.S. The court ruled that since the entire transaction had taken place in Italy, he had to be sued over there. Catch-22. Crassi got off scot-free, but his reputation suffered irreparable damage. Both he and Belmudo had been burned because they were already playing a crooked game. The kickbacks to Crassi were evidence of this. Their satisfaction didn't come from jobs well done; it came from lining their purses. They were made to order for an operator like Destazia. Remington took its lumps because we were blinded by the opportunity. Destazia had painted the Trojan Horse of vistas. When you're an entrepreneur, you don't look a gift horse in the mouth. You look behind its ears, peer up its nose, and take it around the track a few times. Madame Destazia, in offering to make us the top shaver in Italy, had followed a practice of Chairman Corleone. She had made us an offer too good to refuse. When someone comes along offering to give you the world, that's when the alarm bells should sound off and the red lights should start flashing. You shouldn't shy away. However, make sure you have all your questions answered before proceeding. We should have insisted that Madame Destazia back up her curriculum vitae with tangible references. We also shouldn't have varied our terms. If we had monitored the program more closely, we might have avoided a mess that hurt everyone involved. Everyone except Destazia and, of course, the opera company. It ended up giving the good Madame an award as one of its most outstanding patrons of the arts.

A Most Expensive Parking Ticket

Parents often tell their children, "Tell the truth. I don't care what it is you've done wrong, you will only make it worse by lying." It's true. If you make a mistake, own up to it. Tell your boss you spilled hot coffee in the lap of your most important client. He'll understand, even if the scorched client doesn't. Covering up your mistakes with lies won't change reality. It can only cost you your self-respect, the respect of your peers, and your job.

I recently saw an example of this in one of my companies outside of the United States. The fellow involved was a good fellow and a dynamite salesman. Let's call him Tim Burke. His boss—Mr. Tiptop—was a meticulous fellow, living and dying by the book.

Mr. Tiptop had a rule. If you were out on a sales call and were stuck with a parking ticket, it was your bad luck. One day, Tim was calling on a major client. This meeting lasted longer than he had anticipated. When he got out of it, he found that his car had been ticketed. The fine was $25.

Mr. Burke had not made a sale at his meeting, so perhaps frustration colored his reaction to the ticket. Whatever the reason, he decided that Remington was going to pay for his mistake.

Tim knew, of course, that he could not claim the money in his expenses. At least, he couldn't enter it as reimbursement for a parking ticket. So he got around this technicality by claiming he had taken a buyer, Miss Sales, to lunch that day. He recorded the cost of the meal—wouldn't you know it was $25—and put in an expenses chit.

Have you ever heard the blues song that proclaims, "If it weren't for bad luck, I wouldn't have no luck at all"? It's called "Born Under a Bad Sign." Tim Burke may not have been cursed at birth, but he was sure living under a bad sign on this particular day. It so happened that his boss had been on the phone that afternoon and had spoken with the very buyer that Burke had claimed he was taking to lunch. The call had nothing to do with Tim. Mr. Tiptop was just making some general inquiries about the account. At the end of the chat, Miss Sales mentioned that Tim Burke was supposed to be calling on her that day. At four o'clock.

When Tim handed in his voucher, it listed the bogus lunch. Seeing it, Mr. Tiptop thought, "Now this is odd. I spoke to Miss Sales at two. She had just come back from lunch. She made no mention of having it with Tim and in fact said she expected to see him at four. Either she is a crazy, a world-class eater, or Timothy is fibbing." He called Miss Sales and asked if she and Tim had gone out to eat. No. Summoning Burke, he asked him to explain the entry. Tim hemmed and hawed, but finally told his boss the truth. Tiptop let him off with a stern reprimand. An embarrassed Tim left the office, thinking the incident was behind him. It wasn't. All business associations are built on trust. With this small infraction, Burke had planted doubts in his boss's mind. He had undermined their relationship.

Over the next few months, Mr. Tiptop kept a careful eye on Tim's expenses. He was looking for the slightest discrepancy. It didn't take long to find one. The company was holding a sales meeting in another city on a Monday morning. Tim was booked into a hotel room for Sunday night. For reasons that remain fuzzy, Tim missed his Sunday flight and didn't arrive at the hotel until Monday afternoon. His room was given to a different individual. By the time Tim joined the meeting, it was already half over. Burke should have called his boss and admitted his error. Instead, he panicked.

Tim was supposed to be in town on Sunday evening for a Monday morning meeting. Tim was expected to include a receipt for his room in his expenses report. The absence of that statement could tip off his boss that he had missed his flight. Burke covered up by taking the bill for the hotel meeting room and placing it in his expenses report. The idea was to trick the company into believing it represented the charge for his own unused quarters.

This thin charade held up for about five minutes. In going over the expenses for the entire meeting, Mr. Tiptop wondered why the company hadn't been charged for a meeting room. The hotel was not a philanthropic organization; they had always billed Remington in the past. He called the establishment and asked what had happened. The hotel manager replied, "Oh yes, you've been billed as usual. In fact, Mr. Burke picked up the statement and said he would take care of it."

Tiptop then phoned several people who had attended the conference. The truth came out. This time there was no reprimand. Burke was told to clean out his desk. Neither of his missteps were terribly serious. A $25 parking ticket and a missed meeting are not two of life's great tragedies. It was the lack of candor that finished Tim.

Another Gift Horse

Wouldn't you suppose that getting a check for over two million dollars was a cause for celebration? Ordinarily it would be. However, a check made out to Victor K. Kiam for something more than that amount was not drawn under ordinary circumstances.

Sitting in my office on a rainy Friday morning, I was going over the copy for our latest Remington commercial. That exercise was interrupted when my secretary informed me I had a phone call. This caller's name was unfamiliar, so I asked that she take a message. The fellow on the line wouldn't settle for that.

He explained that it was an emergency and that he had to speak to me immediately.

Emergency? Thoughts of accidents and ambulances crowded my head. I jumped on the phone and was greeted by a pleasant, modulated voice saying, "Mr. Kiam, you don't know me. I work on Wall Street. I was walking to the office this morning and, well, I don't know how to say this exactly, but were you expecting a check anytime soon?" That seemed a simple enough question, but I didn't have an answer, the volume of business is so great it's often impossible for me to keep track of every minor transaction. I said, "It's possible. Why do you ask?" He replied that he had found a check made out to me. The caller had snared it just after a stiff wind had sent it fluttering up Wall Street.

After first thanking him, I said that the check could be for almost anything and that he should send it to our accountants. I was all set to switch him over to them when he said, "Well, Mr. Kiam, I really don't want to put it in the mail. You see, it's for a very large amount." I asked him how big a check it was. In round, dulcet tones, he chimed, "It seems to be for two million, two hundred and sixty-three thousand dollars."

You can appreciate how the figure gave me pause. I don't care how busy we were, if someone owed us that much money, we would have known about it. The note was a cashier's check. This meant it could be cashed anywhere by anyone, so long as it had been endorsed by me. I needed to think. Asking the fellow for his office phone number, I promised to call him back in twenty minutes.

At this point, I had two alternatives. I might get back to this man, give him a generous reward, and then cash the check in a hurry. Couldn't do it. I knew darn well that I wasn't due a check for that amount from the bank. This would have been accepting the money under false pretenses.

The second alternative was far more viable. I called a friend in the banking business. When I first phoned, he thought I was pulling his leg. Couldn't blame him for that. Having been assured I was serious, he said, "The first thing you must do is have the check picked up from this guy. Now as long as you're certain that this isn't some legitimate payment you've forgotten about, you should also call the bank. I suggest one of their agents should make the collection. If you like, I'll also send over one of my lawyers and a security guard to witness the transaction."

The transfer took place and was duly recorded. That afternoon, the bank's security chief called, thanking me for my prompt response in the matter. He also asked that I not mention the incident to anyone. The bank was apparently conducting an internal investigation and was unwilling to risk the scorching glare of publicity. It knew that would damage its inquiry. When I asked if I could give a reward to the man who had found the check the chief said, "No, that won't be necessary. You stay out of this. We will take care of the gentleman. Then I think it would be best if you forgot this ever happened."

How could I do that? I mean this was a check for over two million dollars, not forty-four cents! Over the next four months, I had my lawyer periodically call the bank to find out what had occurred. We couldn't learn a thing. Finally, the truth came out as part of a major scandal. Employees at a particular branch of this prestigious institution had been issuing cashier's checks in the names of famous people. They would be endorsed and then cashed. The scam had netted these con artists almost twelve million dollars before they were apprehended. A bit of Sherlock Holmes in me prefers to think I had a tiny hand in their capture. I must say I still can't believe these people thought they could get away with it. The incident only proves that some people are greedy enough to try anything. It also taught me a lesson in the disadvantages of being too well known. Of course, I suppose the perpetrators may have been giving me a backhanded compliment. After all, I didn't notice them signing the Philips president's name to any of those checks.

The Galloping Venture Capitalist

Some years after leaving Remington, Harry Stokes was considering an investment in a company that produced ship fittings. He was receiving some assistance in this enterprise from a young venture capitalist named Tom Barron. Harry was very impressed with this man. He often told me, "Vic, if you're ever looking to raise some money for a project, this is a fellow you should meet. We're getting together with him next week and I would like you to be there." I always treated advice from Harry like the Sermon on the Mount. Though Harry didn't know it at the time, I was already involved in a project requiring some venture capital.

My deal was in the formative stages. It involved purchasing a company called Maui Divers, a maker of fine coral jewelry. Located in Hawaii, they had a government license to operate a submarine. This sub carried two passengers. It would patrol the ocean floor searching for coral. Reaching a reef, it would use two crablike claws to cut the coral. The now severed prize would be dropped into a basket attached to the sub and carried off to be transformed into delicate pieces of jewelry. The government license was exclusive. No other company was allowed to mine that ocean for these exquisite skeletons.

The venture-capital group looking to back this investment was giving me a rough time. I felt they wanted too much equity in return for their money. Their stubbornness and Harry's recommendation made Mr. Barron a very attractive figure. I accepted Stokes's invitation.

As it happened, Barron and I were practically neighbors. He owned a brownstone less than six blocks from where we made our New York headquarters. Barron kept his business offices on one floor. When I got there, the joint was jumping. Secretaries were bustling back and forth; the phone never stopped ringing. It was all very impressive.

I was greeted by Mr. Barron. A tall, bearish-looking fellow, he smoked a cigar and appeared rather soft-spoken. When he did speak, you got the idea that he was giving you "The Word." He was like an oracle. Before the meeting with Stokes and his partner got underway, we discussed the Maui venture. Barron agreed that the project had possibilities. He said he would examine it further and get back to me with some suggestions.

About this time, a deal came along that stole my attention from Maui Divers. It was Remington. That project consumed most of my time for the next few months. After its completion,

I ended up getting involved with Harry and his nautical venture. Stokes was living in Tucson, Arizona. His partner lived in Connecticut. Barron had provided the financing. Since Barron's home was practically right next door to my own, I began to see Tom on a regular basis. We would often breakfast together while discussing the ship-fitting venture.

Besides going over the Stokes project, Tom was always bringing me other ventures. One of the first was a company that imported fine European wood carvings. Its owner was a man who had no formal business training. He had done amazingly well on his own. Looking to expand the operation, he now needed both financial and managerial help. I thought he had a heck of a business, but I wasn't interested. This didn't deter Tom. It seemed as if he was bringing me a new idea every other week. I have to admit I loved his energy and enthusiasm.

One day he called me at my office. He said, "Victor, I'm selling my country home and I'm taking out a second mortgage on my brownstone. I have a super deal and I need capital fast. You've got some idea of the different things I have my finger in. I am fully extended at the moment. The mortgage is more than enough to cover what I need, but I won't get the money until that deal is closed. That will take too much time. I need about $20,000 to tide me over." I was about to tell him that my own finances were tight—the Remington purchase after all was not a small one—but he had already anticipated me. He said, "Victor, I wouldn't want the money from you. I'm going to apply for a loan to be paid back in six months. I was wondering, first, would you recommend a bank and, second, would you be the guarantor for the loan?"

I had just received a loan on behalf of our Friendship Jewelry Company from a New Jersey bank. I called the loan officer and said, "I know this fellow who wants to borrow some money short term. He's in venture capital and he's working with some friends of mine. At the moment, he's borrowed up to his ears and is not sure he can get any more credit. Would you look over his papers? He's getting a second mortgage soon and the loan will be paid off. If you won't lend him the cash directly, I'll guarantee it." That was not a bright decision on my part. By offering to cosign for the loan, I was giving the bank the perfect out. The loan to Barron was risk-free if they had me ready to take full responsibility for the entire amount.

The loan officer agreed to interview Barron. He called me the day after the meeting. "You know," the banker said, "this is an impressive fellow. He's into so many different things. He showed me his projects, we've looked at the value of his house. We'd like to give him the loan, but with all the projects he's got going, we would indeed like you to be the guarantor." I acquiesced. At the time it wasn't a hard choice to make. Tom seemed to be running a well-organized and thriving company. I trusted him. In fact, I trusted Tom too much. Just as a matter of sound business procedure, I should have obtained a lien against his house. It would have given me access to his money if he failed to make good on the loan. That's hindsight. Instead, I cosigned the loan without obtaining any legal means of redress if Barron defaulted.

I didn't pay any further attention to the transaction. Remington was commanding all of my time and concentration. Eight months after the loan had been approved, I was reviewing my finances. I wondered, "How come we haven't heard anything on that Barron loan? Tom hasn't been around since he got the money. I have no idea whether it's been paid off or not. I better call the bank."

As it turned out, the loan officer was about to phone me. Not only did the bank records show that the loan's principal was still outstanding, they also indicated that Tom hadn't paid any interest in over four months.

I got off the phone to call Tom. Instead of reaching him, I was connected to a recording informing me that Mr. Barron could no longer be reached at this number. He had left New York and had also left my favorite entrepreneur holding the bag.

We conducted a search. I found an old telephone book that listed the number for his house in New Jersey. We did reach a party there. They informed us that they had just recently bought the home from Mr. Barron, but that the former owner had not left any forwarding address or phone number. I contacted Harry Stokes and his partner. They didn't know where Tom was either.

Getting back to the bank, I explained that Barron could not be found. I asked them to conduct their own investigation. With their resources, they could scour many of the nation's banks. If they found an account bearing Barron's name, we'd know where he was. Their explorations couldn't turn up a single clue.

As cosignatory, I was on that hook for the full amount of the loan plus any interest due. However, the bank couldn't press me for the funds until they had conducted a search, "with due diligence." They had to exhaust every avenue in trying to find Tom Barron.

A short while after this incident came to light, my son Tory entered the Harvard Business School. One holiday he came home lugging a poster that had been up in school. It read:

TOM BARRON
AMERICA'S TOP VENTURE CAPITALIST
WILL BE
ADDRESSING
THE ENTREPRENEURIAL CLASS
OF THE
HARVARD BUSINESS SCHOOL

Tory, knowing nothing about the loan, innocently asked, "This is a fellow you knew, isn't it, Dad?" I said, "You're damned right I knew him! He stuck me! When was he up there?" It had only been the previous week.

I called the Harvard Business School. They didn't have Barron's address. He had conducted his business with them over the phone. They gave me a number. When I called, the phone was answered by a person who claimed never to have heard of Tom Barron. Welcome to the twilight zone.

A couple of months go by. One morning, I am reading a copy of a business magazine. It contains an article entitled something like "America's number-one venture capitalist is riding high." Guess who the article was about? Bingo! It was an interview with the enigmatic Mr. Barron. The article showcased all the marvelous deals Barron had engineered.

The publisher of the magazine happened to be a friend of

mine. I got in touch with him and asked how I could reach Barron. He checked with the fellow who wrote the story. Another false lead. Apparently, Barron had made all the arrangements for the article by phone. He had sent the magazine a packet of autobiographical material bearing no return address. The actual interview took place in the magazine's New York office. I had seen this film before. Claude Rains plays a wacky scientist. He enters an English inn dressed in bandages. Whenever he wants to indulge in a little bit of mayhem, he whips off the gauze and vanishes into thin air. I was chasing the Invisible Man!

He didn't even give us the luxury of a few clues. In the interview, he mentioned several companies he had funded or brought public. When you called information for their phone numbers, you discovered they were nonexistent.

These dead-ends both frustrated and tantalized me. I was determined to find this guy. Finally, we got a lead from a most unexpected source. I came home one evening to find my wife Ellen reading a circular. It invited Ellen to be profiled in a new book spotlighting female entrepreneurs. The book's author? Yes, it was the Invisible Man himself. This brash SOB had the nerve to ask my wife for an interview!

The request listed some of Mr. Barron's previous tomes. You've seen these sort of books. They all have titles like *How to Make Your First Three Million Before the Age of Eight.* His books were published by some company in California. I immediately called the publisher and asked for Tom Barron. The phone was hung up. When I called back, no one answered.

While my quest was going on, the bank was dunning me for payment on my guarantee. Interest had pushed the loan up to $27,000. I took the circular and the accompanying letter to the bank and reminded them that they were obliged to try to find Barron before coming to me. "Your man is somewhere in Marin County," I said. "Go get him."

Believe it or not, the bank finds him. It demands immediate satisfaction. Barron pays them all the interest due, but not a penny of principal. The bank then calls me and says, "Mr. Barron is contesting the loan. He claims he's made principal payments that we haven't recorded." How's that for a stall? Of course, the bank sees through this ruse. They know if Barron had given them a penny he would have a canceled check and the bank would have the transaction in its files. Despite the transparency of this ploy, the bank was now forced to dredge up its records, send copies of payment to Barron, and wait for him to reply. It started to look as if this thing would never end.

Six months of correspondence between the bank and Barron begin. The interest starts to pile up again. Finally, the bank decides to sue Barron.

I went to a meeting in England thinking the bank had finally got a handle on this thing. I had intended to be gone for a month. An emergency put a crimp in my plans and forced me to return home early. The matter was serious enough for me to take the Concorde for the return flight. As I got on board the plane, I saw Tom Barron and his wife already seated. I suddenly felt like a benign version of the policeman in *Crime and Punishment*.

I'm sitting in the back of the jet, completely out of their view. I don't do a thing during the flight. After landing, I go up to him as he's waiting for his luggage. We talk. I ask, "Tom, what the hell is going on with this loan?" He gives me the same story he's been giving the bank. He's paid most of it, but the records are in error. I told him what he could do with that fine tale, and then I said, "Tom, just pay what you owe. When you walked out on the bank, you walked out on me. We've been friends. Don't cheat a friend." I grabbed my luggage and left.

Calling the bank on the following day, I told them Barron was in town and apparently quite solvent. His wife was draped in mink and they had flown in on the Concorde. They thanked me and said they'd get right on it. The result? I got a notice from the loan officer only a few months ago. Barron's company had gone bankrupt. Over twenty million dollars of investors' funds had floated up to the ozone. There was even talk that charges of fraud would be brought against my former buddy. The bank did not want to stand in what had become a long line of outraged creditors. They had completed their due diligence. I had to pay back the loan.

I was taken in by Mr. Barron. He gave every appearance of being a man worthy of trust and respect. I thought he was an entrepreneur. I was wrong. Don't make the same mistake. Ninety-nine percent of the people you'll meet in business will be honest. Just be aware of the exceptions.

You may now be asking yourself, How can I protect my interests and my ideas? Your concepts—no matter how innovative—aren't worth anything unless they give birth to a tangible enterprise. In order to sell the venture or to acquire the capital needed to launch it, you'll have to share the idea with others. Document every move you make! Whenever you frame the idea in a letter, send it via registered mail and be sure to have copies sent to your lawyer and/or business manager.

Learn from the experience of Mike Shanley. Shanley had created a national promotion that seemed perfect for a certain large American corporation that we will call the Omnipotent Corporation. He brought the idea to its marketing team. Omnipotent looked it over for about a month and then rejected it, writing, "Though this is a fine idea, we just can't see doing anything like this at this time." Since the idea was tailored for Omnipotent and was inappropriate for any other sponsor, Shanley put it in his turn-down file and forgot about it. Six months later, he's watching TV. An Omnipotent commercial comes on, singing the praises of its latest national promotion. It's the very idea Shanley had proposed. They are even using the name he had suggested.

As soon as he recovered from the shock, Shanley called his lawyer. Mike had documented his idea. The initial proposal and all subsequent correspondence had been sent with a return receipt requested. In addition, he had held on to the letter of rejection. Armed with this evidence, his attorney approached Omnipotent and came away with a fat settlement for his client. Mike had been wise. Without documentation, he wouldn't have collected a dime.

There are other methods of protection. Some of them—like taping your business conversations—invade gray areas of legality and should not be done. They may support your case, but could also be inadmissible in a court of law. Why take chances? Invest a few dollars in a good attorney and have him outline the various precautions you can take. It will save you a lot of head-aches.

One other thing you should remember. The four episodes described in this chapter all had at least one thing in common: the central charades were spun of the flimsiest gossamer. You often won't be fooled unless you allow yourself to be fooled. Always remember that all that glitters is just glitter. Then you'll take time to find the true gold. For example, if I had looked behind the Barron facade and demanded tangible collateral, this tale would have had a different ending. No matter, I guess it could have been worse. I lost over $20,000 but I came away a wiser man. As for Mr. Barron, I have no idea what has happened to him. Perhaps he's off somewhere with Madame Destazia. Writing an opera.

5

Your Reputation:
More Precious Than Gold

Those people who refused to play their entrepreneurial hand according to Hoyle forgot a very important tenet. For the entrepreneur, nothing is more valuable than his good reputation. Without one, you'll be hard pressed to do business for very long. It is your coin of the realm! A good reputation can help open the doors to investment capital, and will make your product or service more desirable to the public. It will also allow you to sleep soundly at night. Never underestimate its worth.

When we first started writing *Going For It!,* we hired a service run by a Mr. Goodpromise to transcribe the hours of tape that eventually comprised its text. The fellow we hired seemed to have his act together. He promised to transform tape into finished copy within three days. His rates were competitive, his offices seemed to be in order, and his work samples looked outstanding.

At first, he delivered as promised. The results were dazzling. As the job wore on, however, the copy deteriorated. Whole sections of dialogue were missing. Typos, some of them terribly confusing, increased. Instead of taking three days, the turnaround time had gone to a week. The problems were an annoyance, but we managed to cope. We were still right on target for our deadline and seemed to have neither the time nor the need to find a replacement.

Unfortunately, as we reached the final chapters, things got worse. We dropped off a pair of cassettes. After two weeks, the work still wasn't finished. We phoned Goodpromise twice a day, demanding to know when the copy would be ready. Each time, Goodpromise vowed we would have it in our hands by the next day. All the next day would bring was another rash of excuses. We finally were forced to pay Mr. Goodpromise a surprise visit. When we arrived we found the reason for his delinquent service. Goodpromise, for reasons best known to himself, had let go of most of his staff. He was now doing all the work—ours and others—on his own. Though he had sworn our copy was "80 to 90 percent done," we discovered that it had hardly been touched.

We did the only thing we could. He was paid for what little had been finished, and the cassettes were taken out of his hands. Given to another service, the job was completed in less than three days. The incident gave us a few nervous moments, but we did meet our deadline.

Two years pass. Mr. Goodpromise reads that we are about to embark on a second literary adventure. He calls me and proceeds to paint a stunning vista. He first apologized for all that had happened the last time we employed him. He explained, "I've streamlined our operation. We've got a full staff now and we're completely computerized. You have to come down to the office and see all the technology we have. The place looks like the Houston Command Center." It was an invitation we declined.

We had no intention of repeating a prior mistake. I have no idea why Mr. Goodpromise failed us during our last encounter. Perhaps he hit a financial blip and was forced to lay off staff. Those things happen. If he had come to us at the time and explained his situation, we could have worked something out. We had been that pleased with his earlier work. Instead, he fabricated excuses and very nearly did serious damage to the project. There is no way we're going to trust him with another large job. The shiny new computers and the enlarged staff don't mean a thing. If potential clients are not convinced you can deliver, you're not going to get their business.

By the way, this can work two ways. If you as the client are less than professional in your behavior, you'll have a hard time getting skilled craftsmen to work for you. Let me give you an example. A fellow you met in chapter three, Ted Barnes, owns a copy-writing service. Having seen his work, I can tell you it's first-rate. The text is clear, crisp, and Teddy never misses a deadline.

He was commissioned by a large marketing outfit to write the copy for a thirty-two-page pamphlet explaining the rules of basketball. It was not a large job. Most of the publication would be devoted to illustrations. However, it did come with a tight deadline. No problem. This sort of rush job was Teddy's specialty.

Barnes and his top sportswriter, Chris Zachry, started working on the manuscript. As each section was done, it was sent to the marketing agency's promotions manager. Each day, this manager would call, praising the copy. Then she would ask for some changes. Drastic changes. Teddy would spend half the night making the alterations. He would fax the new text to the agency by the following morning. That afternoon, he would listen in astonishment as the promotions manager would once again congratulate him on a great job and then ask him to switch back to the original text. It became painfully clear that this woman had no idea what she wanted.

Somehow, Teddy got the project done on time. Four days after the deadline, he received a call from the promotions manager. She said, "Mr. Barnes, I was about to send you a check, but we have a problem. One of my staff members has reviewed your manuscript and says it is filled with errors. Since it has already been sent to the sponsoring client and has been put to press, there is nothing we can do about it. We are not going to pay your fee until after the pamphlet has been distributed. If no one complains about false information, we will send you a check."

Errors? The first thing Teddy wanted to know was "Who on earth reviewed this thing?" He put his argument thus: "The rules and records covered in the text are pretty basic and I double-checked all the material. You know, I have to warn you about something. Lots of amateurs think they know a lot about basketball when they really don't know a thing. It wouldn't surprise me if the person who looked the pamphlet over doesn't know what he's talking about. In fact, I would bet on it." Ted wasn't being arrogant. It was not as if he thought he was incapable of making a mistake. However, he felt he was on pretty sure ground. The fellow who wrote the pamphlet, Mr. Zachry, had covered basketball for over twenty-five years. Hiring him to turn out a pamphlet on the game was like hiring Field Marshal Montgomery to write on North Africa during World War Two.

Ted sent his copy of the manuscript to a friend who covered sports for a major New York newspaper. The reporter reviewed it and couldn't find a single factual mistake. Barnes again phoned the promotions manager and challenged her claims. During the discussion, it was learned that the supposed mistakes were spotted by a nineteen-year-old office boy of dubious sports background.

Ted demanded he get paid immediately. The promotions manager refused. When he called to complain to her superior, he was told, "I'm sorry but it's her decision to make. I have to back my people up in situations like this." Teddy was forced to accept her terms. Though the fantasy had occurred to him, he couldn't very well go to her office and force her to write a check at gunpoint. Eight weeks passed. One afternoon, Ted received another call from the promotions manager. She said, "Mr. Barnes, I have that check for you. Thank you so much for doing such a terrific job. The client and his vendors are all very pleased." She went on to say how she looked forward to working with him again. Amazing! Teddy thought he was dealing with a modern Jekyll and Hyde. It was as if the earlier accusations questioning competence had never been made.

Shortly after this, that promotions manager offered Teddy another assignment. He turned her down. Ted later told me, "The money was pretty good, but I didn't need it that badly. It just wasn't worth the headaches. If they ever replace her, perhaps I'll work for them again. But I'm not touching another job from them as long as she is there." I can't blame him. That promotions manager blew it. First, her early flip-flops were unprofessional. In administering a project, especially one that has to be done in a hurry, clarity is a must. Second, she should have called Ted the moment she sensed there might be a problem with the copy. This would have given him the opportunity to either allay her fears or make the necessary corrections. Finally, you should never be too quick to accept the word of a neophyte over a hired professional. If that office boy was indeed so knowledgeable, why wasn't he hired to do the pamphlet? This manager came across as an amateur. Too bad. Her behavior has, at least temporarily, cost her company the services of a crackerjack copywriter.

A person like that promotions manager can cast a foul light on her entire company. It doesn't matter that she might be an exception in what might be an otherwise first-rate crew. Unless its members are given a chance to prove otherwise, they are going to be tainted.

Be aware that this form of guilt by association can adhere to you in a number of ways. One of the first products to be sold in our retail shops was a telephone. The phones shown to us as samples seemed to be top-quality items. However, after they were delivered, we soon discovered the manufacturer had let us down. Customers started bringing the phones back and we soon had a small list of complaints. I tested a few of the instruments and discovered that their grumblings had been well founded.

Remington acted quickly. It didn't wait for any more returns. Recalling every phone, we gave each customer a refund and an apology. There was no alternative way to handle it. Remington could not afford to have a shoddy product in the stores. We couldn't allow one dud's failure to reflect on our basic line. Without this philosophy, we risked having consumers think, "Remington? Yeah, I bought that lousy phone from them. I'm not going to get stuck again. If their phone was that bad, how good can their shavers be?" The entrepreneur who doesn't do everything he can to stop that sort of customer reflection before it starts is committing corporate suicide.

This concern for your venture's image must be shared by your partners, co-workers, and employees. In the moments when they are dealing with a customer or an account, they *are* the company. It doesn't matter what position they hold. The larger your organization, the more crucial this becomes. When I first took over Remington, I inherited Paul Saltzman as credit manager. This gentleman's life has not been gentle. He had lived in Germany and had felt the lash of Nazi atrocities. He was married and had a college-aged son. That boy was the source of his greatest pride.

We experienced a rapid growth during those first two years. As a leveraged buy-out company, it was critical for us to keep a steady cash flow. We needed our accounts to pay their bills on time. In this regard, Paul was a godsend. You couldn't hope to find a more diligent fellow. A reserved, pipe-smoking gentleman, he seemed to charm our accounts into meeting their obligations. At least, that's what I thought.

The reality was somewhat different. Underneath the placid exterior, my credit manager was hiding a very low boiling point. Paul would lose his cool whenever he called on a delinquent account. It was almost as if the unpaid funds were coming out of his own pocket. As an entrepreneur, I would usually encourage such zeal in my employees. But this fellow was taking it to an extreme. He would imply that the customers were cheating him. If they disputed his allegation, Paul would rip into them with every foul word you could imagine. I mean he would curse up a blue haze.

This had apparently been going on for some time before we finally learned of it. Our sales manager had started to hear the first rumblings. In a typical exchange, he would call on a buyer and be told, "You know our credit manager has asked me to tell you he's having a difficult time with Paul Saltzman. He can't believe the way this man talks to him." The buyer would then usually continue by citing specific instances.

I was given a full report. When I asked Paul what was going on he said, "Nothing. I'm just keeping pressure on them until we get the money." I said, "That's fine, Paul, but we don't want to antagonize these people. They're important to our success. When you call them be firm, but polite." He said he would tone down his approach.

I didn't hear any complaints about Paul for about a month. Then one morning, the president of one of our accounts called me. He said, "Mr. Kiam, I know I'm one of your smaller customers and it is true we have fallen a bit behind in our payment schedule. But I don't think that's any reason to continue this campaign of verbal harassment. We will pay you soon. Now, when I told this to your credit manager, he found this most unacceptable. In fact, he responded with a stream of four-letter words that has left my ears buzzing. I like your company and your shaver. Think you're both doing a heckuva job. But if this gentleman continues to berate me or my people in this fashion, you can forget about doing business with us." I apologized profusely to the man and then headed straight for Paul's office. I was accompanied by his immediate superior, the company controller.

I told him, "Paul, we have a problem. I can't have you abusing our customers. I don't care how much money they owe, this must stop." I turned and left. As soon as I got back to the office, I took stock of the situation. The strange thing about this was that the outbursts never occurred anywhere else but on the phone. Saltzman's letters were models of business decorum, punctual and polite. In person, his demeanor bordered on shyness.

The furor suddenly died down. After several complaint-free months, it seemed as if Paul had a handle on his problem. Suddenly, tragedy struck. Paul's only son died. He was out for a while on compassionate leave. When he came back, his former behavior resurfaced. In fact, it became more intense than ever.

We recognized the seriousness of the situation. I also understood that his personal trauma had to be exacerbating his condition. What could I do? With what he'd just gone through, I couldn't fire him. I gathered the sales managers and regional directors together and asked them to smooth things over with their accounts. They were to explain what our problem was and then ask our clients to bear with us.

This kept our accounts from bolting, but it didn't seem to help poor Paul. His haranguing became intolerable. We finally insisted that he seek psychiatric help with the company paying for his weekly sessions. That seemed to do the trick for a little while. Then the dam broke again and we were forced to let him go.

Sad. We had all the compassion in the world for him, but

a company's reputation with its accounts was being jeopardized. That relationship was the lifeblood that supported several thousand jobs. We just couldn't allow it to be damaged any further.

Mr. Saltzman was given a good reference. We said he was a hard-working, aggressive credit manager. I left out any mention of his erratic deportment. I just couldn't bring myself to bad-mouth this tortured fellow. He was in his mid-fifties. Finding a new position at that age would already be hard enough. Trying to do it after having left a company beneath a cloud would be damned near impossible.

Let me give you an example of how damaging an injured reputation can be for an entrepreneur. A good friend of mine is head of a Wall Street brokerage house. He had called me extolling the virtues of Norman, a man with an exciting idea. He wanted to start a cable TV network that would allow consumers to do their shopping at home. You would see the products and their prices on screen. After listing the choices' code numbers, you would use your credit cards to order the items by phone. These purchases would then be delivered to your door.

I met with Norman over lunch. I absolutely fell in love with his concept. Considering an investment in the venture, I did a background check on him. Norman had been the president of a cellular phone company. That company had raised over five million dollars for its launch and promptly went broke. The alarm bells started ringing. I called the fellow who introduced us and said, "The guy has a fabulous plan, but unless you can find out why his other venture failed so quickly, I'm not interested. There seem to be too many similarities between that phone company and his new business."

It took a week to get the full story. Apparently, the phone company had an excellent product and an expert staff. It failed despite these virtues for one simple reason: Norman was a lousy administrator. He didn't know the first thing about running a company.

I went back to Norman and told him I would invest in his venture as long as he agreed to one proviso. He could not be the chief executive officer. He found my terms unacceptable. He insisted on heading the company. We parted. I can tell you that I was not surprised to learn later that he never was able to launch his idea. Several investors showed heavy interest until they got a close look at his background. Then they made the same demand as I did and received the same reply.

Norman could have overcome his stigma if he had been willing to compromise. No, he wouldn't have been the CEO. But if we had turned his dream into a success, his failing with the phone company would have been forgotten. He could have parlayed this triumph into other ventures. Instead, he was a man who couldn't get out of his own way. He tripped over his own ego.

This is not the first time I've seen this happen. Mack Lardner was a man with a promising communications company. He took the enterprise public and raised $8 million. One year later, the company was bankrupt.

The blame rested with Lardner. For him, being a CEO meant first-class travel around the country, chauffeured limousines, exorbitant expense accounts, and plush offices befitting royalty. It was almost as if the business was an afterthought. Compounding this, Lardner just did not know how to run a business. When the company went under, tales of his extravagance surged through the industry. He is currently trying to launch a comeback. It's been a struggle. Though each one of his new ventures is attractive, no one will take a risk on them as long as he insists on being at their helm. Investors have told him this. He just doesn't seem to get the message.

This was not the case with Lyle Adams. Lyle had been a sales manager at Playtex. He was lured away from that position by a lucrative, two-year contract with the Revlon company. One afternoon, he was called into Charles Revson's office just as the pact was about to expire.

Lyle felt he had done a pretty good job. He had just returned from a successful business trip and figured this meeting would be the opening of negotiations on a new agreement. It wasn't quite that. Mr. Revson opened the discussion by asking, "Lyle, how long have you been with us?"

"Two years."

"I see. And what's the length of your contract?"

"Two years."

"Uh-huh. Well, I guess your contract is about up, Lyle."

That was the whole meeting. By the time Lyle got back to his office, his name was already being removed from the door. Revson never even told him why he was being dismissed. Now unemployed and middle-aged, Adams had a dickens of a time trying to find a position. Getting fired by a company at the end of your first contract is not the sort of thing that inspires confidence in a prospective employer.

Luckily, Mr. Adams is nobody's fool. He realized that the chances of his getting work on an upper executive level were slim. He came up with an entrepreneurial solution. Adams called on a young, growing company. He took a position that offered a sizable pay cut and a backward step on the corporate ladder. None of that bothered him. Lyle Adams was an entrepreneur. He had confidence that, given a chance to perform, he would work his way back toward the top. His vibrant self-belief was rewarded. Mr. Adams is once again ensconced in the top tier of a major corporation. Had he been too prideful to assess his situation honestly, he might never have recovered from the Revson firing.

I've seen a powerful example of this in my own company. A few years ago, I was introduced to a bright fellow who was in the midst of a private hell. He had been the executive vice-president of a company that had gone bankrupt. That company's failure was bad enough, but to compound the issue, its president was tried and convicted for engaging in illegal business practices. He was sent to prison.

The vice-president was as honest a man as you could want to meet. He wasn't charged with any crimes. When he claimed he had no idea what his superior had been up to, no one directly involved with the case doubted him.

Despite this and the man's outstanding credentials, he was unable to find another job. Potential employers saw a shipwrecked enterprise, a CEO imprisoned for fraud, and they figured the number-two man had to be in on it no matter what the law believed. This fellow went almost a year without coming close to being hired. At fifty-four years old, things were looking mighty bleak.

I was convinced that this fellow would be an asset at Remington. I was curious about why he had stayed around while the cesspool built up around him. When I asked him for his version of what had happened he said: "I was as surprised by what that man did as anybody. The chief financial officer reported directly to him, so I had no way of discovering what was going on with the company funds. If I had known sooner, I would have resigned. But I found out the same time as the banks. By then, his shenanigans were public knowledge. The company folded and I went with it. I didn't have a chance to get out with my skirts completely clean." I checked his story out and was satisfied. The position I had for him was not as lofty as the one he had held. It paid only about 30 percent of his previous salary. As executive vice-president, he had been running an entire company. Now he would be in charge of one small division.

He took the position and did one bang-up job. Not too long ago, he was offered a slot with a consulting firm at more than double what we were paying him. Because he was a realist, willing to start all over again, he is on the fast track back.

Contrast this with another acquaintance of mine. This fellow had been chairman of a good-sized organization. The company hit rough times and he eventually found himself out of a job. This failure haunts him whenever he applies for a top position. He refuses to prove himself all over again by accepting a lower-level job. My misguided friend has been unemployed for over five years. He is unable to face the fact of his recent poor history.

The key point to remember is that the entrepreneur whose reputation has been sullied has to find a way to stay active. You might be the Fred Astaire of the business world, but in order to prove it to others you need a stage on which to dance. Don't worry about salary as long as it's enough to pay the bills. Coming back at a lesser job shows you've got some fortitude, that you're not a quitter. What sort of impression do you think my friend makes when he tells potential employers that he has been out of work for five years? Do you think they believe he's been on sabbatical writing a novel?

Reentering the job market at a lower point gives you a chance to build up a record that will obscure any of the black marks that have fallen against you. It also allows you a peace of mind that will be an advantage when you are finally negotiating for a higher position. When that fellow I had hired was approached by the consulting firm, he didn't have to jump at their first offer. He already had a job. He was clear of debt and his current bills were being paid on time. He could now deal from strength. The position also kept his self-worth afloat, adding to his confidence.

If you are ever in a situation where you have to undo a tarnished image and are hunting for a position, use this fellow as a model. Put your pride in your rear pocket and opt for opportunity. Don't fuss over salary, perks, or titles. Do look to take on as much responsibility as you can. It will allow your performance to be easily measured and will let you strut your stuff for your employers. Most important of all, get the job!

Honest self-assessment can often help you avoid scenarios that are ripe for reputation gouging. George Lourie had started a leather goods company with several old cronies. One of his partners had a request. He wanted his twenty-eight-year-old son-in-law Carl brought in as executive sales manager. Apparently Carl had been a district sales manager for a leading brewery. George didn't think this young man was ready for such a large responsibility. He had never held a position this lofty before, and he was new to the business. George's partner wouldn't take no for an answer. He guaranteed the kid was up to the job and he promised to work overtime teaching him the ropes.

This might have worked out, except there was something neither George nor his partner understood. Carl thought much less of himself than his father-in-law did. He knew that he wasn't qualified for the title he was about to receive, but he was afraid of offending his in-law by turning it down. He reluctantly joined the company.

It didn't take very long for Carl to have his insecurities justified. Not knowing the business, he found himself unable to communicate with his salespeople. Most of them were an older bunch who had been raised in the leather business. They resented having to work under this upstart and they were not shy about displaying their animosity. Carl was not up to matching their little verbal broadsides. What little confidence he did have in himself began to deteriorate quickly. He started drinking.

Word gets around fast in any industry. Carl would show up loaded at sales meetings and appointments with accounts. He became known as the industry drunk. Scheduled to run a presentation for a mammoth client, he showed up so inebriated he had to desist after fifteen minutes. He turned the floor over to an assistant, stepped outside, and nearly passed out. Carl was fired the next day. I'm not sure what has happened to him. I do understand he's been unable to get any sort of executive sales job.

Just as a bad reputation is poison in business, a sterling one can give you a tremendous advantage. When I tried to come up with the financing for Remington, I had pretty good credit. I had borrowed money to start businesses before and had paid it back. Having worked for successful companies, I also had a pretty good résumé. Each one of them was known as much for its integrity as for its ability to produce a healthy profit margin. The ventures I had launched on my own had generally done well. This record did a great deal to make up for whatever funds I lacked. It showed I was a good financial risk and a business builder. Without it, I doubt the money for the Remington project would have been available.

Having told you all this, let me throw you a curve. There will be times when you will have to look past a reputation. Yes, you did read that. It's not a contradiction. Notice I said look past, not ignore. As an entrepreneur you might discover that the reason a person received a bad name in one company might be the very thing that compels you to hire him. I've had this happen. I was looking for someone to run a Remington acquisition. Several candidates applied for the position. One fellow, Bruce Collier, stood out. He had worked as head of the retail department for a well-known conglomerate. We called it for a reference and the response couldn't have been more negative. His former boss wouldn't state it in direct terms, but he clearly implied we should stay away from Bruce. When I asked him why, he replied, "Even though his record might not show it, he's a loose cannon. He was always questioning company policy and proposing new ideas. He also worked too many hours. His co-workers hated him because he made them look bad. Nothing but a problem." Hmm, a guy who bucks the status quo, thinks creatively, and works too hard? My kind of executive! I finished the conversation by making sure Bruce didn't have any serious vices or any recent burglaries on his record and then thanked the old fussbudget for his time. Then I called Bruce to offer him a job. I'm not sorry I did. From day one he's been a tremendous asset to the company.

You all know the adage about sizing up a person by the company he keeps. That holds true in business. Ann Richards is the marketing director for an international fashion company. This firm has enjoyed a lofty reputation for quite some time. About a year ago, the founding executives sold the company. The new owners had some peculiar ideas about running a business. Rather than continuing to build on what was already a prestigious foundation, they instituted a flock of cost-cutting measures. First they replaced many of their skilled craftsmen with less talented individuals who were willing to work at reduced wages. Then the efficient administrative staff, never an extravagance, was cut back. Finally, they became lax in their operations. Much of the company's merchandise is imported from Europe. Any fashion item entering the United States must carry its fiber content clearly labeled. It's the law. This company had become so negligent, 50 percent of its imports often failed to show this required marking. All these items had to be reworked. By the time the merchandise was shipped, stores had been forced to cancel whole advertising campaigns. Ann would then be forced to chuck entire promotions and pricing plans into the wastepaper basket.

Clearly, her new bosses weren't interested in building their enterprise. They were looking to make a fast buck. As a result, the company is slowly sliding into decline. Ann is in her mid-twenties. This is her first upper echelon position and she savors her title. But she also knows she is now hooked up with a loser. When she asked me for advice, I told her to do her damnedest to correct whatever problems she could, and to start looking for a new job. Leaving now, she goes out with a curriculum vitae filled with positives. She will be able to say that she tried to make the best of a horrid mess, but that the situation was beyond her control. A marketing director can have little impact on corporate policy when the CEOs are such foul-ups. It's doubtful that any knowledgeable person will attach this company's eventual failure to her, and her refusal to stay with this band of clowns will only enhance her record. However, she must move quickly. If she is still on board when the company hits its nadir, she will be tainted by the thick coating of the owner's mismanagement. It will be very hard to remove this particular smudge. In choosing a company to work for, always associate with winners. You'll learn more. If you go on to another position, you will be able to leverage off your company's success. Employers want to hire those who have been part of a triumph.

I'd like to end this chapter with one final example illustrating the power of a good name. I had bought a company that distributed industrial components through mail-order catalogs. It was called Pic Design. It had been running low on capital for quite a while, and run far behind on deliveries. As its credibility suffered, its volume fell off drastically. It was finally on the edge of insolvency.

We grabbed it just as it was about to tip over. I thought the basic company was sound and that an influx of cash would put its workings in order. I also knew the enterprise badly needed a new image. We decided to rename it "Pic Design, a subsidiary of Remington Technologies." Nothing changed but the title.

Since the Remington turnaround, our company has become known for its high standards. We are the shaver manufacturer that exercises 100 percent quality control. As you've seen, we're also an organization that refuses to be associated with shoddy products. Our money-back guarantees tell the public that we stand behind our merchandise. It's a pledge of good faith that has never been betrayed. By adding the Remington monicker, we were letting the public know that we were standing behind Pic Design. Someone must like our history. In less than fourteen months this nearly bankrupt company is back on its feet. Business is already up by 25 percent. Yes, we've stabilized the company's performance. Our customers now know it's a reliable supplier. But we couldn't have rebuilt consumer confidence if the public hadn't been willing to give Pic a second chance. We bought that confidence with the Remington name. What kind of value can we put on that?

6

Entrepreneurship:
More Than Just a Business, a Way of Life

People often think of entrepreneurship as applying only to business. To them, it's nothing more than the art of building a successful enterprise or deal. This is a misapprehension. For me, entrepreneurship is a way of living. My bromide, "Business is where you are," means we should keep our focus on the business at hand. No matter what the size of the store or company you are calling on, during the time you are there it is the most important account in the world. You are totally committed to it from the moment you walk into it until the moment you leave. You shouldn't rush through a shoddy presentation at a small drugstore simply because you want to hurry off to pitch Macy's. This adage is just another way of underlining the importance of prioritizing. It is a philosophy that has helped me accomplish a good many things in business. It has also assisted in keeping my life from fraying at the ends.

The most important priorities in my life have been family, business, and tennis, in that order. There are even times when tennis creeps into the number two spot. A fourth priority would be the advancement of education. An educated society offers a higher standard of living for its people. So allot some time and financial support for educational organizations.

In terms of hours, business does demand the greater portion of my time. It has to. When I'm attending to it, the job commands my full concentration. Despite this commitment, I've always known that business isn't everything.

To some entrepreneurs that statement may seem like blasphemy. There's always been a stereotype about successful businessmen. Supposedly, the powerful CEO is so driven by ambition, his personal life is usually a shambles. The person at the top is often depicted as someone lacking compassion, a robot with a ledger for a heart. The film *Wall Street* with its Prince of Darkness, Gordon Gekko, reigning from the film's dark center, certainly contributes to that caricature.

A great many people are now convinced that this sort of all-devouring android represents a business norm. However, in my opinion, the person who leaves life's real treasures by the wayside in some all-out assault on success, fame, and wealth is missing out on so much. I have been married to the same wonderful woman for over thirty years. We've raised a fine family. I couldn't be more proud of any of them. The happiness they've brought has taught me something and I'm here to tell you that *winning at the workplace is a shallow triumph if you're losing at home. Those who can maintain a healthy bottom line in both environments are achieving the greatest victory of all.* There is no reason why the entrepreneurial principles that engender success in business can't be applied to achieve a happier personal life.

Marriage and the Entrepreneur

I was just looking at a copy of the magazine *Forbes.* It's the issue celebrating the Forbes 400, a listing of America's richest men. Looking through it, I noticed that almost every one of them has been divorced. This is tragic. If a person is willing to put in the effort, I don't think this failure rate has to stand so high.

You should lay the foundation for a solid relationship as soon as things turn serious. Share your dreams with your prospective mate. More importantly, let him or her know the sacrifices those hopes demand. You are not going to be home at six for dinner every night. Social obligations will go unmet. Quiet, relaxing weekends are going to become less frequent. This might not seem shattering now, but after five or six episodes of missed dinners and canceled invitations in a two-week period, the other half of a relationship might blow his or her cork. If the person you love is unable to cope with your lifestyle, it's best to find out before you make a deep commitment. If you can't work out a compromise, you will either have to cease being an entrepreneur or leave the relationship.

Ellen and I had to make adjustments after we married. Socially, she is much more outgoing than I. She has a lot of friends and would like to have them over for dinner. It is tough for us to entertain all that often with my schedule. She adapted to that. For my part, when she did plan a rare night with friends, I made sure I was available. Occasionally, we would be invited to a large function. I hate big parties. Who do you generally meet at these affairs? Someone you've never known before and will never see again. You have a light conversation about things of little if any interest. Bores me silly. When I do socialize, I prefer it to be at an intimate gathering. However, if we are asked to a large get-together, and it is something Ellen really wants to do, I go without complaint and do my best to make it a happy time. She pitches in by seeing that we don't get hooked into too many of these galas.

Here's a good example of compromise. Early in the writing of this book I found that the Christmas holidays were soon to be upon us. This is naturally a very important time of the selling season so my duties at Remington are heavier than usual. It is a Saturday afternoon. My wife and I would love to be finishing our Christmas shopping together. However, I have a deadline to meet and I've got to stay home to write this book. Ellen is disappointed, but she understands. She is once again in charge of buying gifts. Meanwhile, I'm working like mad to clear my calendar. Come Christmas Eve, I don't want business or the book to encroach on our celebration. It's all a matter of give-and-take.

The entrepreneurial life is often a roller coaster. Your mate should be prepared for that. There is no reason why you shouldn't discuss your business with the one you love. Keep him or her informed about your losses, triumphs, and plans for the future. You want your loved one to be a partner in life. How long would you stay in a partnership in which you weren't allowed to know what the company was doing or to see the books?

A fellow recently told me his business's tale of woe. Sales were markedly down and he had to fire some of the people in his division. His own position was tenuous. I asked him if he had told any of this to his wife. He said, "Oh, I never discuss business with her!" Is that fair? What on earth is going to happen if his enterprise falls apart? He should prepare her now. She needs to know and he is going to need her moral support.

I've always discussed my business with Ellen. It takes up so much of our life, I don't see how we could have avoided the subject. I value her cool head when I'm trying to come to a decision. I also need her support. Entrepreneurs often take on high-risk endeavors. When they are in jeopardy you don't need a partner harping on how bad things are. You want someone who will see you through the dark days. This partner holds your hand, offers realistic counsel, and never loses faith in you. Depending on the severity of the situation, he or she might even pitch in to help in a more active manner.

For a time, Benrus went through a particularly rough period. The company was in trouble because we were undercapitalized. Orders were way down. I had to cut my salary in half. Ellen and I began to formulate a survival strategy. We started by making a list of personal cost-cutting measures. Our expenses would have to be rolled back if we were going to get through this. Things were so grave, we were considering selling the house. I didn't want to have to take the kids out of school and this seemed the only way to raise their tuition while meeting our other bills. Having had a long run of success, it was all very traumatic.

One night during this horrible time, I woke up to find my wife in the bathroom sitting on the edge of the tub. She was working away with a pad and pencil. I asked what she was doing. She explained, "A woman I know teaches dance. She's about to retire and close her school. I think I could take it over from her.

I'm making a list of friends whose children might want to attend."

Oh, did my heart want to burst! Ellen wasn't wasting energy fretting over our predicament. She was ready to do whatever she could to help make ends meet. We righted the Benrus situation and that school never did get opened. However, on Ellen's next birthday, I gave her a gift from the heart: a pair of dancing slippers. It was my tribute to her for being such a rock. Throughout that entire bleak time, she never lost confidence in me. How can you lose with someone like that beside you? If I ever entertained any self-doubts, I could call on her strength. Then the spring would again jump into my step and I'd be hungry to find another Everest to leap over.

Entrepreneurs are often on the move and that can present a whole new set of problems to a relationship. I've seen marriages in which an enterprise forces the spouses to live in separate universes. A man or woman, climbing to the top in an industry, is flying off around the world. They have friends in New Zealand and China. They can quote the tariffs and duties in Kenya. Their spouses are lucky if they occasionally visit another state. They don't know anything about the international marketplace or the best restaurants in Tokyo. These people are at home in some little town trying to balance the family budget while raising the children. They might be involved in a small business. Their only contact with a foreign land occurs when they receive the local travel agency's annual calendar.

If they don't find a way to bridge the differences in their lives, they are going to have a problem. After a few years of this, the globe-trotter and spouse both look up and say, "We're growing apart." The next thing you know, they are spending time with marriage counselors or, in the most tragic of circumstances, filing papers for divorce.

You can help avoid this by bringing your partner into your realm. When you get home from a trip, share as much of your experience as possible. Bring back literature, pictures, and anything else that will give your mate a sense of the country or city you've just visited. Don't spare any details; take time to present a full view. When you're away you should phone daily. To hell with the expense. Let the other person know they are still a vital part of your life's fabric.

I recently saw one marriage flounder because the husband never bothered to call home. Whether he was in the office or off on a trip, he just couldn't pick up the phone to see what or how his wife was doing. The guy just didn't think it was important. This behavior was symptomatic of a generally uncaring attitude toward his wife. It wasn't that he didn't love her. He did. He was just too caught up with his business to be sensitive to her needs. When his spouse started to talk about divorce, he suddenly realized he hadn't been giving her enough attention. It was too late.

If you do have to travel and you have the opportunity, you should take your mate with you. Especially on the more exotic trips. I always try to have Ellen accompany me on certain travels. This does two things. First, you and your mate get to spend time with each other on an adventure. Second, your partner gets a taste of what your life is like on the road. That is not inconsequential. I know many wives whose husbands spend a lot of time in various lands. They are stuck at home tending to the mundane demands of daily living. Having never been on the road with their husbands, they create fantasies. They think, "That guy is in London. He's probably eating at the best restaurant and schmoozing with exciting people. What am I doing tonight? I'm trying to convince Bobby to eat all of his spinach. Then I have to go over his homework. And of course the cleaning has to be done. I'm going to be exhausted. I'd love to sleep late, but I have to get up early tomorrow to drive the kids to school. Meanwhile, that guy is across the Atlantic having a hell of a time! The rat!"

It does happen. I've seen resentments fester over this very issue. These can be avoided. If you take your spouse with you on a trip, he or she will find that this view bears little semblance to reality. With a schedule that is anything like mine they will first experience the delight of waiting for your baggage and then plodding through customs during the wee hours. Then they will see you reaching your hotel at 2 A.M., getting up four or five hours later for that first meeting of the morning, and working all day long. No chichi friends. No fancy restaurants. If you can eat at all, you do it on the run. You have to take care of business. When you get back to the hotel, you're so exhausted, you can barely open your room door, much less trip the light fantastic in some fashionable disco. You plop into bed and swiftly drift into the land of sweet nod. If you're lucky, you had enough energy to get undressed before making that well-deserved excursion.

How's that for a jolt of reality? When your spouse gets a dose of it, the envy and resentments will cease. They will realize they are in a partnership. You both have jobs to do and one is not necessarily more pleasant or exciting than the other. Only the locales are different.

The dynamism of your whirlwind pace might have another benefit. It could inspire a mate to get involved in a business of their own. I can't think of a better prescription for a happy marriage. It doesn't have to be a huge enterprise. A small mail-order business or some other cottage industry can provide more than enough challenge and excitement. With it in place, you both feel fulfilled. Your conversations are spiced by tales of triumph, disappointment, worry, and hope.

Ellen and I have been involved in several ventures together. She is currently running the Friendship Collection. We constantly talk over business. She has always had a keen interest in whatever I am doing. I give her accomplishments the same attention. In fact, I am more tickled by her successes than by anything I could possibly do. Our common interest and participation in businesses enhance an already solid rapport. It adds a little more sizzle and glue to the marriage.

Because entrepreneurs often live and work on the edge, humor is vital to the success of any relationship. I don't believe we have had a major fight in our marriage. There are two reasons for that. First, we don't bottle things up. If something is burning us, we let off steam before exploding. It's another case of "Business is where you are." If expressing your dissatisfaction is the business of the moment, deal with it then and there. Second, we both have a sense of humor. Neither one of us is afraid to laugh at ourselves.

This last quality certainly came in handy when I made a change in my commercials. The first Remington ads featured me in a suit behind a desk. Then I decided to be a bit more daring. Since no one actually shaves while wearing a jacket and tie, I appeared in a commercial wearing my bathrobe in a bathroom setting.

When Ellen took a look at this ad, I thought she would kill me. Oh, did she let off steam that night. You would have thought the living room was a sauna. She said, "How could you, a distinguished businessman, appear on TV in a bathrobe? Have you seen any other CEOs or politicians prancing about dressed like that? What kind of image are you creating?" She really let me have it. You would have thought I had bared my buns in *Oh! Calcutta.*

Despite her worries, the commercials did quite well. However, we did get some letters claiming the ads were still not quite realistic enough. These writers pointed out that most people don't even wear bathrobes when they shave. I took an informal poll and found out they were right. What was I going to do now? I wanted a commercial with as realistic an ambience as possible. I was an entrepreneur always ready to break new ground. I decided to shuck the robe.

I shot a commercial with one towel wrapped around my middle and another draped around my neck. I made sure the top towel covered at least half of my manly chest. I didn't think the world was ready for a full exposure.

I neglected to tell Ellen about this development. Gee, I don't know why. I guess I forgot. I also told the rest of my employees that if they should talk to her, they should forget also. I knew the secrecy wouldn't last for very long. You didn't have to be the head of the CIA to figure out that you can't carry out a covert operation under the glare of a national ad campaign.

One night we were watching the evening news. They cut to the commercials. What entrepreneur was brought into our living room via the miracle of the airwaves? Yes, it was Mr. Kiam himself, half-nude from the waist up, extolling the virtues of the microscreen shaver. People across America were salivating. I was sinking in my chair. Knowing that the reckoning was near, all I could do was stare at the set. I didn't dare look at Ellen.

The commercial was a thirty-second spot. It seemed to run for two hours. When it ended, Ellen didn't say a word. The news continued. Again nothing. We watched the show to its conclusion and still I didn't hear a peep.

I'm thunderstruck. I finally worked up the gumption to ask, "Honey, did you notice the new ad during the news?" She had. When I asked her what she thought of it, she said—and this really rocked me—she liked it! I said, "Ellen, I just don't understand this. When I switched from a suit to a bathrobe, you blew your cork. Now I'm in nothing but two towels, and you're not angry at all. How come?" She replied, "Because it won't be on for very long." When I asked why she thought that, she answered, "We both know that commercials are supposed to sell products, right? Well, nobody is ever going to buy a shaver from a guy with a body like that!" The next sound you heard was that of a time bomb being defused by laughter.

We Are Family

If you're blessed with kids, I know it can be hard to find an equitable balance between work and family. Most things worth having never come easy. But I believe your task will be much simpler if you apply your entrepreneurial creativeness to your domestic life.

For instance, Ellen and I have three children, Lisa, Tory, and Robin. When they were growing up I didn't have as much time to spend with them as I would have liked. I was often on the road from Monday to Friday. Because we considered it important, we gave the weekend to the kids. They picked out our activities. Whatever they wanted to do—go ice-skating, visit the zoo, take in a movie—became the marching orders for the day. One ritual we performed almost weekly was our Saturday morning soccer game. My son and our dog would play against my daughters and me. Ellen and I also took time to teach them how to ride bikes, how to swim, and eventually how to water-ski. Unlike some dads, I couldn't give them little pieces of me every night. But those big chunks of father they got on the weekends made up for it. It created a bond.

On those occasions when I was able to come home at night, it was often very late. The kids would be ready for bed. With the help of a friend, I was able to steal some precious moments with them. The friend was a fellow named Squeemy the Rabbit.

Squeemy was my creation. On the way home, I would construct adventures for this eccentric hare. Squeemy was a spy in one of the tales. Needing a disguise, he covered himself in pink toothpaste. Everything went along fine for him until he walked in front of an open fire hydrant. The splashing water washed away his disguise. Now he had to escape before he was found out. Not exactly the Brothers Grimm. These were simple stories that amused the children just as they were going to sleep and gave me an opportunity to interact with them.

I don't think the children ever resented my absences. Part of the reason for that was communication. As soon as they were able to understand, they were told why Dad had to go away so often. We didn't make the demands of my position a mystery for them. When you're breaking your back to make an enterprise go it's going to cut into your time with family. Isn't your family one of the main reasons you're making that sacrifice? It's an act of love and you shouldn't be afraid to let your children know that.

I also eventually discussed the various projects I was working on with the children. If I had a success, I shared it with them. If one of my plans went bust, they found that out too. That was especially important. I didn't want them to think I walked on water. I wanted them to know that though I had tried and failed, I was going to keep trying. They learned that you don't allow a setback to unravel your dreams. You mustn't be an icon to your children. If they know you are not superhuman, that you understand failure, it will be so much easier for them to approach you when they are troubled by a mistake. They will know it's not the end of the world. There is nothing lonelier than a worried child who feels he or she has no one who understands their distress.

When our kids had a problem—schoolwork, peer-group

pressure—we gave them our undivided attention. Business is where you are, and your family is your most sacred business. When I hear about communication gaps, I have to shake my head. You both talk, you both listen. Really listen! If one of your children is telling you about the difficulty she is having with math, don't be thinking about tomorrow's meeting or have your nose buried in the *Wall Street Journal.* They need your focus. No matter what your successes enable you to bestow upon your children, the most important thing they can receive is yourself. Give it completely.

In some cases you might even be able to allow your children to participate in your venture. When Ellen and I started the Italian jewelry business, eight-year-old Lisa was our "chief shipping clerk." We ran the company from our home. Since I worked during the day, most of the business was tended to at night. Ellen and I would price and label the items on the living room floor. Lisa would pack the jewelry, then weigh the boxes for postage. She became a part of the business.

This was especially exciting for her because she was doing something none of her friends had ever done. It was also another chance to spend time with Ellen and me. As a by-product, Lisa developed a natural business acumen. When she had only a small number of boxes to pack, she would say, "I guess the company isn't doing so well this week." We'd then tell her why we were sending out fewer orders. She gradually got the gist of what went into running a venture. As I think you'll see in a later chapter, we planted an entrepreneurial seed back then, one that is still growing.

I also made it a point to time my own vacations from work with the kids' holiday from school. We would go away as a family. When the children started to play tennis, we spent most of our vacation time going to their tournaments. On weekends we took them to their matches. The entire family shared in the exhilaration of victory and the disappointment of defeat. We eventually began to play with and against each other. That sport became a marvelous mode of communication for us. Tory and I got so involved with it, we became a nationally ranked father-son combination.

You can watch a relationship evolve when you and your son or daughter participate in a competition. When Tory and I first started playing, I was the better athlete. I had to compensate for the weaknesses in his game. After his sixteenth birthday, his game started to soar. We became equals on the court. Time spent preparing for and participating in matches became quality time. You are both committed to a common goal and a common excellence. You have one more thing to discuss over the dinner table. As you learn to adapt to each other as players, you adjust to each other as people. I can think of few things that can promote togetherness between parents and children more than the sheer joy of playing a game.

The amount of interest you show in your children tells them how important they are. Any person who doesn't believe in himself isn't going to be much of an entrepreneur. An entrepreneur takes risks, is decisive, and is not afraid to call attention to himself and his work. This demands a high degree of confidence. The entrepreneur understands this and knows the value of a positive self-image.

Your children may have no interest in business. However, life is an entrepreneurial venture, the largest game of all. I've seen so many melancholy adults, trapped in existences that will never measure up to their adolescent dreams. These are people blessed with innate talent, even genius, but lacking the confidence to express it.

Imagine if Pavarotti were afraid to sing or Evelyn Waugh too fearful to write. Forget the loss to ourselves and think instead of the private hell in which these suddenly pathetic individuals would be forced to wander while haunted by their smirking, elusive muse. Could there be any greater pain? If so, I wouldn't want to know it.

Considering these tragic scenarios, a failed salesman comes to mind. At initial glance, you would think this fellow had it all. Good looks, a quick mind, and what seemed like admirable poise. Would you believe none of these attributes could help carry him through a presentation? Whenever he called on a customer, particularly a large one, his muscles would tighten, his voice would rise an octave, and a torrent of damning perspiration would sweep over his body. As the physical symptoms of this anxiety attack heightened, he would blank out whole sections of his proposal.

Everyone thought these occurrences were merely a manifestation of the jitters suffered by many rookie salespeople. They assumed they would vanish after a week or two of comforting experience and a few sales. The condition only worsened. The fellow resigned after only six weeks on the job.

In private conversation, we later got an idea why this fellow was so insecure. Apparently, he had a domineering father. Throughout his childhood, nothing the son did could ever please his dad. High grades in school, a certain prowess in athletics, and an excellent moral character failed to make an impression. The young man lost sight of his value because he had never had it affirmed by the most important figure in his life. As a salesman, each customer he called on became the father he could never please. His best efforts—outstanding performances too, I might add—had always met with rejection. The pain inflicted by this particular cruelty was so crushing it crippled the young fellow's attempts to succeed. The violent physical reactions were insulating him from another disappointment. He had, after all, touched excellence so often, only to come away with fingers burnt by paternal indifference.

We have to give our children love and encouragement. One without the other is nothing more than a brightly wrapped empty box. We always made it a point to let Lisa, Tory, and Robin know we had the utmost confidence in them. When Lisa had the idea to publish a newsletter centering on preschool education, we didn't tell her the idea was too risky or that she lacked the necessary experience. We urged her to run with her dream. If she wanted our advice, we were there for her, but we didn't stand over her shoulder monitoring her ups and downs. We were content to root like crazy from the sidelines unless we were called into the game.

Robin was working in sales and marketing for the Friendship Collection when she was approached by a medium-sized cosmetics company. It offered her the position of marketing manager. This was an impressive entry position. She would report directly to the company's vice-president and would be in charge of her own product lines. The job gave her a chance to participate in sales and product development and couldn't help but broaden her business experience. Having worked for Friendship and for a prestigious New York department store, she was already used to seeing things from the perspective of the retailer. Now she would look through the eyes of the manufacturer. We hated to lose her; she had been a valued employee. But Ellen and I both encourage our children to make their own decisions. We also knew this was an opportunity she couldn't pass up.

Unfortunately, three weeks after she joined the company, the vice-president in charge of marketing quit. His resignation left Robin and a second young lady, both relatively inexperienced, to develop the company's marketing strategy. As a result of their company's lack of organization, they were also required to solve problems outside of the marketing realm. Late shipments, mismarked items, and other glitches were all brought to Robin's attention. She and her associate weren't given either help or guidance. They were left on their own.

It soon became apparent that both girls had been put in a position that required long hours and astute financial acumen. Robin was working twelve hours a day, six days a week in order to solve the problems and develop viable programs. Although she enjoyed the challenge, it was gradually wearing her down. The company never got around to replacing the marketing director. As each week passed, Robin felt a bit more overwhelmed. She soon realized she needed a greater knowledge of accounting and finance in order to meet the demands of her position. She could not get this training while on the job. There just wasn't any time.

Robin took a pragmatic look at her situation. She was working for a disorganized enterprise. Its problems often seemed endless. In seven months, it had been unable to hire a new marketing director. Left on her own, she had no one to teach her the ropes. She also recognized that she needed a better grounding in finance and accounting. Weighing these facts, she made an entrepreneurial decision. Robin left her position. She was looking past the short-term illusion of job security. I am proud to say she took a long-term step and went back to school. Enrolling in a curriculum that includes financial planning and basic accounting, she is turning her weaknesses into strengths. She will resume her career as a more well-rounded and knowledgeable individual. By going back to college Robin is giving herself the ammunition to achieve excellence. She's going for it.

When it came time for Tory to choose a high school, I had a preference. Tory was not very keen on my choice. We didn't argue the point and I didn't pull rank, ordering him to like it or lump it. Instead, we calmly discussed our differences. Tory wanted to stay in a local high school because of its outstanding tennis program. The school team was about to be upgraded by the arrival of young John McEnroe, already a known star on the tennis circuit. The institution had high academic standards, so I had no quarrel with that and I knew Tory—as he pointed out in our conversation—had aspirations to become a tennis pro. After listening to the cool and reasoned explanation for his choice, I supported it.

I'm not just taking time here to commit the crime of many parents: bragging about one's children. I'm simply trying to point out the power of a lifetime of encouragement. A great athlete, now retired, had become a coach. He gained a reputation as an outstanding trainer of young players. When asked his secret, he replied, "Simple. I teach them the fundamentals. If they have the reflexes, they can execute the basics. Then I tell them how great they are. It's amazing. If you keep telling a person how great they are, eventually they start to believe it."

Call it positive thinking or anything else you like, we let our kids know that the only thing they couldn't achieve were the things they didn't try. I don't want anyone to think I'm presenting the Kiams as a model and I wouldn't attempt to give specific advice on how to raise a family. By comparison, running a business is a much easier task. You want to lend guidance, give advice, and, when necessary, enforce some discipline. But to that mix add a heaping cupful of independence. Let your children know that all limitations are self-imposed. You're an entrepreneur. You want your enterprise to be manned by dynamic go-getters and risk-takers. You shouldn't want anything less for your family. I often say a new venture is like a baby that has to be nurtured. Well, your young children really are your babies and they're more important than any profit-and-loss sheet. We mustn't ever lose sight of that.

Choosing the Family Business

If you run your own company or business, your child might someday opt to join you in it. As long as it is their own, unpressured choice, I heartily endorse the decision. It is also one that should not be made lightly. There are easier things in this world than having Mom or Dad as a boss.

Tory took quite a while before deciding to join Remington on a full-time basis. During the summers he would work for our New York sales representative. Carrying a briefcase full of brochures, he would call on accounts—mostly drugstores—and try to persuade them to beef up their Remington lines. He wasn't walking out of stores with $10,000 orders; he was lucky to sell one or two shavers to each account.

After graduating from Harvard University, he was hired as a financial analyst by the brokerage house Drexel Burnham. He learned a good deal in the two years he spent there, but somewhere along the line he decided that Remington could be an exciting opportunity. However, his career with us nearly ended before it began.

He had accompanied me on a book tour of Australia. I received an unusual amount of publicity during the sojourn. It seemed everywhere I turned, someone either had a microphone or a camera stuck in my face. It was a circus of non-stop interviews for newspapers, magazines, television, and radio. People were actually asking me for my autograph. It was great fun, but we hardly had a moment to ourselves. Tory found the scene a bit overwhelming. They didn't teach you to be prepared for this sort of commotion in business school. Midway through a visit to Melbourne, my son excused himself and took off on a walkabout near the Great Barrier Reef. He said he needed to clear his head.

We agreed to meet on Bora-Bora. Away from the cameras

and questions, Tory was able to share his thoughts with me. He was troubled. He said, "I don't know how I feel about all this publicity and your obligations to the media. I don't know that I want to run around making speeches. If this is what Remington is going to be, I'm not sure I want it. Dad, you're a pretty hard act to follow." I told him I could understand how that might appear to be the case, but that a lot of his perception was an illusion. I explained, "This isn't a normal situation. It's a fluke created largely by the TV commercials and *Going For It!* This stuff has very little to do with our business. It's just icing on our cake. The real business of Remington is a lot of slogging away, doing the nuts and bolts work to build up the company."

He was still a bit shaken. He wondered if joining Remington would be the correct move. Tory was particularly concerned about his identity. Throughout the tour, Tory thought everyone looked at him as being "Victor's boy." They didn't know anything about him and they didn't seem to care who he really was. He felt they had pigeonholed him. That irked him. He didn't want to go through life thought of solely as "Son of Kiam." I can't blame him. It sounded like some sort of damned monster movie. He wanted to be his own individual, not an addendum.

I said, "You have an opportunity here that is available to few people. It might not be the company for you. Who can say? But I think it would be foolish to walk away from it without giving it a try. You're a young man. A year is not a long time at your age. If at the end of the year, you're not satisfied with the company or you feel your identity is still threatened, go off and do your own thing. I'll support any decision you make. And if you decide you don't even want to test this opportunity for a year, I'll support that too."

I wanted him to join us. But, just as he had the right to choose his own high school, I had to let him choose his own business life. It doesn't matter how much you encourage a child's independence or boost their self-confidence, all that talk is just talk, nothing more, unless you allow them to stand on their own when it comes to crunch time.

Tory decided to come on board. As a parent, you are always looking for common interests to be shared with your kids. When that interest happens to be your enterprise, an entity that has become so much a part of your being, you have built the ultimate bridge over the so-called generation gaps. You are going to partake jointly in the marrow of life, participating in its triumphs and disappointments.

Be aware, though, that this can entail certain difficulties. You should do everything you can to avoid the appearance of nepotism in the treatment of your child. This can be done in a variety of ways.

I make a conscious effort to keep our Remington relationship on a businesslike level. When Tory enters the office, he ceases to be a son. He's another valued Remington employee treated the same as everyone else. In fact, I bend over backwards not to make it easier for him. For example, his pay scale is much lower than it should be. I probably shouldn't say that. In a later chapter, I'm going to discuss getting a raise. Armed with that information and this admission, he might come at me for a few more dollars. I wish him luck. I keep his salary down because I don't want anyone to think he's riding into work on a gravy train. Teamwork has been such a vital element of the Remington success. All it would take is a dose of jealousy to dent the spirit we have created in the company.

A charge of nepotism would have a similar effect. Tory came up with an entrepreneurial solution to head off any such claims. In business school, Tory had been taught the importance of learning everything you could about any company that employed you. He was also told that executives should build a rapport with the other employees.

Knowing these principles had succeeded at Remington, he decided to implement them in another, rather creative way. When Tory joined the company, he didn't come in as part of management. He started as a factory worker and held various positions on the work floor. He helped run the machines that manufacture our blades and sat on the assembly line. He put in time in every section of the factory. His paycheck and hours matched those of his fellow workers.

At the end of half a year, he knew more about the actual manufacture and shipping of our shavers than I did. Tory learned so much, not just about Remington but the people who make it work. I doubt anyone appreciates the job they do more than he does. For their part, the factory people found that here was a young man who wanted to achieve his own success, who was willing to pay some dues. There was no animosity when we moved him into a junior executive position. He has been with us for two years and has become quite an asset. If he wants to, he might even be president of the company someday.

But like any entrepreneur, he'll have to earn it.

A Shaggy Dog Story

I have found that even the small traumas of your daily domestic life can often be ironed out with some entrepreneurial creativity. For instance back when I was still with Playtex, we bought a dog for the kids, a Shetland sheepdog we christened Omar. He became a fourth child. Everywhere we went, Omar went. We took him to Central Park and let him play games with the children. One morning, they were tossing a ball to him in a large field on 79th Street. I was talking to a friend of mine. The only other person around was a sallow man with a small whippet.

At some point, the kids' shouting pulled us out of our conversation. I looked over to see what was wrong. Omar had disappeared. He had gone running after the ball, turned behind a bush, and hadn't returned. Omar was well trained. He would usually appear at the call of his name. Scattering about the field, we shouted in all directions. We even got in a cab and called for him throughout the park, but it was no use. If Omar could hear us, he wasn't answering.

We didn't drop our search. I had each of the children cover a different block on the way home. Though highly unlikely, it was possible that Omar might have started back without us and got lost. We asked passersby if they had seen him. No luck.

We called the ASPCA and gave its officials Omar's description. That night, the family was worried sick. Neither Ellen nor I could get to sleep. As I lay awake, I thought, "This dog means so much to us, I have to approach this the same way I would go after a prized account. I've got to put everything I have into finding Omar." The next day, I went to Playtex and told my boss I was taking a week off to find my dog. He looked at me as if four screws had just dropped off my head. I told him, "Sure, I know it sounds crazy, but I've got to do it."

I then immediately went to Young and Rubicam, our company's ad agency. I told an executive, "I want to run an ad campaign to find my dog. Anything you can do to get me on TV, radio, or into the newspapers is fine with me. I'll do anything." We took out ads in every New York newspaper, advertising a $500 reward for the return of Omar. No questions asked.

The ads ran on a Tuesday morning. That evening, I got a call from a private detective who said he was an expert in finding lost people and animals. He thought he might have some ideas on how to find Omar. We arranged to meet.

This fellow was like someone out of a Raymond Chandler novel. He showed up with a snap-brim hat and an ill-fitting trench coat, and he talked out of the side of his mouth. Throughout our interview, he kept cleaning his nails. With a stiletto. He told me, "There have been a lot of dog-nappings in your area. The dogs are sold in an illegal show in Pennsylvania. They are then used for medical experiments. I'll check into those. In the meantime, I would suggest we hire a crew of kids to put notices concerning Omar in the lobby of every building from 59th to 96th streets. Make sure the notices include a good, clear picture of the dog."

I did as he asked. I also got a list of all the veterinarians and animal hospitals in the tri-state area, that is, in New York, New Jersey, and Connecticut. I sent Omar's picture to each one of them along with a letter asking if anyone had brought in such a dog. We followed up every possibility. When someone mentioned that cab drivers often pick up stray dogs, we put our next ad in the taxi news.

Young and Rubicam got me on a local TV show called *New York, New York.* I went on the air to make an appeal. Prior to my appearance, the show featured a guest who had baked the world's largest pizza. I was sitting next to it off-camera. The fumes from the onions and peppers wafted about me. It was so intense my eyes began to water. By the time the interview started, I had tears cascading down my cheeks. It sure gave my appeal an emotional quality. New York just opened its heart. I was deluged with suggestions and clues. Unfortunately, none of the respondents had Omar. We followed all their leads though. One woman said she thought she saw Omar in a vacant lot in the Bronx. We scurried up there and spent the better part of an hour searching. Nothing.

We got the police involved. They told us that dog-napping rings often operated around the park. These crooks would use a small dog as a decoy for other pooches. Oh no. I thought about that sallow-faced man with the whippet.

Omar's disappearance occurred while Harry Stokes and I were trying to prevent the Riklis takeover of Playtex. At the upcoming weekend I would have to attend a crucial meeting which had been fixed with the owners of the Schlitz Brewery. This was the meeting which I chronicled in chapter two. There was no getting around it, so with what little time I had left, I hurriedly made arrangements with the police to set a trap. We would rent a dog, have Ellen and the cops go to the park on Saturday, and attempt to decoy any would-be dog-nappers into making a move. Ellen would keep me abreast of the progress by phone.

She called me Saturday evening. The plan couldn't have been a bigger dud. First, the rental agency misunderstood my instructions. I wanted a medium-sized dog of excellent pedigree, a pooch that looked as though it would sport a heavy price tag. I wanted a dog that the thieves would find irresistible. The agency sent us a six-foot-long Great Dane. You should have seen this animal. He had teeth that made the shark in *Jaws* look as if he were all gums. An armed Al Capone, accompanied by his entire mob, wouldn't have tried to steal this dog. Even the police were terrified of him.

It was too late to get a replacement. The Dane was brought to the park in a squad car. Lights were flashing. Sirens were screaming. If there had been any dog-nappers about, you can bet that display would have scared them off. Naturally, this thin charade didn't turn up a thing. When I heard the details, it nearly put me at my wit's end. I thought, "What are we going to do now?"

We concluded our meeting with Schlitz that evening. Having returned to the hotel, I started to pack for my trip home. I wanted to get back and continue the search for Omar. Just as I finished with my suitcase, the phone rang. It was Ellen. She said, "He's back! We have Omar back!" I could scarcely believe it. In the last series of ads, she had raised the reward to $1000. Someone saw the ad and called to report he had the dog. He had been driving near the park on that Saturday morning. Omar had been prancing about in the streets, and this driver nearly hit him. After checking to see he was okay, he waited for someone to claim him, but nobody came. Omar never wore his leash and collar while playing, so he wasn't carrying any ID. Concerned for the dog's safety, the good fellow took him home.

Flying back to New York, I didn't care if the Schlitz deal came through or not. I was ecstatic to have Omar back. I doubt we would have if we hadn't made his return a priority. The episode proves something I've always believed: you can achieve anything, in business or out, with the application of entrepreneurial initiative. Think about it. What were the odds of retrieving a dog lost in a city as large as New York? A lot of people would have given up after our first couple of attempts. Who could blame them? But we got Omar back, because we refused to allow any alternative. I've run a few companies and have made a couple of acquisitions. My wife still thinks the effort I put behind getting Omar back is the most impressive entrepreneurial feat of my career.

Don't Do Business with Friends

A happy domestic life does extend beyond the realm of family. You want to build lasting friendships. You can protect these relationships by keeping your social and business lives separate. This one isn't written in stone. Sometimes you can't avoid doing business with friends. If your lifelong buddy wants you to be a partner in the idea of the century, it would be foolish to reject him out of hand. Just be wary. I've seen many a friendship done in by a deal.

Damage can sometimes be done by the most well meaning of arrangements. In 1961, Ellen and I met another couple while on vacation. We played bridge with them and went out on a couple of dinner dates. They were a lot of fun. The husband's name was Joe Pagan and he was the head of an advertising agency.

Some time after we had returned home, Mr. Pagan called me. We exchanged the usual pleasantries and then he asked if I could come to his office on the following morning. He wasn't specific, but he did say he wanted to discuss an interesting proposal. My calendar was clear until the afternoon, so I agreed to see him.

I didn't have a clue as to what his agenda was going to be. Midway through the meeting, I was even more puzzled. He kept talking around things. Finally, he started to approach the subject at hand. He said, "Vic, you have a very attractive wife." I thanked him. Then he continued, "But she's not as young as she used to be." That didn't sit too well with me. I bristled, "None of us are, Joe. What are you getting at?"

He stood up and took on a professional air. Putting his fingers beneath his lapels, he said, "You were in the cosmetics business. As you probably know the maturation process takes its toll. As you get older, your face starts to take on some lines. Often they can make you look older than you really are." I replied, "Yes, yes, I know that, Joe. *Now what on earth are you getting at?*"

His words came out in a rush. His agency was representing a cosmetics company. It was coming out with an astringent guaranteed to tighten the skin and reduce the lines in a person's face. The agency needed a model to do a high-brow TV commercial. It was going to be used during a gala to celebrate the opening of the Lincoln Center and would be seen nationally. Pagan thought Ellen would be a perfect choice to star in the commercial. He said, "I can't call her and go into that spiel about aging and wrinkles, but you could. I promise you, if she does the spot, she'll get paid a handsome fee."

Ellen had been a model before we got married. I thought she might be interested in Pagan's proposal. I had a dickens of a time, though, trying to figure out how to broach it to her. I waited until breakfast the following morning. I opened by saying, "Honey, you look sensational." She thanked me. Then I said, "You know both of us are getting along in years and . . ." She cut me off with such a look. I was treading on unsteady ground now. "What's that supposed to mean?" I replied, "Nothing. It's just that you have this great maturity now. You have this look of experience. You know, your face isn't young and innocent anymore. You're a mature woman with all the attractiveness that goes with that."

As vistas go, I had the feeling this one was drowning me in my own paint. She asked me what on earth all this drivel meant. I told her about my conversation with Pagan. When I first described the product, her eyes began to narrow. She thought I was suggesting that she needed it. I calmed her and said, "No, I love the way you look. Wouldn't change it for the world. It's just that they are doing a commercial for the Lincoln Center opening and want you to star in it. It will run all over the country. If it's a hit, you can make a small fortune in residuals. And it's bound to be fun."

Ellen wasn't buying it. I asked her not to make up her mind so quickly. Joe didn't need an answer until the following afternoon. There wasn't any reason why she couldn't sleep on it. "Besides," I told her, "you don't have to commit to anything over the phone. You can go to the agency and see what they have planned. If you don't like what they have in mind, you don't have to go through with it."

I don't know if my remark made any difference, but by that evening she had decided to give it a whirl. She and Joe arranged to meet. When she gets down to his office she discovers she isn't the only woman competing for the role. The room is crowded with professional models and actresses. This placed the idea in a whole new perspective. Here was a job Ellen had been reluctant to take, but the sight of all those competitors stoked her fires. Now she was hell-bent to get the part! When my wife sets her mind on something, she invariably finds a way to achieve it. By the end of the day, she was cast in the ad.

They shot the commercial the following evening. After makeup, she was photographed for a series of "after" shots. Six hours into the shooting, with the lines deepening from exhaustion, they took the "before" pictures. The filming ended at four in the morning. Bone-tired and *sans* makeup, Ellen was asked to sit through a few more shots before leaving. And I said this would be fun!

We joined some friends for the commercial's debut. They set up the TV in the kitchen, put out a buffet, and waited with us for the big moment. It was one of the first ads of the evening. Ellen, the picture of elegance, comes out of Lincoln Center with her "husband" and bumps into an old girlfriend. The other woman is deliberately frumpy looking. The girlfriend takes Ellen aside and says, "We were in the same class in high school, but you look so much younger than I do. What's your secret?" Ellen then tells her about the wonders of this miracle cosmetic. The friend replies, "Oh boy, I can't wait to get it so I can look as good as you." Then both women rejoin their husbands and move off at the fade. We all thought Ellen did a terrific job and she was pleased with the way it came off. All we had to do now was sit back and wait for the residuals to start flowing our way.

About a week and a half after the commercial airs, I get a call from one of Ellen's best friends. I asked how she was doing and she said, "I'm fine, but I'm not sure if Ellen's going to be. Have you seen this morning's *New York Times*?" When I told her I hadn't she sighed, "You better see it before she does. Turn to page twenty-three." When I did, I nearly had a heart attack. There was a full-page ad underneath the headline, "Now you can have a facelift without surgery!" Ellen was featured in the accompanying photos. They had the "after" shot in which she looked like a film star. For the "before" photo, they used the final shots taken at four in the morning. They even doctored the prints, deepening the lines to make her look as awful as possible. Ellen joined me just after I had looked at the photos. I'm trying to figure out a diplomatic way to break this to her, but there isn't any. Handing her the paper, I said, "You're going to see this sometime. It might as well be now."

She was embarrassed by what they had done to the photo and how they had used both it and her. I wasn't ashamed; I was furious. If Pagan had been there I would have thrown him out the window just to see how high he bounced. That was my first reaction. After cooling off, I thought there might be a better way to handle this. I asked Ellen to bring me her contract. It contained a release for the TV commercial. It did not, however, say anything about a print ad. Pagan and his agency were in trouble.

I called Joe and said, "For God's sake, how could you run those photos without Ellen's permission! You've got to pull those ads!" He said it was already out of his hands. Only the client could halt the campaign. I started screaming so hard I nearly swallowed the telephone. Pagan tried to soothe me. He offered to call the client, explain the "mistake," and have the advertising lifted.

Joe got back to me that afternoon. He meekly explained that the program had been launched nationally and had become a juggernaut with its own life. There was no way to stop it. I screamed, "Oh yes? Well, here's something else you won't be able to stop. I'm going to sue your butt and your client's." Pagan replied, "Don't do that, Vic. Ellen's going to do very well with this commercial and . . ." Refusing to let him finish, I yelled, "We don't give a damn about that. You signed an agreement and you violated it. Now take care of this or you can see me in court."

I hung up on him. That evening, I told Ellen about our conversation, promising that we would sue if something wasn't worked out. She was just as upset as I was, but she didn't want to take Pagan to court. When I asked her why, she said, "He's our friend." I explained, "Honey, we can't look at it that way. He made a business deal and went back on it. This thing is going to run everywhere now. If he was our friend, he should have looked out for you." Despite my reasoning, Ellen wouldn't be dissuaded.

A month later, her mother, abroad on vacation, sent us a European fashion magazine. The ad was running over there.

Faced with this fresh upset, I asked her to at least speak to our lawyer to see if there was any way to end this thing. She did. He told her that a lawsuit was her only recourse and repeated my view that it shouldn't be looked upon as a personal vendetta. He added, "As a businessman, I'm sure Mr. Pagan will understand." Even with his assurances, Ellen still wouldn't press the suit. That incident occurred over twenty-five years ago. We never did sue. However, I haven't spoken to Joe Pagan since that last phone call. I see him at parties and just turn my back on him. I don't believe I'd have the same violent reaction if this had been just another business deal. Yes, I would have become hot, but in time I would have forgotten about it. But this was a "friend." When a friend pulls something like this, the hurt is lethal. Goodwill and trust are drained from the relationship. Not too many deals are worth this risk.

The Proper Fit

Many people seem to think they have to make their lifestyle fit their entrepreneurial venture. It isn't always so. Depending on your priorities, you can make it work the other way around.

Fred Nichols was a man who had a big hand in our getting the original financing for the Remington turnaround. After the purchase, he joined the company as its treasurer. I enjoyed Freddy. He was easy-going, considerate of others, and a top professional. Each evening, before going home, he would drop by the office. We'd discuss the company over cups of coffee. Sometimes he'd stay an hour, sometimes only five minutes. The amount of time was unimportant. What mattered was the feeling I got for Freddy. Here was a fellow who genuinely cared about the company and what we were trying to accomplish. Having been through the early struggle to purchase Remington, he treated it as if it was his own. He was committed to its success.

One afternoon, Freddy asked if he could see me on an important matter. We went into my office and poured ourselves our ritual coffee. He sat in his chair for minutes without saying a word. Then I noticed his eyes were watering. When I asked him what was wrong, he still couldn't get any phrases out. He was choking with emotion. I told him to relax. Finally, his story gushed forward. Having been divorced, he was about to re-marry. His bride-to-be had three children. Freddy had three kids of his own. She was a practicing midwife and had to work odd hours. As you know, babies usually pick the most unpredictable times to enter the world. When she was on a call, someone had to be home with the children.

A friend of Freddy's owned a company that manufactured boat-in-a-bottle kits. These kits were bought by hobbyists who used them to build bottled replicas of the *Mayflower,* the *King George V,* and other famous ships. It was a small venture run mostly through mail order. This friend was now about to retire and had offered to sell his business to Freddy.

It was perfect for him. The whole enterprise could be run out of his home and was an answer to all of his problems. Despite this, he was torn. He didn't want to leave the company.

I was also being pulled in two directions. I didn't want to lose Freddy. He had been a valuable right arm. But I also knew he had found an ideal situation. I told him, "Buddy, you have been one hell of a man here. You've given me quite a void to fill. That's all right. This is your shot. I know you'll make it go. If by any chance it doesn't work out, you'll always have a home here." We hugged each other and then we both cried.

I'm happy to say he had a big success. He bought a big rambling house in a small town in Maine. His workshop is on the top floor and his bride is the local midwife. He is not in the fast lane. The needs of his loved one put some limitations on his business options. Yet he is as much an entrepreneur as when he was playing for higher stakes with Remington. More of one. Now he's building his own business. He's faced with the same decisions that I or any other CEO have to make, only on a smaller scale. Most importantly, Freddy is a man with his priorities in order. He wanted a happy home life. He also wanted to have a success in business. Freddy is the ultimate entrepreneur. He got both.

Always the Entrepreneur

The entrepreneurial spirit should enliven every waking minute. I know a businessman who is involved in several successful ventures. Whenever he goes to a restaurant he tries to choose at least one dish, even if it's just an appetizer, that he has never tasted before. When he and his wife celebrate each other's birthdays, they invariably go out to eat. They always pick a place featuring an exotic cuisine.

On his last vacation he hiked along a river to its source, scaled mountain cliffs, flew kites at midnight, attended his first opera, and even went skinny-dipping in a mountain gorge. The water was about forty degrees. Brrrr! That will get your blood moving in the morning. Didn't faze this fellow. He's always trying to experience new things. On my own vacation two years ago, I stoked coal on a barge going down the Mississippi. When I first went to Japan, I couldn't leave without trying their legendary Kobe beef marinated in beer. What was the point of these exercises? Adventure. At heart every entrepreneur is Indiana Jones.

When we talk about an entrepreneur, we're talking about a swashbuckler who sops up huge portions of life with gusto. This person can approach his or her life away from the office with the same energy, creativity, and enthusiasm they bring to their enterprise. This should be easy for the entrepreneur. He or she is a doer, an activist who refuses to be a passive victim to bogeyman Fate. Throughout this chapter, domestic obstacles and problems were often overcome by the application of a little entrepreneurial initiative. Do you want to spend more time with your family? Create time. You've just seen that it can be done. If you are willing to go the extra mile—and all entrepreneurs are—you will negotiate the compromises that bring bliss to relationships. You have the power to make life work. You don't have to settle for a shining business record but a damaged home life. You can make your lifestyle fit your business, and vice versa.

My friends, you can have it all!

7

Going For It Around the World:
The Global Entrepreneur

If your enterprise grows large enough, you might be able to expand into the international marketplace. With all the complexities of worldwide trading, I wouldn't want to attempt to give anyone specific advice in this chapter. To really help you, I would have to know the complete background of your particular business. However, I would at least like to paint the broad strokes by sharing some of my own globe-trotting adventures.

A Lesson Learned in Panama

The entrepreneur looking to perform on the global stage has to be ready for just about anything. Back in the sixties, as president of Benrus, I was approached by a man who wanted to distribute our watches in South America. I checked out the man's credentials and came away impressed. He was South America's largest distributor of Seikos and did a great deal of business with a major U.S. electronics company. Checking with both companies, we found they had enjoyed a long and happy relationship with him. Further investigation revealed that he enjoyed excellent credit.

I was going to meet this fellow in his native Colon, Panama, and show him a full range of our samples. This trip would be combined with a rare vacation. The plan was to spend time in

Nassau with my family and a few friends, and then fly into Colon for my get-together with the distributor.

Arriving in Nassau, I naturally had to pass through customs. The inspectors looked through my package containing the seventy-two boxed samples and suggested the watches be placed in bond. They explained that this would allow me to avoid paying a duty on the samples. I could place the samples in their case while I was in Nassau and then pick them up before leaving for Miami en route to Panama.

I took their advice. The container holding the boxed watches was wrapped in impressive steel bands, defying even a modern Houdini to break into the package without disrupting the seal.

When I came to pick up my goods, it looked as if everything was going to go according to plan. I received the samples out of bond, took off for Miami, landed safely, and then caught an Air Mexico flight to Panama City. Once there, I was met on schedule by the distributor's driver and whisked off to Colon. The samples case, still bound in steel, had been placed next to me in the backseat.

Arriving at my hotel, I had dinner with my host and arranged to meet him at his office the next morning. The opening negotiations went without a hitch. The distributor wanted our product and he thought the opening prices mentioned were quite reasonable. I was now ready to apply the coup de grâce with a mesmerizing presentation of our samples.

Reaching into my display box, I held up the watch case so that its contents could be seen only by him and then slowly opened the top lid. This was a deliberate tension builder. I wanted him to savor the magnificence of this miracle of modern timekeeping. My host's eyes fixed on the case's contents and his eyes widened. "There," I thought, "I've really made an impression." Before I could get through patting myself on the back, the distributor did an odd thing. He started laughing. I didn't see the humor of my presentation until I turned the case around to face me. There, in the indentation that should have held my sample, was a gorgeous, perfectly rounded rock!

I was dumbfounded. Plowing through the rest of the cases,

we discovered that all the samples had been similarly displaced. Someone had lifted the watches. Whoever it was, they had been farsighted enough to realize the package would be weighed as it passed through customs. The stones were obviously meant to substitute for the lost weight of the samples. Pretty clever, but it turned out that I had something of a last laugh on the unknown perpetrators. Those watch samples had been nothing more than empty cases. They lacked the innards needed to keep time.

The thieves' presumed discomfiture gave me little solace. I left Colon without an order. I was able, however, to arrange to meet with the sympathetic distributor during his next trip to the States. It was at that meeting that we eventually came to an agreement.

I learned two valuable lessons during that adventure. One was not to trust bureaucracies. As an entrepreneur, I should have known that. If I hadn't placed all my faith in those steel bands or the customs officer's official seals, I could have uncovered the loss of the samples immediately. I was also taught the error of false confidence. No matter how strong your presentations have been in the past, you must be sure to review every aspect of it before each new airing. Had I bothered to check my case on the evening prior to the meeting, I would have spared myself some embarrassment.

A Most Amazing Alchemy

When selling internationally, you'll sometimes discover that a product unable to find a market in one country can be successfully introduced in another. The air purifier we discussed in an earlier chapter was one example of this. My adventures with a popcorn maker provide further evidence.

Remington hadn't planned to manufacture popcorn machines. The fact is we fell into the business on the wildest fluke. One afternoon, the managing director of our English company received a call from the American embassy's commercial attaché. This fellow was phoning to see if we made popcorn makers. When told we didn't the man sighed and said, "Oh, that's too bad. The Department of Agriculture and the Popcorn Institute of the United States are trying to promote the worldwide sale of popcorn. We have a surplus of corn back home. If we don't unload it soon, the grain will start rotting in the silos. We thought it would be a good idea to introduce a top quality popcorn-maker in the U.K. in order to increase the demand for corn. Someone suggested Remington as a possible manufacturer. Your products are well known in this country and they have excellent distribution. We thought it would be perfect if you would launch the program on an exclusive basis." When I heard about the conversation, I knew the fellow had not called to ask a question. He could have found out if we manufactured popcorn makers without phoning our managing director. I got the clear impression we were being invited into a new business.

We were interested in learning more about the project. A meeting was set up at our embassy in London. The director and I represented Remington. The attaché was joined by members of the Popcorn Institute, an American association dedicated to increasing the international sale of popcorn.

During our discussion, it was made clear that Remington was being brought quite an opportunity. The PCI representatives told us that they had garnered popcorn orders from the major food stores in the United Kingdom. A mammoth promotional campaign was already approved and in place. All it needed was the additional marketing support of a top quality popcorn maker. The PCI was willing to spend over a quarter of a million dollars on a U.K. test market for the popper. It would put up additional promotional dollars if that experiment proved successful. They also produced statistics bolstering their contention that the machines would find a warm welcome in England. At the time, high-fiber foods—and you would have to place popcorn in that category—were enjoying excellent sales in the U.K. The medical industry had apparently released a number of reports praising the effects of a high-fiber diet. England had also always been a large consumer of commercially produced popcorn, albeit this version was often covered with caramel or some other sweetener. We thought it was a pretty good bet that Britons would like a chance to make their own popcorn at home.

These facts and the promise of substantial advertising support were too much to ignore. If Remington could successfully open the market in England, it could then move on to the rest of Europe. My goodness, we had the chance to become the emperors of popcorn! With a possibility like that staring us in the face we had no choice but to agree to manufacture and distribute a popcorn machine.

Having researched the market prior to our gathering, we had already determined that a hot-air popper would be the route to follow. It didn't use oil in the cooking process. This meant the corn came out less greasy and was lower in calories. A lab study had also shown that the hot-air machine could pop more kernels in less time than other models. We actually had a fellow pop corn on every type of machine available. After it was done, he would record the number of unpopped kernels for comparison. The hot-air popper always came out on top.

Remington had one other advantage in this enterprise. By studying the many popcorn machines on the market, our engineers were able to design a superior model by integrating the best features of the other brands. In a short time we manufactured 40,000 machines that met our high company standards.

Since popcorn is really an American product, everyone agreed it was appropriate for this new popper to make its debut during a press reception at the American embassy. We had Glyn Christian, the well-known British TV chef, handle the cooking. What an amazing fellow. No one would have dreamed he could create so many recipes featuring popcorn. We served popcorn with sautéed mushrooms, popcorn with Italian spices, Cajun popcorn, popcorn with exotic cheeses melted over it. We must have fed forty varieties to over 400 people including international dignitaries and the press. They couldn't get enough of the stuff and their insatiable appetites were ample proof that the party had been an unqualified hit.

I hardly had time to munch a morsel. Most of my afternoon was spent with TV reporters seeking interviews. That was fine with me. I wasn't there to eat. Getting exposure for the corn and

the popper was the whole purpose of the gathering. One reporter from the BBC expressed some skepticism over our
party's success. Confronting me on camera, he said, "The people here are gorging themselves, but most of them travel a great
deal and have been exposed to this style of popcorn before. I
wonder if you can sell your popcorn to the average Brit."

My reply was a good five minutes on the miraculous benefits
of popcorn and the Remington popper. I also pointed out that
popcorn was so delicious, it didn't need the sweet coatings that
distinguished much of England's popcorn. All it needed was just
a pinch of salt and possibly a bit of butter.

When I was done, the reporter said, "Since you believe in
your machine's popcorn so strongly, let's see if you can sell it
to the man or woman on the street. Where are you bound for
after the reception?" I told him we were spending the next three
days in Manchester. He replied, "Super! Find a spare hour or
two and we'll send a crew up there. We'll pick an outside location and film you trying to sell your popcorn."

There was a challenge I was ready to accept. I always feel
that if I believe in a product, I can sell it. I thought our machines
produced the best homemade popcorn you could buy. With my
experience as a salesman, I was certain I could convince a few
British citizens to try this luscious treat.

Three days after the reception, the BBC man arrived at my
hotel. He brought a pushcart laden with my machines and a
chef's outfit to be worn by me. I was told that the cameras would
keep filming until I had made a sale. He then escorted me to a
location that had already been picked by his crew. It was the
Manchester spot known as the "Shambles." I had never seen so
many derelicts in one place. Most of them were either scroung-
ing cigarettes, sleeping off a drinking session, or getting one
underway. There were liquor bottles strewn all over the place.
It wasn't quite the test-market site I had had in mind. It just
didn't appear as if it could yield the proper demographics.

Decked out in my apron and cook's hat, I pushed my fancy
little cart to the nearest corner. My four popcorn makers were
cooking away. I knew I couldn't possibly sell any popcorn to the
derelicts. It was unlikely they would have the twenty cents needed

for the purchase. So I was forced to go after pedestrians as they passed through the Shambles. This was not easy. No one wanted to linger in this place for very long. I found myself in a series of foot races, trying to catch up to anyone who remotely resembled a potential customer. I ran up to one prosperous-looking man and said, "Would you like to try some great popcorn, cooked American style with salt and butter? Only twenty cents!" He wouldn't look at either me or the popcorn. Instead, he just brushed by, nearly knocking the bag from my hand. A few moments later, I got the attention of a young woman. She wasn't any more receptive to my pitch than that first fellow. For the next fifteen minutes, no matter what I tried, I couldn't make a sale.

Finally, I came across a nanny accompanied by a little girl. Having had no success dealing with adults, I decided to capture the youth market. I placed a few kernels in the child's hand and encouraged her to try them.

Before she could place one in her mouth, her nanny slapped them from her hand and yelled, "You mustn't ever take sweets from strange men!" I must say that last comment made me a bit huffy. I replied, "Madam, this outfit might look silly to you, but I can assure you that I am not strange and this is not candy. It is American popcorn. It's much better for this girl than any sweet. Here, try some yourself."

The nanny accepted a small handful. After tasting it, she turned to the child and said, "Yes, all right my dear. You may have some." The little girl grabbed a few kernels and placed them in her mouth. I could feel the tension rising. Was she going to like the popcorn? Would she beg Nanny to buy her some? I couldn't take any chances. I wasn't merely trying to sell a bag of popcorn; I was defending the honor of God, country, Remington, and the Popcorn Institute of America! I had to get this order! As soon as she started chewing, I began painting a vista, saying, "There now, isn't that wonderful? So delicious and healthful! I bet you've never tasted anything as good!"

To be quite frank, the child didn't look pleased with this culinary experience. She appeared to be chomping on a wad of Styrofoam and kept making the most extraordinary faces. I was afraid she was going to spit my delectable creation into the camera lens. Working fast, I turned my attention to the nanny. I was pretty sure she had enjoyed her little sample. I asked, "Wouldn't you like to take a bag of this healthy snack home with you?" She eyed me suspiciously and asked, "How much is it?" I'm an entrepreneur. I had already discovered that the product wasn't moving at twenty cents, so I came up with an instant marketing ploy. A one-time only, half-price sale. I offered her a bag for ten cents.

I can't tell you how grateful I was when this lovely woman handed over the money. I had finally sold a bag! It gave me the same satisfying jolt I had received when I sold my first account as a young salesman with Lever Brothers. The cameras moved in to record the historic transaction. I looked into the lens and said, "As you can see, while it might take a little time, Britons will love this popcorn once they give it a chance."

In the midst of my triumphant words, a derelict approached the cart. He was a battered fellow, wearing a dilapidated overcoat and sporting a number of fresh scabs on his forehead. I couldn't tell if he had been in a fight or had just fallen down. His eyes were bloodshot, his face dirty with week-old stubble. When he opened his mouth to speak, his breath nearly blinded me. Grabbing my sleeve, he said, "I'm hungry, could you give me some of that stuff you're making?"

How could I refuse? With the cameras still rolling, I handed him a bag. He stuffed his cheeks with a fistful of popcorn and commenced chewing. Unfortunately, he had no teeth. As he put the popcorn in the right side of his mouth, the half-gnawed, slimy white bits would drool out on the left. It was one of the most disgusting sights I had ever seen.

The piece was part of that evening's news. Wouldn't you know it, they showed my big sale, but they ended the story with the shot of the hobo spouting corn. I held my head and thought, "Great, just the thing people want to see after dinner. That picture is going to sell a lot of machines."

As it turned out, the popper was about to have greater worries than this humorous news story. A month after leaving England, I received a telex from my managing director. It read, "The popcorn program is in trouble. Please phone."

I reached him that afternoon. He said, "I received a call from the attaché at the embassy. There has been a drought in your American regions and there is no longer any excess corn to sell. The Agriculture Department and the Popcorn Institute are pulling out of our agreement."

This meant Remington was stuck with 40,000 popcorn makers and no promotional support. Our entire marketing strategy depended on that government-financed advertising and the mammoth influx of American popcorn into the British market. Boy, I'll say the popcorn program was in trouble. When I asked my director how we could salvage something out of this debacle, he replied, "Why don't we buy popcorn from an American company and give it away with our machines? We can build a promotion around that."

That sounded like as good an idea as any. We purchased a truckload of popcorn from Orville Redenbacker and hired women to demonstrate our machines across England. Without the advantage of any advertising, we managed to unload about 30,000 of the poppers—at cost. We didn't make a single penny from their sale. In fact, we were actually operating at a loss. The cost of the popcorn and the demonstrators cut into our margin and there were still 10,000 machines sitting in our Bridgeport factory. We couldn't sell them in the U.S. They weren't equipped with the proper voltage. Frankly, we didn't know what to do with them.

A few months after this episode, our Middle Eastern distributor was visiting our plant. Passing through the lab, he noticed one of the machines. The guys in the lab had been using it to make popcorn during their lunch break. The distributor was taken with the gizmo and asked for a demonstration. After watching it go through its paces, he asked if the machine could be adapted to cook other foods.

That was a good question. We'd never thought about it. When we asked him what, specifically, he had in mind, he explained that everybody in the Middle East ate nuts during their Sabbath. Hosts continually had to heat up these treats in the oven whenever guests arrived. This roasting was time consuming and involved the use of messy oils. Our distributor thought the hot-air machine might offer his countrymen a more trouble-free cooking alternative.

After careful examination, our engineers found that the machine could be easily adapted at a low cost. We just had to add a minor attachment and a nut tray. This done, the transformed corn poppers were then shipped to the Middle East as nut roasters. The result? Not only did we sell our remaining inventory at a profit, we ended up with a new business. The Remington roaster is still being manufactured in, and sold throughout, the Middle East. It is a very popular item. This should show you that a product that is a dud in one country can be a winner in another. It also proves that a good entrepreneur is not just someone who can turn a lemon into lemonade. On occasion, he can make peanut butter out of popcorn!

Sir Clive and the C5

Sometimes even a bit of global maneuvering cannot turn the most worthy lemon into lemonade. About two and a half years ago, I was visiting the U.K. on business. While there, several of us happened to attend an exhibition at Earls Court. A model greeted us in the building's lobby. She stood next to the C5, an electric mini-car manufactured by Sinclair Vehicles, and was passing out leaflets extolling the vehicle's virtues.

The car is actually an electric tricycle, built low to the ground, and able to carry only one driver-passenger. It has a single front wheel with two more in the rear and a steering bar that's positioned beneath your legs. I thought that it could serve as a wonderful transport over short distances. For instance, my wife and I have an apartment in Florida that we use as a vacation hideaway. It is located on a development that is barely four miles long. That mini-car looked like it would be the ideal leisure vehicle for traveling within that complex. I could drive it whenever I went to the nearby tennis court or had to pick up a newspaper. That would free our regular car for Ellen's use. She could take it whenever and to wherever she wanted and not have to be concerned about dropping me off or picking me up.

We asked the model what she could tell us about the car. All she could do was hand me a pamphlet. She didn't know what kind of mileage it did or how often the battery had to be recharged. She didn't even know where or how the thing could be purchased. This was an egregious error on the part of her company. You should never allow anybody to present or demonstrate your product unless they are thoroughly schooled in its use and benefits. You want them to know the item as well, if not better, than you do.

I asked some of the fellows connected with our English company to find out where I could buy the C5. Locating the distributor, they had a car shipped to our factory in Bridgeport. I was like a child on Christmas morning when it arrived. I couldn't wait to tool around in it. A quick spin to the local grocery store convinced me that the C5 had been a sound purchase. I wasn't alone in this assessment. Almost everyone who saw the mini-car wanted to buy one. As I was soon to find out, this was not a reaction shared by consumers across the Atlantic.

Sir Clive Sinclair, the C5's inventor, was having a devil of a time trying to sell his cars in England. His company had been marketing this battery-powered vehicle as an alternative to gas-gulping automobiles. Ads showed the C5 making its rounds through urban traffic.

This was a mistake. Several factors militated against the C5 being able to replace more traditional vehicles. For one, the car could only do about twenty miles an hour, so it wasn't practical for highway use. In addition, it was built so low that a flag had to be attached to a high pole connected to the car's rear. This served as a warning to other vehicles. Without it, drivers might not be aware that your car was in front of them. They could easily run over you before realizing what they had done. Knowing that the flag was the only thing standing between you and disaster did little for your peace of mind. Of course, this flag also offered no protection if a car in front of you suddenly stopped short. Your C5 could slide beneath the larger vehicle, possibly causing injury. Finally, the car's body was made of a light but durable plastic. This lack of bulk could make a driver, used to the armor of metal automobiles, feel particularly vulnerable.

The British press crucified Sir Clive for manufacturing a product that lacked a practical use. Admitting it was not a replacement for conventional vehicles, Sir Clive defended the C5 as an important first step toward the manufacture of a truly all-purpose electric car. This hardly silenced his critics in the media. One ran a picture showing the C5 attempting to fight through city traffic wedged between two trucks. It was not an inspiring sight. In fact, it was downright frightening. It gave the impression that the mini-car and its driver were about to be crushed by the two elephantine vehicles.

I was in England at the height of the bad publicity. Though I had never met Sir Clive, I knew of him as an innovative leader in the computer and electronics industries. I felt it took a lot of guts to come out with a product this innovative and wanted to phone him with some encouragement. One entrepreneur to another. It seemed a good time to let him know that he had at least one very satisfied customer.

Sir Clive wasn't in to take my call. I left a message explaining who I was and congratulating him for making such a fine product. Two hours later, one of his officers phoned me. After thanking me for the unsolicited praise, he asked if he could meet with me that evening.

He arrived at my hotel accompanied by a small delegation of Sinclair executives. They didn't waste much time getting to the marrow of their purpose. They had hardly removed their coats when one of them asked if Remington would like to help their company market the C5. I told them it was a possibility we could explore. Sold in the U.S. as a leisure vehicle rather than an urban auto, the C5 would not have to endure the ridicule it had suffered in England. I suggested that this fresh start could make all the difference in its acceptance by consumers. Buoyed by my response, the executive arranged for Sir Clive to meet with me at our Connecticut factory. That encounter resulted in an agreement allowing Remington to distribute the C5 in the U.S. The mini-car would be sold in community developments, such as the one I visited in Florida, and on college campuses. We thought the vehicle would have an appeal to students. The cars would also be offered to some select retailers.

The first shipment from England brought us about 1,000 C5s. We used 150 of them in a southwestern test market. Sold at various prices, we found the mini-car received its most favorable response when retailed at $400. A higher price hampered sales significantly; anything under that made it an unprofitable venture.

Sir Clive had agreed to sell us each C5 for $250. Even with the cost of shipping, this left us with an adequate margin for advertising and fair profit. Unfortunately, the value of the American dollar began to erode rapidly just around this time. Our analysts projected that this sudden free fall could find us paying $350 for each C5. Such a slim margin would leave us little breathing room.

Though the increased price would multiply our risk, we were still ready to leap into the market. We had that much belief in the venture. Then our insurance company squelched the deal. They had issued us a policy for the test market at a relatively low cost. Insuring a nationwide retail launch, however, was going to require a more extravagant plan.

The insurance company thought the vehicle would pose a high risk if used on the open highway. There wasn't anything we could do to allay these fears. Therefore, when the company agreed to issue us a policy, protecting us from liability, it was for a princely annual premium of $500,000.

We just could not cover that. It had already been established that the C5 could not be sold to retailers for more than $400. Such a high premium would have wreaked havoc with our margins. What a predicament. We could have sold a lot of C5s without making a penny of profit! Unable to negotiate a lower rate with the insurance company, I had to call Sir Clive and tell him our deal was off.

Being an entrepreneur, Sinclair was not about to accept failure easily. He came back to us with another plan. Apparently, an Israeli company had recently expressed interest in manufacturing, distributing, and exporting the C5. Sir Clive had convinced them they could build the car for $250, returning us to the original profit margin. An Israeli insurance company had already offered to underwrite a policy at rates that would not be ruinous.

After meeting with representatives for all sides, we drew up a trilateral agreement. The Israeli company would manufacture the car, Remington would distribute it in the U.S. and Canada, and Sir Clive's company would receive a royalty for each C5 sold. It was further stipulated that the car had to be manufactured for $250 or less. Any rise in price, unless first approved by Remington, would immediately void the contract.

When it came time to sign the document, Sir Clive could not get the price limitation into the contract. The Israelis didn't want to be on the hook if their costs became dramatically inflated. I could understand their hesitancy. No one wants to be locked into a potential loss. But without that guarantee, Remington could not risk the deal either. It's a shame. Properly marketed, I think the C5 is a splendid product. It's too bad its story couldn't have had the same happy ending as the popcorn maker.

Know Your Market

If you are able to do business in a foreign country, you should realize that each nation can have its own peculiarities when it comes to doing business. Learning what the nuances might be in advance can help you avoid some unusual pitfalls.

For example, suppose you had been in the American watch business in the sixties and seventies and had wished to compete for government or military contracts. Benrus had been involved with several of these open bids. We found you had to do more than just tender the lowest bid or offer the best quality. Federal officials required that you buy a certain brand of jewel to be used in your watch movements. If you didn't, your offer wouldn't receive any consideration.

An American Indian tribe mined the mandatory stones. Their products were called Turtle Mountain Jewels. I'm sure the law demanding their use was well intentioned. Unfortunately, the jewels had one minor flaw: they didn't work. They were the wrong shape and tended to crack rather easily. If you inserted them in a movement, there was no way you could guarantee how long they would keep the thing running. You also couldn't vouch for the watch's accuracy.

Luckily for us, the government contract only stipulated that we had to buy the jewels. It didn't mention anything about using them. Benrus would purchase the appropriate number of Turtle Mountain Jewels for each of our watches. If we had a contract for 10,000 watches, each requiring seventeen jewels, we ordered 170,000 gems. Then we would place them in storage and use better-quality stones. At one point, we had over two million gems locked in a warehouse. We tried to use them on some of our Wells jewelry, but they just weren't good enough. They ended up as fodder for our disposal. It used to break our hearts to see such waste, but this was the price of doing business while handicapped by a well-intentioned, misguided policy.

Knowing the special needs of a country can help inform many a decision. When I first took over Remington, we were looking to cut all the fat out of our operation. Anything that could save the company money and perk up its cash flow was examined. One of the first things to catch our eye was a shaver that operated on a dry cell battery. It hardly seemed practical. This model had the same power and cutting efficiency as our more convenient Remington rechargeable. However, after eight to ten weeks of regular shaving, the batteries would have to be replaced. It didn't sound terribly economical to me, and looked like something Remington could live without.

I was ready to put this item on the list of possible cuts, when two things grabbed my attention. First, the shaver was sold almost exclusively in the U.K. Second, this battery-powered Remington accounted for over 25 percent of our English shaver sales!

It's always been very important for us to keep a strong profile in the British Isles. I wasn't about to kill a product that was enjoying such a great success over there. Curious to discover the reason for this extraordinary, isolated performance, I called my English managing director. He explained that bath-

rooms in many older British dwellings do not have electric outlets. A man tackling his beard after his morning bath or shower
had no place to plug in his shaver. Using an extension cord to
reach a socket outside of the bathroom was too much of a
bother. If we took away the convenience of the dry cell shaver,
our customers would probably either jump to a competitor or
go back to shaving with a blade. Those possibilities made up my
mind. We continued manufacturing the battery-powered Remington and eventually offered it in our catalogs to our American
customers. They've been buying it as a backup shaver to be used
on long trips or outdoor outings where an electrical outlet might
be hard to find.

Often the quality standards for products vary from country
to country. The Friendship Company was importing a large
number of jade items from China. At least, we thought they were
jade. The invoices said they were jade. The Chinese customs
officers didn't dispute this claim. Every country we shipped them
to accepted them as jade. Every country, that is, except Great
Britain. The U.K. has a higher standard. After we brought these
items into the country, British authorities claimed they didn't
qualify for jade classification in the U.K. We showed them our
bills and duty slips but couldn't persuade them to abandon this
stand. Hit with a $10,000 fine, we were ordered to call our
jewelry "carved Chinese stone." We had a fabulous jade ele-
phant that had been racking up tremendous sales throughout
England. As soon as we rechristened it, the numbers took a
nosedive.

Chinese silver gave us another problem. The Oriental version of sterling and what the English regarded as sterling were
apparently two different metals. Friendship was not allowed to
advertise any of our earrings, bracelets, necklaces, or other silver items as sterling in the U.K. Again, this dented our sales. We
tried to persuade the Chinese manufacturers to adapt to the
British system of standards, but they wouldn't consider it. We
were trapped between two conflicting perspectives.

I couldn't fault either side. The English authorities weren't
about to lower their high standards for anybody. On the other
hand, in China we were dealing with a country that had gotten

along rather nicely as a closed society for more than sixty years. As far as the Chinese were concerned, they knew what jade was. They had been using it to produce breathtaking *objets d'art* when our ancestors were huddling in caves. They couldn't see any reason why they should acquiesce to what they felt were the wacky requests of some uneducated Westerners. If we had only known the difficulty the contrasting views would cause, we wouldn't have allowed ourselves to get stuck in the middle. We would probably never have attempted to bring the products into Britain. It just wasn't worth the hassle.

Your advertising can be restricted by the laws of certain nations. Though I speak French, I wasn't allowed to use my own voice for Remington TV ads airing in French Canada. You had to be a member of the Union des Artistes in order to do commercial voice-overs. I could appear in the ads, but my voice would have to be dubbed. The law was very strict about this. The authorities had even gone so far as to dub the voice of Catherine Deneuve in her Chanel commercial. This despite the fact that the actress's native language is French!

In order to comply with their regulations, I offered to become a dues-paying union member. We were informed that union membership was closed. My commercials couldn't run unless we allowed somebody else's words to be placed in my mouth. Stonewalled at every bureaucratic turn, we reluctantly complied.

The dubbed spots had been running for almost two years when I gave an interview to the Montreal *Gazette.* Most of the questions centered around an economic analysis of Quebec. At one point the reporter asked what it was like for an American to do business in French Canada. He also wondered if I would ever open a Remington factory in one of the provinces.

I responded that while I enjoyed the French-Canadian people, I found the climate for business most inhospitable. When the reporter asked why, I replied, "I do my own commercials in my own voice because we have found it heightens the realism. We tested dubbing in languages other than English when we first took the spots abroad. It was so much less effective. Seeing this silver-haired gentleman speaking their language flawlessly and with the proper accent made people doubt I was the American who had actually bought this company. They thought I was an actor from their own country. When they hear my voice speaking their language less than perfectly, there isn't any confusion. I'm obviously a Yankee with enough confidence in his product to put his name, money, and reputation on the line. That's the whole thrust of our ads. Your government and its union regulations are destroying the image we are trying to portray."

The article ran that weekend. Less than a month later the union called inviting me to become a member. I've been using my own voice in French Canada ever since. I guess that says something about the power of the press and the power of entrepreneurial perseverance. I just wouldn't let the issue die.

Remington encountered a similar problem about three years ago. I had already done a German commercial and had hoped to run it in both West Germany and Austria. The German government had no objections, but the Austrians balked. Apparently most of the commercials that ran in Austria were made in Germany by Germans. Native Austrian performing artists weren't fond of this arrangement. It cut into their own employment. In response to their difficulty, the Austrian government passed a law identical to the one we had found in French Canada. Only native voices could be heard in commercials shown in Austria. Citing this restriction, the authorities refused to air our spots.

Attempting to resolve the problem, I flew into Austria to meet with the proper officials. I made the same argument I had in Canada. A slickly made commercial featuring a Victor Kiam speaking flawless Austrian would undermine the integrity of our spots. They countered by saying my demand would deprive an Austrian announcer of his employment. I sympathized with their position but could not accept it. I would even have agreed to a version of the Turtle Mountain solution, paying an Austrian actor his usual fees if they would just let me use my own voice. They would not change their minds.

I wasn't going to give up until I had made my case before

the country's highest authority. Telling the officials that their insistence would render my commercials useless, I asked to speak to the director-general of the Austrian Television Authority.

We met the next day. The fellow in charge was a pleasant man. We discussed the shaver and chatted about the general state of Austrian TV. After a few minutes of this, I bore down on the purpose of my visit. I said, "I doubt you're aware of it, but the law you have forbidding me to speak in my own commercials is both oppressive and discriminatory. Forgive me for speaking so harshly, but that's my honest view."

The director-general thought I was overreacting. He couldn't believe that dubbing my voice could cause us any real harm. I replied, "I can understand your skepticism, but this tenet eliminates opportunities for certain entrepreneurs. Remington is a comparatively small company. The electric-shaver manufacturers I compete with are international juggernauts. They are impersonal monoliths; their commercials don't rely on a personal message."

I then proceeded to lay out the history of our commercials, how they demonstrated that the little guy has a chance to fulfill his own dream. I further explained that Remington had a reputation for honesty in advertising. I was the only one who could tell my story because it was *my* story. If an announcer did it, the public just wouldn't buy it.

The director-general hemmed and hawed a bit and finally said, "But, Mr. Kiam, we have this rule. I can't change it just for you." Mr. Director-General, I thought, welcome to the wonderful world of entrepreneurship. I told him, "I don't want you to change the rule; it's a good law if it protects your citizens' chances for employment. Augment it. Make an exception for those people who own companies and would like to make their case before the public. How many of us are in that position? I doubt the amendment I'm suggesting will have anything but an imperceptible impact on the television artists' industry."

He agreed that my case had some merit and offered to bring it up at a meeting the following week. Shortly after that gathering, the rule was amended and we were able to go on the air as originally planned. If I had accepted the first no, gone along with the status quo, we would never have been able to use my voice. In that case, I doubt we would have run the commercials at all.

Brought to You by the BBC

I love British television. It's so much more freewheeling than the TV I've become used to in my own country. For instance, on one British show I was asked to be part of an "expert" panel. The evening's topic centered around the legalization of prostitution. I'm still not sure why they picked me for that particular subject. It wasn't clear whether they wanted me to discuss the possibilities of money-back guarantees or to determine the industry's Intangible Balance Sheet. I would guess that each of the prostitutes who appeared on the show did have a USP.

The *Ruby Wax Show* certainly gave me a jolt. I was one of her first guests. Ruby's approach to hosting was, shall we say, unorthodox. In preparation for my own appearance, I had made it a point to catch her act. It was the craziest show I had ever seen!

On the evening I tuned in, her studio audience included a 500-pound man dressed as a woman. He was one of the less eccentric people in attendance. Ruby's guest that night was the American actress Katherine Helmond. Sometime during their discussion, Ms. Helmond mentioned that she was friendly with a certain British celebrity. That woman's name escapes me now. Apparently Ms. Helmond was going to meet this luminary after the show.

Ruby asked, "You're seeing her tonight? Do you know where she is now?" Katherine replied that the woman was probably dining at a well-known London nightspot. The next thing you know, Ruby races from her chair, commandeers her camera crew into a car, and takes off. She was going to try to get a live, impromptu interview with this unsuspecting star.

The cameras continued to roll as she pulled up to the nightclub. A bouncer tried to block her entry, but Ruby was an entrepreneur. She was not going to be deterred. Pushing him out of the way, she stormed through the door, made her way to the star's table, and announced, "Hello, I'm Ruby Wax and we are on television right now." The celebrity looked stunned. She screamed, "Oh my God!" and leaped to the sanctuary of the ladies' room.

Ruby went after her like a heat-seeking missile. Yanking her reluctant cameraman, she charged into the bathroom and headed straight for the star's stall. Restaurant employees ended up having literally to drag her out of the ladies' room. I couldn't stop laughing, but Ellen started to have some second thoughts about my upcoming appearance. She wondered if it was a good idea for me to go on such a wacky show. I can tell you right now there is nothing like this on American TV.

I considered her concerns but decided to do the show anyway. After all, I'm an entrepreneur, a risk-taker, right? I got to the studio and was disappointed to find that there weren't any 500-pound transvestites waiting to enliven my audience. Instead, I got a fellow dressed in nothing but a G-string and tattooed from head to toe in tiger stripes.

They had scheduled me as the evening's second guest. Dressed in a bathrobe and clenching a long cigarette holder between my teeth, I was supposed to run through my commercials in several different languages. Then we were going to talk about the various Remington products. I showed her the VicVac and demonstrated how it worked. Then I pulled out the Fuzz Away, a new product used to shave pills off your clothes.

Ruby was enthralled with this item. I was about to show it off when she said, "Let me try it!" Taking it from my hand, she turned her back to the audience, hiked up her dress, and peered between her legs. Then she bolted back up, turned to her audience, and announced, "No, the fuzz is still there, folks!" Oh, if I hadn't been howling so hard I would have died from embarrassment. I couldn't believe she had said that. Pulling such a stunt would have earned her a week's suspension on an American network. It didn't bother me though. However, if I'm ever on her show again, I'll be sure to leave the Fuzz Away home.

Doing Business in the Land of the Rising Yen

I've always been impressed with the industriousness of the Japanese people. For them, doing the very best job they can is a
matter of honor. With Japan moving to the forefront of the
global marketplace, you can see how this attitude has paid huge
dividends.

Remington has had its own company in Japan for the better
part of this decade. Before entering the Japanese market, we
sought the help of a consultant, an expert on trade in that area.
Ninety-nine percent of the time, I won't use consultants. I've
always maintained that they are like castrated bulls. They can't
perform; all they can do is advise. However, in this case, we
needed someone familiar with the territory to draw up a market
profile. His research convinced us that we could create a niche
for ourselves in Japan. With that information in hand, I went
over and paved the way for our entry. If you're thinking of
entering a foreign market you can also use a consultant or trade
organization to help with your research. But once the facts and
figures are in, you have to go to that country and handle your
own negotiations. You can't allow a consultant to run with that
ball. No one can sell your company, product, or idea better than
you. No consultant or advisor can know your business or your
competition as well as you.

Our initial foray into the country came as part of a joint
venture with a Japanese company. Fifty percent of our board of
directors were Americans representing Remington. The remaining half was made up of our Japanese partners. Having
worked closely with its people, I have come to know the nation
well. In a time of huge U.S. trade deficits, we are one of the few
products made in America and sold in Japan. To succeed over
there you have to be more than just a good businessperson. You
have to understand the people, and be able to adapt to their
culture and its nuances.

For instance, my Japanese managing director and I once
called on the buyer for one of Japan's largest department stores.
This was at a time when Remington was first trying to open up

Japan. It was crucial that we have a big success with this initial test of the market. I wanted to make a sale to every store we called on. Netting this large account would certainly give our program a terrific opening boost.

The buyer, let's call him Mr. Tanaka, greeted both of us warmly. He asked me how my flight from the States had gone and how long I was going to be in his country. My managing director, Hank Saito, served as translator for both of us so there was no communication gap. A few minutes after our arrival, Tanaka's secretary brought in rice cakes and tea. Everything seemed to be going splendidly.

When the buyer asked what he could do for me, I told him we were launching our shaver with a mammoth market test. It was going to be backed by a national advertising campaign, with heavy concentration on television. Mr. Tanaka was shown product samples, along with graphs and charts describing our entire promotion. I thought it looked like a first-class presentation. If I had been the buyer and this campaign had been brought to me, I would have leaped at the chance to put in an order.

When I finished, Mr. Tanaka was all smiles. He looked at me as if I were the Easter Bunny and Santa Claus all rolled into one. Speaking through Mr. Saito, Tanaka agreed that we had a wonderful program. He asked some questions about pricing and congratulated us on the craftsmanship of our shavers. Then he bowed deeply. The meeting had ended.

I couldn't wait to ask Hank how large an order we could expect from this man. As soon as we got out of the office, though, I sensed something was amiss. The polite smile had faded from my director's face. I said, "Hank, what on earth are you looking so glum about? I don't think I've ever had a better meeting with a buyer." Shaking his head, Saito said, "That may be, Vic. But we didn't get the order." I couldn't believe it. I asked, "Are you sure? That just can't be. What did Tanaka say?"

Hank explained that it wasn't important what Tanaka said, it was what he didn't say that underscored our failure. He hadn't given us the name of his wholesaler. The significance of this was lost on me until Hank explained how the Japanese system works.

Unlike stores in the U.S. and Europe, Japanese shops have no room to carry any inventory. Space is at a premium in this overcrowded country. So wholesalers will hold a store's merchandise and use it to stock each retailer two or three times weekly. These wholesalers are the only route into the retail market. Without an introduction from a buyer, a manufacturer cannot do business with a wholesaler. This means he has no way of getting his product into the consumers' hands.

Was Mr. American Entrepreneur about to accept this rejection with Oriental detachment? I should say not! I suggested we go over Mr. Tanaka's head and speak directly to the merchandise manager. Yes, it was the Gray's drugstores strategy all over again. Hank kiboshed that bright idea. He said, "That would never fly. No matter how delicately you handled the buyer's boss, things just aren't done that way in Japan." From the grave tone in his voice, I knew this was a status quo I could not undo. However, the situation was not hopeless. Hank had hatched his own entrepreneurial plan.

He made an appointment for us with the branch manager of our bank in Tokyo. Hank explained our predicament to this fellow, who promptly called the manager of the store's bank. We didn't get an immediate solution. Instead, we were told to wait in an adjoining office while the two bank officials worked on our problem. Some ninety minutes later, our bank manager came in with good news. His colleague had just called back. We were to meet with the store's president at nine o'clock on the following morning.

This meeting was held at an office located about a mile from the store. I gave the president the same presentation I had given his buyer. When I concluded, there was more bowing and smiling before we left. As we made our way to the elevators, I must admit I was more confused than ever. That must have showed. Laughing, Hank looked at me and said, "Don't worry, Victor. We got the order." I asked if this meant the president had proffered the wholesaler's name. Hank shook his head and replied, "No. But we have permission to see the buyer again at two o'clock this afternoon. Only he can make the final decision." Terrific. This was the same guy who had turned us down only yesterday. I wondered why things should be any different twenty-four hours later.

Hank assured me everything would be all right. That afternoon, we kept our appointment with Mr. Tanaka. I suddenly felt like I was participating in a Noh drama. Both Tanaka and his secretary acted as if they had never laid eyes on us before. Everything happened just as it had the previous day. The first thing Tanaka asked me was how my flight to Japan had been and how long I intended to stay. The secretary once again brought in rice cakes and tea. And then he asked what he could do for us.

I made my presentation as if it were for the first time. He asked the same questions about pricing. When we were finished, we bowed and made our way out of the office. As soon as we got clear of that room Hank said, "I told you everything was fine. We got the name of his wholesaler." We were in business! I later asked Hank why the transaction had taken such a circuitous route. He explained that we couldn't have seen the store president without going through the banks. We needed the introduction. I had understood that, but I couldn't see any difference between my going to the merchandise manager, as I had first suggested, or our speaking to the store president. As I would find out, there was a very big difference. It was all a question of face. Obviously, the store president had interceded on Remington's behalf. But having us repeat the presentation allowed Tanaka to create the illusion that the order was his decision and that he hadn't been influenced by his superior. This allowed us to make our sale while Tanaka retained his honor. To the Japanese, nothing is more important. The entrepreneur who forgets this won't do much business in Japan.

He should also know that the Japanese are an intensely loyal people. Remington's operations in Japan are now in the black. In our first few years over there, however, we had quite a struggle. We were getting murdered by the strong dollar. The company lost over half a million dollars in our first year.

Six months into the following year, that trend continued. I began looking at cost-cutting measures to ensure our survival. Eventually, I had to consider our payroll.

Mr. Osaka, our company president, had come to us with a financial background. We no longer had much financial business to worry about and Hank Saito was actually running the company's day-to-day operations. It appeared as if Mr. Osaka, who was costing us over $75,000 a year, was expendable.

Since he would be taking on added responsibilities, Hank was the first one to learn of my decision. He suggested holding a board meeting before taking action. That was fine with me. I must admit my mind was pretty well made up, but I knew the move would require board approval. I was hoping our Japanese partners wouldn't oppose the dismissal too strenuously.

We met the following day. The board consisted of six members: myself, two other Americans, and three Japanese. One of these was Mr. Osaka. He sat there while I made the case for his dismissal. That was awkward. I felt like Lucretia Borgia discussing a choice of poisons with her intended victim.

I tried to handle it as best I could. I praised Mr. Osaka for his past performance—easy to do since he was a fine executive—but explained that circumstances necessitated his removal. When I was finished, the three Japanese directors talked amongst themselves in their native language. It seemed like a calm, reasoned discussion. I thought they were helping Mr. Osaka come to terms with the inevitable. Therefore, I was somewhat surprised when Hank Saito asked if we could adjourn the meeting until the following day. Hoping to keep things as harmonious as possible, our American contingent agreed.

We met the next morning. Hank Saito opened things up by announcing, "We have taken your points under advisement and agree that we must cut back on spending. We have had a discussion with the company staff. They have volunteered to take a 10 percent pay cut so that Mr. Osaka can remain as president. Mr. Osaka, Mr. Morita, and I will also decrease our salaries by the same percentage." I almost fell out of my chair! I said, "If that's OK with you, that's more than fine with me. I wasn't happy about having to let Mr. Osaka go in the first place. I'm glad you came up with this most entrepreneurial answer to our problem."

Does that story tell you something about the Japanese? It taught me that they operate as a team. When one person in the company is having difficulty, it becomes a joint problem. No wonder there doesn't seem to be an obstacle they can't overcome. I'd like to finish this chapter with a little story that might provide some further insight into the Japanese businessman's philosophy. I was dining in a Tokyo restaurant with several prominent Japanese executives. They were showing me quite a time. They honored me with a seat at the head of the table and saw to it that our waiter tended to my every need. When it came time to order our meal, they all recommended that I join them in enjoying a great Japanese delicacy. How could I refuse such gracious hosts?

The dish was brought out and placed before us. I wasn't certain what it was, but it seemed to be some sort of fish. As I started to eat my portion, I noticed that everyone at our table was watching me with rapt attention. I chewed a morsel, swallowed, and smiled my approval. It was a succulent dish. They didn't say a word. They just kept looking at me. After several moments of this, they finally heaped the fish on their own plates and started to dig in.

I asked one of my hosts why everyone had been staring. Had I committed some sort of culinary offense? Was I supposed to lead everyone in a Japanese version of grace before indulging my palate? He assured me I had done nothing wrong. Hardly able to hold back a grin, he explained. "You see, Victor, this is a very special fish. Only a select few chefs in our country are licensed to prepare it." When I asked why that was, he continued: "Because it is blowfish. It contains a powerful poison that must be extracted before cooking. If this is not done properly, just a few bites can be injurious, even fatal. My colleagues were just checking to see if you would survive before they partook of their own meal." Oh my lord! I guess I should have been offended. Instead, I was impressed. I figured, "No wonder this country is doing so well. These Japanese are even entrepreneurial about dinner." After all, in essence they were trying to measure the chef's intangible asset: his ability to remove the toxin from the blowfish. They just happened to be using me as their balance sheet!

8

Brainstorming

I'd like you to come into my office. Don't worry. You're not about to be called on the carpet. I just thought we'd lean back, throw our feet up on the desk, and do some brainstorming. We'll share some ideas on elements of entrepreneurship. We won't worry about a formal structure. Let's just free-associate and talk about any topic that jumps into our heads.

Getting a Raise

Some time ago, Senator Edward Kennedy was trying to capture the Democratic Party's presidential nomination. During an interview with newsman Roger Mudd, he was asked why he wanted the country's top post. He couldn't answer the question. It's not just that he couldn't find the right words; he couldn't find any words at all. It made it seem as if he either didn't have any concrete motivation for competing for the office or that his reasons were too trivial to share with the public. You can imagine how this went over with the nation's voters. They figured, "If he can't make a better case for himself than this, why should I give him my vote?" Almost immediately after the interview, the Kennedy campaign went into a tailspin from which it never recovered.

Senator Kennedy had committed the same blunder made by thousands of employees every year. He had asked for a raise—in this case, a job promotion—but couldn't show his employers, the voters, why he deserved it.

I've seen this happen countless times. A person calls on his boss and says, "I've been here for a year and I think I should have my salary increased." You ask them how they have earned the pay hike, and they give you an answer as substantial as the senator's. I don't understand it. If you were selling a car to someone, what would you do? Go up to a potential customer and say, "Buy this car because I want to sell it"? No, you would paint a vista detailing every attractive aspect of the vehicle. You'd talk about the great mileage it offered, safety features, its affordable price, and all the other items that turn on the consumer.

Whenever you make a presentation, you go in armed with facts, figures, charts, graphs, and anything else that will support you. In both instances, you come as prepared as possible. If you're looking to get a pay raise from your employer, you should bolster your request with the same thoroughness.

As a first step, take the time to make your case on paper. Document everything you have done for the company over a specific period of time. Be honest with yourself. A list peppered with hyperbole won't withstand the slimmest executive gust. One overstated item can cast doubts on your entire paper's credibility. You can guard against this by drawing up a private comparison between yourself and a fellow employee in a similar position. See how you stack up against this person. Are you producing a measurable amount more for the company? Remember, this is a *private* comparison. This list is for your eyes only and shouldn't be used in your actual presentation. Its only purpose is to provide you with a perspective.

Once you've established that you have indeed made a substantial contribution, put together an outline for your employer. No matter how much you've done, don't overload your boss with paper. The emphasis should be on the quality of your performance, not the quantity of print you can produce. One or two pages should be enough. It should look something like this:

MEMO TO: Mr. Boss

RE: Past year's performance of Mr. E. M. Ployee, Director of Promotions

Over the past year at Boss and Sons, Mr. Ployee has created the following programs:

1. *The International Submarine Band Memorial Dinner:* an event that opened up forty new accounts for this company and attracted nationwide news coverage.

2. *The World Cup Sweepstakes:* a promotion that boosted our sales 33 percent during its six-week run. It was so successful we already have a variation of this idea in place for next year.

3. *The Krazy Widget Giveaway:* a premium promotion of a new product. We gave away one Krazy Widget sample with each purchase of a container of Hammond's Miracle Hair Restorer. An enormous hit— it increased sales by 40 percent and provided the base for the successful launching of our Krazy Widget bracelets.

In addition, through a judicious use of vendors, Mr. Ployee has managed to bring in our ongoing promotions at 20 percent below their usual cost, saving this company over $100,000. Even with these savings, the company's past high standards were maintained and in some areas surpassed. Looking at the near future, Mr. Ployee has already arranged to have Krazy Widget featured as a November cover story for *Nuts and Bolts Magazine* (circulation: 3,000,000 national, 8,000,000 worldwide) and has a commitment from Sylvester Stallone to feature Hammond's Miracle Hair Restorer prominently in his upcoming film *Rocky V: Rocky Meets Frankenstein* (February release date).

In closing, I would like to point out that, over the last year, Mr. Ployee has represented the company in several community service and charitable projects including the Cancer Fund and the Annual Community Christmas drive. In December, he received the company's annual safety award for officially suggesting the installation of a safety net beneath the tightrope in the corporate gymnasium. He has been with the company for three years and receives a base salary of $40,000. Based on his performance, he would like his remuneration reevaluated.

What have you done with this summary? You have cast a brilliant spotlight on your achievements and have drawn a vista bright with future promise. With this document drawn up, make an appointment with your boss and present it to him at that meeting. Bring two copies so you can both go over your claims together. You have now given him something tangible to wrestle with. If you went in without proof and said, "Mr. B., I think I've done a lot for our company over this last year and would like to discuss a raise," he could dismiss you simply by saying, "Really? Well, I don't agree with you. Your raise is denied."

He can't easily dismiss that piece of paper. He might dispute some of your claims, in which case you would reach into your briefcase and bring out any records you have to support them. Remember, you're going to come with all your cannons loaded. By the time your meeting is over you will have obtained one of three things: a raise, an understandable refusal ("Yes, you're doing great, and I know you're not aware of this, but the company is about to have some rocky times"), or a clue that you might want to seek employment elsewhere. The offhand refusal, without reason, means your good efforts are unappreciated and might mean they will be forever undervalued.

Common sense should tell you the proper time to request a raise or a promotion. If you or your department recently made a blunder, you're not going to call on your boss no matter how good a year you've otherwise had. He could use that recent failure to undermine all your other accomplishments. If your meeting is about to begin and he seems to be in a bad mood, make an excuse and cancel. Reschedule for what you hope will be a more opportune time.

Whatever you do, don't look for a pay increase or a promotion when you know the company is going through some difficulty. That advice might seem so obvious as to be unnecessary, but I've known employees who used these critical moments to attempt a form of blackmail.

When I was chairman and president of Benrus, we were constantly up against the problems caused by undercapitalization. Things got particularly chancy just prior to a Christmas sales period. Needing additional capital to buy goods for that busy time, we were forced to re-do our loan agreement. The fellow negotiating the terms for us was one of my key executives. The banks were playing hardball, but he was giving as well as he was getting. I was confident his efforts would reap the money and the conditions we needed.

In the midst of these dealings, he came to my office to discuss his progress. After filling me in, he floored me by saying, "I think the company would be better off if you didn't spread yourself out so thin. You should divvy up your responsibilities. Why don't you continue as chairman and put me in as president of the company?"

Nothing else he said was specific. There wasn't even the hint of a threat uttered, but I got the clear inference that if I didn't agree to the change and the accompanying raise in pay, our loan agreement would be in jeopardy. Without that capital, Benrus could very well go under.

Now this fellow knew our backs were against the wall and he was almost certain that he was the only person in the company—at that particular time, anyway—who could handle these negotiations.

He was right on that score. Anyone else in the company would have been out of his element. I wouldn't have felt completely confident taking over the discussions; I had been too busy with the marketing side of the business to give it my full attention and it really wasn't my area of expertise. I couldn't hire a financial professional to replace him. It could have taken weeks to find someone. That new person would have had to spend several grueling days steeping himself in the company background. Once he was finished, he would have had to start the negotiations at ground zero.

What on earth could I do? Benrus couldn't afford that kind of delay; we needed a commitment for the money as quickly as possible. I also knew that firing one of Benrus's high-ranking officers at such a crucial juncture in the negotiations wouldn't be the best way to hold the bank's confidence. This fellow had every right to believe he was indispensable. He had entered my office with a loaded gun and had drawn a bead on my heart.

I was tempted to accede to his wishes, but I knew that wasn't any way to run a business. What sort of entrepreneur would I be if I bent with every threat that walked through the door? Putting on a jaunty air, I called his bluff. I told him that if he was unhappy with his present position and was unable to complete the negotiations, I would be happy to step in for him.

Thank God, he backed down. The loan agreement went through in time. As soon as it did, this fellow's importance to the company dropped considerably. Unable to trust him, I grew to depend on him less and less. He never got close to the position he craved and left Benrus shortly after this episode.

I'm going to let you in on a little secret, something he didn't know. I thought his idea of separating the two top spots in the corporation did in fact have some merit. Indeed, I had been toying with that very idea for a good while. I wasn't quite sure if it was the thing to do. I was still wrestling with the decision when he came to my office. Had he approached me at a less critical time, I would have given the matter serious consideration. He would have been one of my top candidates for the presidency. An able man, he possessed many of the qualities I look for in a top executive. These didn't count for anything once he tried to cut the legs out from under me and Benrus. I suddenly saw him as a selfish, grasping individual, ready to threaten the company's welfare to advance his own cause.

Thinking he could make good with this gambit also showed poor judgment. It was the sort of faux pas that leaves an indelible stain on your record. There was no way he could ever hold another high position in one of my companies. If your company is ever in a tough spot and your particular talents place you in an advantageous position, don't commit a similar error. Cast your self-interest aside and grab an oar with the rest of your colleagues. Then row for all you're worth. Once out in calmer seas, you'll find an appreciative employer ready to grant you your well-earned reward.

Keeping the Spirit Alive

I'm often asked how can you keep the entrepreneurial spirit alive within the corporate framework. I think you do it, first, by hiring people possessing the same zest for hard work as you and then by challenging their talents.

For instance, Remington's chief financial officer used to accompany me on my trips to our Japanese company. He would analyze their operations and their cash flow, do all the usual fiscal chores. About a year and a half ago, I found my schedule no longer permitted my frequent visits to the Orient. Wishing to keep open a clear line of communication, I called my financial officer in and said, "John, instead of having Hank Saito report to me, I'm going to have him deal with you from now on. You've seen the business over there and understand how it works. You are now responsible for the entire operation—the marketing, advertising, and all the rest of it—not just the financial end. You'll give me regular reports and we'll discuss the business's progress. If any questions or problems arise, you can come to me at any time. But the direction for the company will flow through you." I had shifted the responsibility from me to him, while keeping my hand in via the reporting process.

In most companies, the CFO wouldn't even be considered for a position of this sort. People would take one look at his present position and assume that he wasn't qualified to run a company's entire operation. As an entrepreneur, you have to look past the stereotype created by titles and see the worth of the employee.

We try to prevent the corporate tendency toward pigeon-holing by encouraging all our Remington executives to famil-iarize themselves with management areas outside their usual realm. A marketing executive at Remington is going to have more than just a passing interest in the manufacturing end of our corporation. When you're a growing enterprise, you want your management to be flexible enough to adapt to the demands of an always-growing, ever-evolving business. This means your company is prepared to face just about anything. It also adds a generous helping of spice to your corporate life.

Clear goals and incentives can also set off some entrepreneurial sparks. We have a man who handled all our company forecasts. He had never headed up his own product division. I made him product manager for our pool alarms. Along with the increased responsibility, we also gave him 10 percent of the profits from that business. Operating a mini-company within the Remington framework, he experiences fully the thrills and disappointments of guiding an entrepreneurial venture. He gets a taste of everything I go through. It makes him a tremendous asset. With a personal stake in the enterprise, he's more committed than ever to our success.

He's not alone in our company. As a matter of fact, every Remington employee shares in an incentive program. They know they are working for more than just a paycheck. If the company does well, they are going to do well. Consequently, they are constantly thinking of Remington's welfare and creating methods to improve our products. This takes place on every level of the company. Remington has become more than just a job, it's a vital part of their lives.

The atmosphere this creates is electrifying. When you walk through our doors, you can sense that you're looking at more than just a group of employees pulling themselves through another day. You're looking at a company of highly motivated entrepreneurs. Has it made a difference? You be the judge. We were recently named one of the "100 Best Companies to Work for in America." At the end of last year, for the first time since 1952, Remington became America's number one manufacturer of men's electric shavers. This from a company that was teetering on the edge of extinction when we took it over. I'd say that's a pretty good endorsement of our product, our people, and our approach.

A Cure for Growing Pains

More than anything else, entrepreneurs running small businesses often ask me how to raise capital in order to expand. If you're looking to branch out, I assume your enterprise must be doing well. As you already know, I've always been a great believer in leveraging one's intangible assets. One of these intangible assets is your success.

Suppose you had a thriving bookstore and wanted to open another in a different section of town. As the owner of a proven enterprise, you can approach venture capitalists or private investors and offer them equity in your new store. Equity investors are looking for a high return on their money; they are willing to take some risks. Show them what you've done. Your glowing bottom line gives eloquent testimony to your managerial abilities. Draw up a plan detailing how you will have an even greater success. Then sell them a piece of your dream. When your business keeps prospering, these happy investors will be a continual source of cash for any possible future expansions. If you take this approach, try to hold on to at least 51 percent of the enterprises. This will allow you to maintain a controlling interest in the business.

Any time your business grows, you are going to be faced with a number of decisions. For example, a man recently wrote me to ask if he should turn his lucrative part-time business into a full-time enterprise. I've often suggested that the budding entrepreneur should launch an initial venture as a part-time affair. It's an excellent test of your idea's viability, yet it allows you still to have the security of a regular paycheck.

Once this test has worked out, as his apparently had, you've taken the first step to entrepreneurial freedom. You must now estimate how much capital and cash is needed to take the business to a full-time level. Don't scrimp with the numbers! Cash is always king. When you don't have it, it's awfully hard to get. Call in an accountant, someone versed in the ways of small businesses, and have him help you with your figures. Be careful to add 25 percent to your final budget to cover any unforeseen glitches. With this figure in hand, estimate your weekly return from a full-time enterprise. If it is enough money to support you, take care of your overhead, and cover your start-up debt, then I heartily recommend your taking the full plunge.

A graphic design company owned by two young men in London faced another kind of decision when their business started to boom. With this increase, the administrative duties—ordering couriers, billing, handling the daily mail, and answering the phones—were demanding much of these gentlemen's time. They needed an administrator who would tend to these duties, freeing the owners to place their full attention on their work.

Their chief concerns centered around cost. They wondered what would be the more cost-effective move, hiring an experienced pro, who could jump into the job immediately, or a junior trainee. The less experienced employee would work at a lower salary but would require a good deal of training.

As entrepreneurs, they had only one choice. They had to hire the best person they could find. There is nothing wrong with hiring trainees to work within your company. However, an administrator in a service business usually holds a key position. If the company's performance starts to lag because of late deliveries or other tasks that have not been carried out efficiently, a reputation can be severely damaged. Since the administrator is often a liaison between company and account, he or she should be someone able to speak the technical language of the customer. You mustn't place your company in the hands of an amateur. In a situation like this, the established pro is worth the extra investment.

Having decided to spend a few extra dollars, the designers wondered how they could soften the impact on their overhead. Such an expense would have to be at least partially passed on to their customers. Nobody likes a price escalation. However, when they are necessary they should be presented in as straightforward a manner as possible.

I suggested the two men broach the additional costs while presenting contracts to their clients. They could list their usual charges and add a 5 to 10 percent surcharge, depending on the job and the administrator's salary. This would be identified as an administrative fee. As long as the billing is reasonable and the firm maintains its high standards, the customers shouldn't raise a squawk. No one, after all, expects you to lose money while providing your service.

One of the more unusual growth "problems" brought to my attention in recent years came from a dear lady in Sussex. She owned a small cat-breeding business. From 1986 to 1987, her revenues had more than doubled. She had advertised in the past, but, to use her own words, "business grew too quickly, forcing me to stop." Of course, when she ceased using the ads, business fell off. She was about to revive her ad campaign when she wrote to me, asking what percentage of her annual revenues should be allotted for advertising.

With apologies, I told her she was asking the wrong question. She already knew how much money to spend. Obviously her past advertising campaigns had been smashing successes. Why not repeat that formula? When I worked at Playtex and someone wanted to tinker with a proven, winning product or promotion, one of my bosses had a stock response, "If it ain't broke, don't fix it!" Business knocking down her door! Why, I can't think of an entrepreneur who wouldn't love to have this woman's difficulty. Placed in her position, if your business had increased dramatically with your last batch of ads, there is no earthly reason why you wouldn't do again exactly what you had done previously—but with the added advantage that the first bit of advertising has already acted for you as a wonderful test of the market. If business had improved by only a trickle, you would make changes. You might even discontinue the ads; a campaign that can't at least pay for itself with increased business is a campaign to abandon. On the other hand, if your ads generated a strong positive response, such as this woman received, you would be advised to make an entrepreneurial investment and enlarge your facilities before purchasing any more ads. *The person who takes the fullest advantage of success is the person who plans for it.*

You want to be able to accommodate that wonderful increase in business. Don't turn it away! In this case, the question you should be asking yourself is how much can I afford for expansion? You can estimate that figure easily enough. Just forecast how much your business will improve if you go back to your former advertising budget. Then enlarge your facility accordingly. Remember, a great success often brings along a bagful of new choices and responsibilities, from increasing a capital investment to hiring more employees to moving to a larger location. If you believe in yourself and the success of your venture, you have to be ready to grow with your business. You have to keep going for it!

Get Off the Air!

Because I appear in the Remington commercials, I often get calls or letters from entrepreneurs who are appearing in their own ads. They ask me about everything from how their copy should be written to how they can hire a good film crew. I offer them what little advice I can. I also warn them of the perils of starring in a commercial. Once your visage is flashed throughout thousands—and sometimes millions—of homes, your life undergoes a radical change. Like it or not, you become a celebrity. More than that, you become so firmly associated with your product, the two of you become indivisible in the customer's mind. From that point on, your public behavior will cast a direct reflection on your enterprise. Do you think that doesn't carry a heavy responsibility? As a fellow who can't even think about leaving his home while carrying a hint of five o'clock shadow, I can tell you it's no picnic.

A personal disgrace brought to the public's attention can destroy an ad campaign and, if not properly handled, ruin your business. The best evidence of this was brought to me not too long ago. A bank president had been doing his own TV commercials. They featured this rather staid, somber individual talking about how secure your accounts would be in his venerable institution. In the commercial's closing moments, he looked into the camera, his slate-gray eyes dispensing waves of integrity, and said, "You can sleep at night as long as you know I'm here

watching your account. Your money is safe with me." Not bad.
His pitch had a warm, personal approach. It was almost as good
as "I liked it so much, I bought the company!"

The commercial ran for about six months and had received
a lot of favorable comments. I had never met this man, but one
afternoon I received a phone call from one of his representatives. This young woman introduced herself and asked, "Mr.
Kiam, are you at all familiar with Mr. Jones's commercial?" I said
I was. She said, "Well, based on the latest news, what do you
think he should do?" I had to ask her to back up a bit. I wasn't
aware that there was any news concerning her boss. She apologized and explained that the story had apparently not gone
national yet. If it had I would have discovered that Mr. Jones had
been arrested on the previous night for driving while intox-
icated. He had apparently been zigzagging his car all over the
road. The police stopped him and had him submit to a Breath-
alyzer test. He didn't pass. In fact, I'm afraid it sounded as if he
didn't even come close.

I told her I could see where the adverse publicity could be
a problem and I was about to offer some advice. I was thinking
that he might be able to get through this mess if he called a press
conference, admitted he made a mistake, and then set up a fund
to help educate youngsters on the perils of drunk driving. A
compassionate public can be awfully forgiving when a man does
his penance in full view. Perhaps this fellow could make some
lemonade out of this lemon. It would certainly make for a safer
drink than what he had been imbibing.

As I started to offer this sage advice, his employee said, "I'm
afraid the drunk-driving charge is only one of his problems. You
see, after he flunked the test, state law required the police to do
a thorough search of his car. When they got to the trunk, they
found his arsenal." His arsenal! Yes, that's what the woman said.
It seems this fellow was caught with an unlicensed cache of
armaments, including a couple of .50 caliber machine guns, an
automatic rifle, and about thirty pistols. I imagine he kept his
anti-aircraft gun home because it wouldn't fit in the trunk. Well,
at least his commercials were truthful. Your money really was
safe with him as long as he didn't run out of bullets. He had

enough weaponry to hold off Colonel Gaddafi, Rambo, the Ned Kelly gang, and the entire Iranian army singlehanded.

After taking in the whole tale, I said, "I can't give him much advice on this one, but I will tell you what I would do if I were in his position. Get off the air! And do it as soon as possible. Yank the commercial you already have on, and reshoot a new one without this gentleman. You can't have him announcing 'Your money is safe with me' when he is being touted throughout the media as the drunk with an arsenal large enough to raid Fort Knox. I don't think it will go down very well with the public."

I added that, in time, he might be able to return as the company spokesman. In our Warholian world, where everybody seems to achieve their fifteen minutes of notoriety, people tend to forget scandals such as this in about a year. If Mr. Jones could forge a semblance of a reasonable excuse for his behavior and get off with a quiet fine and reprimand, he might even be back sooner. But as long as he was a hot item, he was going to have to distance himself from the bank so far as the public was concerned.

As you can see, appearing in your ads can be a two-edged sword. Yes, there is a certain amount of ego gratification when people recognize you on the street. On the other hand, you are no longer just you. The individual has merged with the company or product. You have to think twice before you do anything out of the ordinary in public. It's almost like being a political figure. Any taint on the person will attach itself to the office. Anything that publicly injures you is going to harm your enterprise.

Turn It Around

The entrepreneur launching a first venture is going to encounter a number of disappointments and unforeseen problems. You mustn't let them stop you! It's a rare business that doesn't have its share of problems. Greet these downward turns with your best face. They are nothing more than opportunities to exercise your entrepreneurial ingenuity.

In *Going For It!*, I introduced readers to my favorite barber, Jack. He's been cutting hair for years. At first he was employed by someone else, but after a while he had an urge to open a shop of his own. Finding what he thought was a prime location, he struck a deal with his landlord, a prominent New York hotel. They agreed that if he made his New York shop a success, he could open similar shops in the chain's other hotels across the United States.

This seemed like quite an opportunity. Jack walked around the hotel while it was still under construction and was mesmerized by its sheer size. At any one time, it would house over 2000 people. Jack would be its exclusive barber. Of course, the hotel's promise made the deal especially enticing. In one small leap, the barber could go from shop owner to franchise CEO.

The chasm that had to be cleared, however, turned out to be a mite wider than Jack originally figured. Jack worked as hard as he could to build his business, but he hadn't figured on a few obstacles. Though the hotel had a prestigious name, and offered magnificent service, it did a transient business. Visitors rarely stayed for more than two or three days and often had their hair cut before coming to town. Businessmen staying at the hotel would come to his shop only for a shoeshine. Those chairs were always full. But the shoeshining profits hardly made a dent in his overhead. Being inside the hotel and unable to advertise his presence on the street, he attracted virtually no walk-in business.

Jack's shop is large and the already high rent has been raised four times since the business opened. Anticipating a huge clientele, he was certain he could meet those gargantuan rates. When his bottom line failed to live up to his projections, Jack began to struggle. He was on his feet twelve hours a day, six days a week. Patches of snow began to swirl about his temples. Dark circles began to creep in under his eyes. After a year of barely making ends meet, no one would have blamed him if he had tossed in the towel. Jack is an outstanding barber, an artist with shears, and he had a small core of loyal customers. He could have found work at high wages with any shop in the city.

Jack, though, wants something more. He's an entrepreneur and he was not about to let his dream disintegrate without taking action. Rather than allow his problems to overcome him, he decided to attack them.

The first thing he had to do was broaden his client base. He had to increase his shop's profile. When it first opened, Jack's business had primarily catered to men. He began offering unisex styling in order to attract businesswomen on their lunch breaks. Brochures, outlining his full range of services, were printed and delivered to businesses in the area.

This increased his walk-in business. In an effort to catch the attention of the hotel's visitors, he persuaded management to enclose an advertising insert in each room's guest packet. That had a slight impact, but he was faced with the problem of timing. Most of these tourists and business travelers would still be getting their hair trimmed prior to their New York arrival.

Readjusting his thinking cap, Jack found another solution. He asked the hotel to provide its reservation list. A week to ten days before a guest was due to leave for New York, they would receive a coupon in the mail. It was an invitation from Jack, asking them to experience the pleasures of a professional New York haircut at a 30 percent discount. This promotion was such a success, he began to circulate the coupons, offering the same price break, to local businesspeople. He would just drop by an office and leave a handful.

There haven't been any miracles, but business has gradually turned around since Jack implemented these ideas. Bills are being paid, salaries are being met, and the shop is keeping busy. Jack is going to make it because he won't allow himself to fail.

If a venture of yours is wobbly, there is no reason why you can't resurrect it as Jack did. All he really did was take stock of his business's assets and liabilities. His talent was the store's greatest asset. The shop's low profile was its greatest liability. By doing everything he could to erase that weakness, he was able to expose people to his store's strength: his skilled hands. Jack's actions have given his dream some fresh hope. Take a look at your own enterprise. Pinpoint the problems and ask yourself if you've done everything possible to overcome them. If you haven't, draw up a fresh strategy with an eye toward eliminating the liabilities. Be as wildly creative as you like. Then gird yourself and jump back into the fray. The adventure is just about to begin.

Building on Your USP

The owner of a ladies' hairdressing salon wanted to increase his revenues. He had already considered stocking the reception area with a wide range of products to be sold to his customers. He wrote to me, asking what other measures could be taken.

As a general rule, no matter what your enterprise is, you must showcase your Unique Selling Proposition (the USP). Discovering your USP is simple. Just ask yourself what your business or product offers customers that places you apart from your competitors. If you don't come up with an answer, then you must create a USP. Do some research. Learn as much about your competition's operation as possible. Try to think of ways you can be different. These additions can come in the form of added services or new products. A longer schedule, offering your customers the advantage of more varied hours, can also help set you apart from the crowd. Whatever you choose, it should be something that makes your venture stand out to your customers in a positive manner.

For example, if you were this salon owner, you might offer a frequent-user coupon. If a customer were to receive a certain number of haircuts over a specified period of time, they would be entitled to get one free. You could also arrange for women to receive a credit for every new customer they introduce to the shop, say, a free styling with every three new accounts. Gift certificates are another option. Customers could buy them as gifts for friends on birthdays and holidays.

If you wanted to increase your range of products as a way of beefing up your USP, you should look at new items that offer an easy fit to your general clientele. For instance, if you sold hunting rifles, you might augment the shop with a knife department or perhaps you would add a line of rugged outdoor wear.

You wouldn't try selling antique jewelry or silk lingerie. What would be the point? Your existing traffic would probably have little immediate use for goods of this sort. People who did want to buy these things would be unlikely to come to your store to purchase them. Stay with what you do best.

For the salon owner, the choices are readily seen. Women who walk through his door are looking to enhance their beauty. Anything that helps them accomplish this task should be considered a potential salon product. Along with cosmetic items, you might offer jewelry, scarves, small portable hair dryers, or even Jane Fonda's home-exercise video. If the space permits, you might hire a reflexologist to offer soothing foot massages while your customers have their hair dried. Show some flair. Anything relating to your customer's obvious needs should be appropriate.

Breaking Old Habits

In Birmingham, England, there is a preventive maintenance company for computers. The company possesses a solid core of highly satisfied customers and does a strong repeat business. As well as offering preventive maintenance they also repair machines. One of their biggest chores is trying to convince their potential customers that preventive medicine is better than a cure and far more cost effective. They needed a method to develop this market, particularly with larger companies, who were set in their ways and resistant to changing from the old "fix it when it falls apart" concept. They wrote to me, just recently, asking for suggestions.

The company's problem isn't new. Entrepreneurs are often bucking against old ideas. There's nothing harder than trying to persuade people to change their habits. The best way to do it is to present them with evidence of past success. Even if you have only three or four clients who have already given you that opening chance, their satisfaction should be put to your advantage. If you were the owner of the Birmingham company, you would already have that band of pleased customers. Those who

have followed your suggestions should be asked to provide written endorsements of your prevention service. Try to get as many
endorsements as possible. Make sure they showcase how your
prevention system is more economical than maintenance, allows
your customers to give more reliable service, and any other
virtues your service offers. Use these endorsements as part of an
artfully drawn brochure, to be handed out to your more resistant customers whenever you make your presentation. That sort
of approach should go a long way toward breaking the ice.

If you are just starting out and find no one will give you that
all-important first break, do what some crazy American did when
he bought a shaver company. It's awfully hard to wrench people
from the archaic ritual of blade shaving. It is steeped in tradi-
tions handed down since the first human sacrifice. This guy tried
to break this savage habit by offering a money-back guarantee
to anyone who didn't find his electric shaver could shave as close
as a blade. That offer told consumers that this fellow believed
in his product so strongly, he was willing to back it with a financial risk. I understand that since that guarantee was first issued,
the shaver and company have done rather nicely! It's not all that
surprising. When you show that much confidence in your service, product, or company, you'd be amazed at how many people
will be willing to give you a chance.

David Versus Goliath

A fellow with a small landscaping business wrote wanting to
know how he could keep up with his bigger competitors. They
apparently had more manpower, allowing them to cover an immense amount of territory in less time than he ever could. Due
to their size, they could order materials in greater volume, keeping their overhead down. This would enable them to keep their
prices below his.

Despite the obvious disadvantages weighing against this
fellow, he had a chance to win this battle. I have found that small
entrepreneurs can compete successfully with larger companies.
To do so they must develop a powerful USP. Put in his shoes,

you would have to ask yourself, "What can I do to make this enterprise different from the rest?" You could, for example, look at your competitors' working hours. When aren't they available? Do they make house calls during the evening? If they generally don't, that might be the time to be offering your talents. You could also invest in an answering service and a telephone beeper. Then let your customers know that you are available 24 hours a day.

Maintaining a high profile is most important. You might perhaps have flyers printed (in other words, brochures offering your product or service on spec), with which—along with your business card—you flood the countryside. You should be very aggressive about marketing your firm. Your flyers must highlight your USP. Draw up a list comparing your company to your competitors. Once again, it's assets and liabilities time. Shore up your liabilities as best you can and then cast a cold eye at the other fellow's negative column. These represent his vulnerable side. They are the areas where you can outperform those larger companies. You can come out on top. Just remember this general rule: if you can't undercut the competition's prices, don't worry. You can always overwhelm your potential customers with hard work and outstanding service.

The Value of Starting Small

Part-time entrepreneurial inventors often wonder how to turn their creations into a viable business. A man recently asked us how he could go about marketing a patented device that fitted onto any standard shovel. It reportedly made digging an easier chore for the gardener.

We were not sent a sample, but since the product was protected by patent, we presumed it had a USP. When you have an invention that deserves your full confidence, you should be willing to make an initial investment in the manufacture of a small quantity. These should then be brought to a number of appropriate local outlets. In this particular case, an inventor could take them to hardware and gardening shops.

If the store owner finds your product attractive, you can arrange for him to sell it at a specified price. You and the shop owner would each get 50 percent of the sale price on each item sold. This will serve as your market test. If the product sells well on this small scale, you can broaden your base by taking it to other stores outside your area. Your success in the local shops can be used to persuade others to carry the item. At this point, you can sell it to them at a set wholesale price, allowing them to mark it up at their own discretion for retail. If your business continues to grow you could even offer it as a mail-order item. A successful market test would also give you another alternative. Armed with the results, you could take your prototypes to a manufacturer of related products and try to persuade him to make and distribute the creation while paying a royalty to you.

Drawing the Line

In a corporate structure, the entrepreneur has to cope with rejection. Highly creative, he will see a number of his concepts spurned merely because they go against the status quo. I've always said you should fight for your idea until your bosses have officially placed it in its grave. At Playtex, I fought like hell for the feminine deodorant to be placed in cosmetics but lost. Once it became clear that the boss's decision was final and the products were placed in the store, I went on to other business. You have to know when the bout is over. If you keep punching out in the name of lost causes, that dead body you are working over may turn out to be your own. This is especially true if you've been given ample opportunity to test your theories.

Let me give you an example. At Benrus, Robert Grim was a fellow in marketing who never took no for an answer. We would have a meeting and someone would report something like "The co-op (advertising bought with a retailer) for the product this year will represent 6 percent of the purchase." Bob would start pounding his fist and say, "No, it should be double that amount. We'll be so much more successful if we spend more money on co-op ads." Then he would outline his reasons.

As this fellow knew, we had a corporate policy that limited our co-op spending, most of which took place on a local level. We were more inclined to invest in national campaigns. However, I have always encouraged my employees to be entrepreneurial. Bob had a degree of flexibility with his budget. When he asked to test market his co-op increase for one key account, we gave him the OK.

The results came back and they were not in his favor. The increased spending had had no impact at all on sales. Despite this, Bob wouldn't drop the idea. He kept bringing it up in meeting after meeting.

I would have admired his fortitude. But, having failed once already, it was incumbent upon Bob to present some compelling reasons for us to give him another crack. He didn't have any. He was just reiterating his now tired and disproven theories. After a good ten minutes of his haranguing, I would finally say, "Bob, for God's sake, we've made that decision. You've nothing new to offer here, so let's all go on to something else." He'd still give me a fight!

Having to face this each time we had a meeting, I began to grow weary of this man's face, especially the part that played host to his mouth. I told his immediate superior that if there was any way he could exclude Bob from future meetings without disrupting the organization, he should do so. I just didn't want to be in the same room with him. If he hadn't been so good at the rest of his job, I probably would have fired him. As it was, his lack of judgment halted his corporate advancement.

The lesson here for entrepreneurs is simple. Bob was given an opportunity and it did not support his claims. At that point, you either have to come back with an improved version of your idea or go along with your organization's thinking. The status quo isn't always wrong.

Not the Shy and Retiring Type

I've often been asked how I feel about corporate policy providing for a mandatory retirement age. In *Duck Soup,* the Marx

Brothers' zany political satire, Groucho sums up my thinking with the title of his anarchistic hymn, "I'm Against It!"

Age is just a number. I know a score of young men who have been walking this planet for over seventy years. I also know a lot of elderly thirty-five-year-olds. Our company attorney just turned sixty-five. A few years ago, he came into my office and announced, "I don't want to retire, provided I'm in good health, until I'm seventy years old. Is that a problem?" I assured him it wasn't. This guy has been with Remington for over thirty years. His background and his knowledge are invaluable to us. Why should I chuck it all away because of a date on a yellowed birth certificate? As an entrepreneur, you don't allow yourself to be swayed by appearances. You're open to everything; nothing is ever mandatory. I just turned sixty. I get more done now in a day than I did thirty years ago. Because of my experience, I can not only work harder than many people half my age, I can work smarter. I've learned the value of prioritizing and can make every minute work for me in a way I never could before.

I don't see any reason why I can't go on like this for five, ten, or even twenty more years. I'm an entrepreneur. I don't put limits on myself or the people who work for me. Why should we stop? Did anyone tell Picasso to put away his brush when he turned sixty-five? Should Sir Alec Guinness stop learning his lines? An entrepreneur is an artist too. When he or she can still hit those high notes, why should anyone care about his or her age?

If the time comes that you voluntarily retire, your entrepreneurial life doesn't necessarily have to end. If you've left your enterprise or your position with a company owned by someone else, I have to assume you've prepared yourself financially. You have some sort of steady income either through a pension plan or some other set-up. Financial pressures, for the most part, are behind you. The children are grown up and have moved out. Don't you know how lucky you are? Your days are completely your own. You can fish, see your grandchildren, scale Mount Everest, or do any one of a thousand other things. You can also track down new entrepreneurial horizons.

Take Bob Leeds. He was chairman of the board of Manhattan Industries, one of the top 500 American companies included in *Fortune* magazine's Fortune 500 listing. He is a bright fellow who likes people and enjoys working with them. Having enjoyed some success, he wanted to give something back to business and the community. Bob thought he might like to try a hand at teaching. He did not have a master's degree in education. However, he did have an immense storehouse of business knowledge and an ability to communicate well.

Bob took on three part-time teaching jobs in colleges in the New York area. He loved it. The challenge of shaping young minds appealed to his entrepreneurial creativity. His performance was so impressive, he was offered a full-time position teaching marketing at the University of Southern Florida. This required an uprooting and an even more intense commitment. Free of any ties to a corporate job, Bob was able to grab hold of this opportunity with both hands. He is now the head of the MBA program at that very university. Older entrepreneurs never die, and they certainly don't fade away. They just keep going for it.

The Entrepreneur and Charity

Successful entrepreneurs are often asked to render service to charitable organizations. This means more than just making a mere donation; it often entails giving a certain number of hours while fulfilling a role within the charity. For example, you might be asked to head up a community fund-raising drive or to take an active role on the board of directors. For those who assume this responsibility, a couple of words of advice.

Don't spread yourself thin amongst a number of charities. As we've said before, the entrepreneur can't be half-pregnant. You approach life with a high-powered, state-of-the-art rifle, not a shotgun. This doesn't mean you can't make financial contributions to other worthwhile causes. Write all the checks you want. Just don't dabble with your time. Fully commit to one organization that works on something that catches your heart.

Once involved with the organization, be prepared to come

up against some of the same archaic notions you've encountered in the corporate world. A non-profit organization is a corporate entity. In fact it generally has more than its fair share of bureaucratic stone-heads and lovers of the status quo. Any time these people are asked to do something differently, they don't see it as an opportunity. They see only the risks.

It's hard to get around these attitudes. In business, if you have a product selling for $5.99 and it's a stable, consistent item, you know you're going to sell a certain, profitable percentage of that product at its current price. Let's say you want to improve your volume. You decide to slice the price to $4.99. Consumers love to see prices drop, so the item will be somewhat more attractive. However, there is a risk involved. If that cut doesn't increase business by an appreciable amount, you have a problem: a rise in volume, but a loss in profits. You can soften your risk with a market test. Selling the product at a reduced price in a small, select area will tell you if the change is worthwhile.

If a charity has run its annual fund-raising drive—its most visible product—the same way for many years, a sudden change offers the same risk you faced with your price cutting. However, the charity usually can't afford the luxury of a try-out. What can it do? Run a miniature test-drive and see if it works? It's very difficult. This risk of failure causes most charities, especially moderately successful ones, to loathe any attempt at serious innovation.

Because of this, I would advise that your involvement should not include membership on a board of directors. Unless you have retired you don't have the time, and the bureaucratic stonewalling of your creativity will prove to be too frustrating. Instead, lend your talents to an organization in an advisory capacity.

I'm not talking about consulting; I'm suggesting more of an activist's role. Find a problem that the charity has been unable to solve. None of their set ideas will have an impact here, because none of them have worked. Give the board a plan showing clearly how you can undo this puzzle. Then you take the responsibility to see that this single project is carried out.

For instance, in 1983 I was asked to head up a United Way

drive in Fairfield, Connecticut. United Way is a conglomeration of major American charities which uses its resources to make a powerful, concerted effort on behalf of its member organizations. For years, the local group had been trying to reach an annual goal of four million dollars. They had yet to do it. When I came on board, I looked over all their past plans and budgets and came up with a few ideas of my own. Then I put a bit of pressure on myself—some extra motivation—by telling the board, "We are going to reach our mark. There's no doubt about it. I hate failure and, to me, making only $3,950,000 would be a defeat. I didn't get involved with this thing to come home a loser."

The plan I formulated was based on the current drive's intangible assets and liabilities. Examining these, I could see that the United Way's campaign material was very strong. An asset. However, it was almost exclusively national in scope. There was the liability. Nothing was prepared on a local basis other than a listing of regional institutions that benefited from the charity. The would-be town philanthropist can't relate to a national campaign. They have a hard time seeing the direct benefits of their good works and contributions. This was a short-coming in need of swift correction.

I suggested the formation of a regional advertising fund. This money was used to buy time on radio stations and space in the local newspapers. We also spent two days filming at the eighteen agencies in our area that received contributions from the United Way. This film was used as part of our overall presentation.

As I had suspected, we found out that most of our corporate contributors knew little about the institutions they had helped support. We arranged for bus tours to take them to the YMCA, Goodwill Industries, Meals on Wheels, and other agencies. They got to see exactly how their money was working. It encouraged them to give more and to solicit contributions from others. We also made presentations to diverse town groups. By the time our drive, with its new emphasis, was over, we passed that four million mark with ease. Having a specific goal and the leeway to institute an untried strategy made this a most satisfying entre-preneurial venture.

Burnout

We've all heard about this. A hard-driving executive has been a mover and shaker with his company for over twenty years. One day, his secretary walks in to find him seated at his desk, staring blankly into space or reduced to a state of tears. He can't bring himself to lift a pen or read another report. A recent TV special showed executives in Japan whose burnout was so severe they had to be hospitalized. They didn't have the strength or motiva-tion to get out of bed in the morning. Most of them looked as if they could barely keep their eyes open. Each of these men was a high-powered figure, holding a lofty position.

I hope this doesn't sound like notes from an ivory tower, but I've never experienced serious burnout and, what's more, I don't know any entrepreneurs who have. Oh, yes, I've worked myself into near exhaustion, but a week's vacation with a few days of banging the ball around on the tennis court and I was as good as new.

You're probably wondering what my secret is. I can tell you I have not stumbled onto a fountain of youth or some magic elixir. Or maybe I have. From what I've seen and read, the executive who burns out is usually the corporate hack. This is a player who enters the corporate ballgame and moves up the ladder until the Peter Principle comes into play. He reaches his level of incompetence and has no place further to go.

You see these lost souls all the time. They trudge off to work in the morning, lugging a briefcase that threatens to anchor them in place, wearing vaguely uninterested looks on their for-lorn faces. What started out as a great adventure twenty years ago has become just another mundane exercise in clock punch-ing. They are not making time, they are marking time, and there is no worse hell on earth. The walls of the office draw closer every day until they eventually squeeze all the remaining juice out of these prisoners. They don't wake up in the morning, ready to charge into battle. Alas, there are no longer any battles worth fighting. No wonder these people retreat into the safe folds of collapse.

Entrepreneurs should never be prone to this breakdown. These are people in love with what they are doing. Their ladder reaches up to the heavens and beyond. There is always another step to climb. They never rest on any one rung long enough to allow boredom to tighten its grip. They are pleased with their success but are always hungry for more. When the day finally arrives when no new challenges seem ready to present themselves, they go out and find some. Or create them. Their vitality is as inviting to the demon burnout as a cross is to a vampire. They are too busy to be bitten.

I recently heard about a fellow, a head of a large corporation, who was asked by an interviewer if he ever thought about slowing down. He seemed to be on the go night and day, often getting only four hours of sleep per night. The reporter wanted to know if this demanding schedule, especially the lack of snooze time, might not lead to burnout. The CEO, a recent celebrant of his seventy-fifth birthday, said, "No, I don't think so. I'm having too much fun for that to happen. Besides, I don't like to get too much sleep. I'm afraid I might miss something." For him, work is no more taxing than breathing. That man has got to be an entrepreneur.

9

They Keep Going For It:
Entrepreneurs I Have Known

I'd like to introduce you to four people from rather diverse backgrounds. They do, however, have at least one thing in common. They are walking advertisements for the wonders of the entrepreneurial life. They have gone for it and won. So can you.

Lisa and the Case of the Undefined Market

Sometimes an entrepreneur has a great idea but can't find a ready market. Don't get discouraged. If your concept has any merit, your perseverance can bring it to reality. Let me give you an example that's especially close to home.

As you already know, my daughter Lisa got her first taste of the entrepreneurial life when she was eight years old and employed by our jewelry company. That entrepreneurial streak has stayed with her. Like all my children, she has always been enterprising, a self-starter, and someone who was not afraid to shake up the status quo. For instance, while only a freshman in college, she started teaching learning-disabled youngsters. Enjoying this experience, she went out and set up a special teaching program in an inner-city junior high school.

The students there were in dire need of guidance. The school suffered from a high drop-out rate and absenteeism was rampant. Many of the students who did attend classes with any regularity were just going through the motions. Fortunately they had a principal who cared. He would do anything to ignite his students. This good man allowed Lisa and some of her classmates to teach whatever courses interested them. For instance, a biology major would tutor these children in the basics of science. Small groups gathered to take advantage of these special classes. Just the fact that someone was showing an interest in them seemed to have a vivifying effect on the students. Strong relationships between teachers and students were gradually formed.

At first, Lisa's college refused to give any college credit to the students teaching these courses. No one had ever done anything like this before, and the school didn't quite know what to make of it. Lisa successfully argued that the students were doing field work in sociological studies, an assertion that won credit for the teachers and recognition for her program.

Her argument was grounded in fact. Having taken a number of education courses, she had a hard time reconciling what she had been taught and what actually took place in the classroom. Consequently, she went for her degree in urban studies and had approached her students from a sociological point of view.

She discovered, for example, that many of these children had trouble reading, not because they lacked the necessary intelligence but because the schools had failed to teach them properly. They had been shunted from class to class with no one caring whether they could read or not. Schools just wanted to get them through the system and out as quickly as possible.

Lisa tackled this situation without any degree in education. That caused her, she says, to "do a good deal of soul-searching. I did wonder if I had a right to teach, if there is such a thing, without a heavy background in education. I came to the conclusion that teaching was really a selling job. I had to sell my students on two things: reading and my love for learning. These kids were now too old to be handed a first-grade primer and asked to start all over again. Such material wouldn't hold their interest. Without a motivation to read, they would be a difficult lot to teach."

Lisa found an entrepreneurial remedy for this problem. She took what she would call a "language and experience" approach. "We brought in material that was related to their everyday lives or that would capture their attention. *Playboy* cartoons, for instance. The boys were very interested in those. We brought in examples of common signs like No Smoking or Yield. Job applications also went over very well with them and were something they had to be able to deal with. We made it a point to keep the structure rather open. We never insisted on tackling only the material we offered. Instead, we would ask them, 'What would you like to read?' and then we'd read that." This approach, born of the creativity of Lisa and her classmates, yielded gratifying results. Not only were the students' performances markedly improved by the program, it also cemented Lisa's deep love for teaching.

This stayed with her even when she took a job as a textbook editor at Harper & Row. One day, some people came to her with an idea for a book. It was, she says, to be "focused on early childhood education. I thought it was a terrific idea, but I couldn't get my publisher to go for it. Harper & Row turned it down, claiming there was no such thing as the early-child market. When we argued that there was, they retorted that the market could not be defined."

That company was not the only one to take this stance. The book industry as a whole was dubious about the prospects for this project's success. They quoted the same misgivings as Harper & Row. Despite this, Lisa was undeterred. The proposal's authors had, she says, "convinced me that there was a market out there. People who ran or worked in day-care centers or took care of children in other circumstances would form the core of the readership."

That sounded good in theory, but you never launch a venture in theory alone. Before proceeding you need facts. You must do the homework that can tell you if your enterprise is worthwhile. Says Lisa, "I started by calling Washington and asking how many day-care centers were located in the United States. They gave me some number like 64,000. Then I called California to see how many of those were in that state. I was told something like 63,000. Now that didn't make any sense. I started to see why it was so hard to define this market, but those high numbers convinced me more than ever that a readership did exist."

Trying to nail down that elusive market, Lisa asked a friend, the editor of a small weekly newspaper in New York, for advice. He recommended that, rather than start with a book, she should consider the possibility of doing a newsletter. Distributed to day-care workers and teachers, it would help establish a mailing list, give a clear demography, and define the existing market. If the numbers were impressive, Lisa and the authors would have the ammunition to do all the books they wanted. The three of them brought in other writers to help them produce the publication.

They called their newsletter *First Teacher.* It featured articles for the teachers and activities that allowed teachers and children to interact. They had hoped to launch the premier issue at the annual National Association for the Education of Young Children convention in Atlanta. Timing proved to be a problem. Lisa recalls, "By the time the first issue was ready for presentation, it was too late to secure a booth at the convention. We asked NYAC officials if they could distribute the newsletters, but they rejected that idea."

Entrepreneurs aren't discouraged by closed doors. If they can't bang one down, they simply build another one. For Lisa this meant "hiring some young boys to stand outside the convention center and hand a free copy of *First Teacher* to everyone who went inside. We felt it was especially important to get it into the hands of those people who were presenting the various workshops that weekend. To meet that end, we somehow secured—I'm really not sure how—a list. It carried each of the presenter's names as well as their hotel address and their room number. Going to each one of their rooms, we shoved a copy of the newsletter beneath their door. It was something. We just wouldn't be denied. Even today, people still remember our campaign down there."

That premier issue of *First Teacher* was good enough to attract 2000 initial subscribers. As the power of word of mouth exerted itself, the newsletter took off. Today, the sixteen-page publication is published eleven times a year. Its readership has grown to over 15,000 subscribers.

In addition, Lisa's editor friend turned out to be a seer. As soon as *First Teacher* established a viable market, Lisa was approached by an editor at Macmillan. "She asked if we had thought about doing books! I said it was something we wanted to do, but we couldn't afford it yet. We didn't have the distribution of a big publisher. She replied, 'Suppose we committed to buying 15,000 of your first run?' I allowed that that would certainly make a difference. With that order, we had finally entered the book market, which was of course our original goal."

Lisa and the *First Teacher* crew have already brought out ten books and are exploring other vehicles involving child education. They have achieved this success because they had an idea they believed in and put all their energies behind its implementation. As it turned out, as with many entrepreneurs, they were pioneers. Entrepreneurs relish the unknown. They see its darkness as a thin disguise for a world ablaze with opportunity. Since the publication of *First Teacher,* the early-childhood-education field has flourished. Whereas conventions used to attract only fifty or sixty exhibitors, some of them now feature over 6000. Publishers who had once been adamant about the industry's "undefined market" are now leaping into it with books and newsletters of their own. *First Teacher* didn't cause this explosion by itself. But Lisa and her friends were among the first to point the way. Like all entrepreneurs and pioneers, they were activists. They didn't wait for someone to bring the market to them. They went out and virtually created it.

The Power of the USP

I was so pleased when I heard this story. Mr. Charles Caffarella is an advertising man in Massachusetts. His business, Caffarella Enterprises Inc., was doing well, but Charles knew it could do better. The question was: How do you go about bringing your company to its full potential? Charles wasn't afraid of hard work;

this fellow is a real go-getter. He would make any sacrifice necessary to make his venture go. However, he felt he needed some
entrepreneurial guidance in setting up a success formula for the
enterprise.

His mother made him a gift of *Going For It!* As Charles
would later write, it was just the tool he had been looking for
because, he says, it "explained *how* you made it to the top, step
by step, move by move." He not only read the book, he took
notes and applied them to his business.

First, he analyzed his company on paper. This required the
drafting of an Intangible Balance Sheet. What were his company's strengths and weaknesses? Mr. Caffarella had a strong
advertising background. People who used his service knew they
were dealing with a first-rate professional. Charles sets high
standards for himself and demands the same of his employees.
In what is essentially a personal-service business, this commitment to excellence is the most valuable strength your enterprise
can have.

His agency's ability to act as an all-purpose company was
another important plus. Besides advertising, Caffarella Enterprises offered related services such as public relations, direct
response programs, strategic planning, artwork and design, and
recruitment. A potential client could have all his needs taken
care of under one roof. If a customer was launching a large
campaign—a promotion comprised of a wide range of elements—this sort of one-stop shopping was a blessing.

Offering a necessary service was another entry in the positive side of the ledger. As Charles had learned in graduate
school, there were three fundamental parts to almost any business: finance, marketing, and operations. Charles felt that
marketing buttressed the other two factors. He realized the financing had to be in place to start an enterprise and keep it
going. The operations had to be professionally run. But, as he
put it, "If you don't have effective marketing, you won't have any
finances to worry about and you won't be able to afford any
operations."

Looking over the plus side of the Intangible Balance Sheet,
Charles knew he was in the right business. It was something he

loved, was very good at, and fulfilled a need. Simply fulfilling a need, however, was not strong enough for Charles. He knew most of the agencies across the state could make that same claim. The one glaring weakness on Charles's IBS was the lack of a USP. What set his company apart from all the others?

The first thing he looked at was his office's location. Though Boston is a beautiful city, it's a tough place to call attention to yourself if you're an ad agency. The town is filled with competitors. It has its own version of New York's famed Madison Avenue. As an alternative office site, Charles decided to move twenty miles south to nearby Raynham, Massachusetts. Located between Boston and another large city, Providence, Rhode Island, it would allow Caffarella Enterprises to draw on both metropolises for clients. Charles's meticulous research also revealed that Raynham was a rapidly expanding area, booming with condominium developments and large industrial parks. There could hardly be a more perfect setting for an enterprise that also wanted to grow.

Separating himself from the crowd gave Charles the opportunity to stand out, but it wasn't enough of a USP. He needed something sexier, something that would capture his potential clients' collective imagination. He went back through *Going For It!* and reviewed the chapter on advertising. One anecdote stood out amongst all the rest. It was our story explaining how we had come to offer the Remington shaver with a money-back guarantee.

That guarantee had actually been inspired by a competitor's marketing campaign. In Britain, rivals of Remington had instituted a trade-in policy. You brought in your old shaver, they would give you $10 off your new one. The brand you returned did not necessarily have to be the brand of the company giving you the rebate. Not bad, but I thought we could go one better. We developed the no trade-in trade-in. If you liked our shaver, you kept it and continued to get the best shave you've ever had. If you didn't like the shaver, you returned it, trading it in for a refund. We did the same thing in America, touting our product as the one that "shaves you close as a blade or your money back!"

This was really more than just a marketing program. It was a public stand, attesting to my pride and confidence in the Remington shaver. That campaign was a big success and, I'm happy to say, we get returns from less than half of 1 percent of all our customers.

Charles had the same confidence in his venture as I have in mine. To his company slogan, "Advertising that Works," he added one more word: "Guaranteed!" Caffarella Enterprises would guarantee all of its labors. If a customer found that the cost of a Caffarella campaign exceeded the additional profits generated by that promotion, the agency would refund its 15 percent commission.

You always want a USP that sings; this one belted out arias. Talk about standing out, nothing like this had ever been attempted in the industry. The press latched on to the marketing strategy and trumpeted the story throughout the state. Businesses flocked to Caffarella because they had no reason not to. They had nothing to lose!

This USP had two things going for it. First, it told the public that Caffarella Enterprises had high confidence in its ability to deliver. In essence, Charles was publicly declaring, "This company can do the job. All we want is the chance to prove it." Second, it put a benign pressure on Charles and his staff to outdo themselves. Once the policy was instituted, Charles knew that "in order to make it work we *had* to be the best." The agency redoubled its efforts to offer maximum service. It thoroughly researched—at a cost of considerable time and expense—each possible client until it had a clear picture of that business's needs. It then designed its programs to address these specific areas.

This hard work paid off. Within weeks of launching the money-back guarantee, Caffarella Enterprises secured over $1 million in new clients. It has picked up virtually every new account it has pitched. With this recent 100 percent closing ratio, Caffarella Enterprises is taking on some of the largest agencies in New England and winning! I bubble up whenever I hear someone has derived so much from my book. It's what the entrepreneurial experience is all about. You want to help others reap the same rewards you have. You want to help build a world of entrepreneurs.

A Crowning Achievement

Rolph McCollister is the closest thing you can have to American royalty. This young Louisiana entrepreneur has been so successful his hometown has dubbed him, "The King of Baton Rouge." Despite the impressive title, Rolph wasn't born into royalty. Like any entrepreneur, he achieved his position by going for it.

He started out hoping to be the next Horace Rumpole. However, after two years of studying law at Louisiana State University, he decided legal briefs didn't hold enough excitement for him. Looking for alternatives, he was attracted to the newspaper business. His father, himself an attorney, had successfully run a small-town newspaper for a number of years and had been asked to start up another. It was to be called the *Enterprise.* Focusing on local news, sports, and other tidbits, it was given away free at grocery stores and on newsstands. Its advertising provided the paper with its profits. Rolph joined the *Enterprise* as a part-time ad salesman and worked his way up to advertising manager. He also augmented his school curriculum with journalism courses.

After joining the newspaper full-time, he found this business didn't spark his engine either. This was not unusual. Entrepreneurs set high standards for themselves and are not easily satisfied. The demands of the entrepreneurial life require you to choose an endeavor that inspires commitment both in your mind and your heart. Many entrepreneurs spend their first few years trying several different ventures until they find the proper fit.

Rolph discovered his in a most unlikely locale: a college basketball game. He remembers, "LSU was in a tournament. The fans of the other school were very vocal in their support of their team. They kept yelling and waving Confederate flags. I thought those flags were especially impressive, because all we poor LSU fans had to wave were a dinky set of pom-poms. They didn't look like much. I thought it would be great to design an LSU flag. When I got back home, I drew up a prototype featuring the team symbol, a tiger. I had a sample made up, took it to school officials, and sold 5000 of them. I made about a dollar for every flag I sold."

More important than the profit, Rolph got a tingle from actually selling a product he had created. The entrepreneur in him had come out. He suddenly realized, "I wanted to be in business for myself. The newspaper job had been a good experience, but it had me doing the same thing day after day. Week after week I was pitching the same routine to the same accounts. In a town like ours where most of the print media advertising was locked up by the major dailies, there was only so much a tiny weekly could do. We had run out of room to grow."

Rolph took the profits from the LSU pennant and invested them in himself. He set up a corporation called Sports Fans of America, designing flags for colleges all over the country. Eventually, he was selling his product to professional baseball and basketball teams. His business was skyrocketing.

He did, however, have one problem. Though he designed his products, he didn't have the facilities to manufacture them. This was done by a well-known company. Rolph had to buy his own flags from them, mark them up, and then sell them to concessionaires at the various sports stadiums. These concessionaires were used to dealing directly with the manufacturer. In order to compete with that arrangement, Rolph had to keep his profit margin slim. Though he was selling a lot of flags, his bottom line was less than it should have been. Whenever you are involved with a new enterprise, you must weigh its Risk-Reward Ratio. If it were a mathematical equation, the Risk-Reward Ratio would look like this:

$$\frac{\text{possible financial benefits of your venture or idea}}{\text{time expended} + \text{money spent} + \text{reputation risked}} = \frac{\text{your}}{\text{decision}}$$

With its low margins, Rolph's first enterprise wasn't giving him the maximum return for his time and money. Recognizing its

shortcomings, this entrepreneur made the best of the situation. He sold the rights of his various trademarked designs to a manufacturer for a 5 percent royalty. With the manufacturer keeping his margins competitive, Rolph wasn't making any more money than before; neither was he making much less. However, he had done something most important: freed his time and attention for another venture.

He decided to take another crack at the newspaper business. The *Enterprise* had been floundering. Rolph was asked to revive it as co-publisher. Unlike his last experience, he was coming back to a challenge. His few years of running his own company had taught him a good deal about marketing. Rolph felt he could apply these lessons to a weekly tabloid and turn it into a success. He recalls: "The flags worked because they were a unique item. I was filling a need with something that hadn't previously existed. I wanted to accomplish two things with the *Enterprise* right off the bat. First, I wanted to increase its revenue by charging for it. If people wanted to read the paper, they were going to have to pay for it. We built up a subscription base of over 11,000, not bad for a small-town weekly. My second goal was to put together a second publication that was like the flags. It would have a strong USP. I wanted it to be something that had never been offered in this town before."

Your USP does not have to be as innovative as the creation of the wheel. As Rolph McCollister so ably demonstrated, you can borrow a USP from another venture and adapt it to yours. He had noticed that a whole new journalistic industry had sprung up across the country. Newspapers touting local business news were doing very well, especially down South. No one had ever published one in Baton Rouge. Rolph thought his fellow citizens might be interested in such a newspaper. Looking to find out how they worked, he picked up forty of these publications and read each one of them. Rolph was then able, he says, "to pick out the best elements of each and incorporate them into something I thought would appeal to Baton Rouge. I noticed that most of them concentrated on news concerning the local businessperson. People like reading about themselves and their neighbors and want to know how someone achieves a success.

In a small town, a lot of diverse businesses impact on each other, so it was valuable to learn what other local companies were up to."

McCollister's *Baton Rouge Business Report* made its debut in September 1982. This was a monthly tabloid devoted to local business news and personalities. It reported on everything from real estate transactions to bankruptcies. If you wanted to know who sold what to whom in Baton Rouge, you bought his *Report.* The first issue was only 56 pages and it was an immediate money maker. People were starved for this kind of news. They just couldn't get enough of it. Now in its fourth year, the *Report* comprises over 148 pages. It has won thirteen national awards. What started out as a two-man operation—Rolph and his city editor from the *Enterprise*—currently has twenty-two employees on its payroll. Had this been Rolph's only success, his story would still be an unqualified triumph.

But there's more. Rolph McCollister is, after all, an entrepreneur. He's not content to cushion his behind with laurels. In chapter one, you saw how Remington parlayed its success by expanding into new, related territories. With his paper enjoying terrific sales, McCollister did the same thing.

We were a manufacturer of an electrical shaver, an electrical grooming product; in branching out, the first thing we got involved with was a hair and beard trimmer, a grooming appliance. McCollister's paper served as a pipeline for the Baton Rouge business community. It was a network strung together by the printed word. Rolph decided to expand that network by bringing its members face-to-face. This led him to the magazine's first spin-off: a business trade show.

Such an event would serve as a showcase for local businesses. For instance, computer companies would set up booths featuring their equipment. Demonstrators would show the public how these items worked. A printer might erect a booth displaying samples of his craftsmanship. A major medical facility, new to the world of marketing, could have its own information center. The show would cater mostly to businesspeople, who were either hoping to attract new clients or find fresh sources for products and services. It would also appeal to the average citizen, curious to see the many wonders of our latest technology.

It was quite an idea. Of course the first thing Rolph needed to pull this off was funding. It's a common problem, the one I'm asked about most when I'm on the lecture circuit. How does a young—McCollister was less than thirty—entrepreneur raise the capital to launch his enterprise? McCollister gives us one good example and I think it can be applied to a lot of scenarios.

McCollister had a powerful asset on his Intangible Balance Sheet (IBS). The strong business ties he had built up through his publication. He used these to help find potential exhibitors for his trade show. Rolph had already reserved an auditorium for the event sixty days in advance. The cost was $2100 for the three-day show. His contract with the landlord stipulated that the rent had to be paid within thirty days of the show's scheduled opening. This gave Rolph about four weeks to raise the required capital.

Rolph did this through an advantageous structuring of his terms. He asked for an immediate down payment from his exhibitors. They put up a certain amount of money for each of their booths. The balance would be due two weeks later, fifteen full days before the landlord was to receive his money. When it came time to pay that rent, McCollister had already collected over $65,000. He hadn't borrowed a cent or used any of his own money. With this cash in hand, Rolph was able to pay for the hall, furnish it, pay salaries to a small staff, spend $20,000 on advertising, and still see a $13,000 profit. All this a month before he even opened the doors!

The show was a smash. The hall was packed throughout the event's run. Exit polls proved that it had managed to attract precisely the sort of crowd the exhibitors needed. Of those who attended, 92 percent were involved in purchasing decisions for their company. They were either office managers, buyers, executive vice-presidents, or CEOs. Rolph couldn't have had a more suitable attendance-profile if he had handpicked each customer himself.

Rolph recalls that he was "particularly impressed with the networking aspects of the show. An exhibitor would come up to me and say, 'I've been trying to see so-and-so for months, and I never could get an appointment. Today, he happened to come by my booth, we started chatting and bingo! I'm supposed to see him next week!' I liked that because it was one of our major aims. We wanted to open up doors for people. That enhances the exhibition's value. One fellow made a contact that led to a $396,000 sale. That wasn't a bad return for his investment, the $595 he had paid for booth space. Someone like that will be in every show we run for years." Rolph's idea has grown since his first convention. From a medium-sized event it has become the Louisiana Business Expo, attracting over 3000 exhibitors.

McCollister has found a way to augment this success with another spin-off. Remember how the Remington warranty-card list led to our catalogs? We took something already in place and transformed it into another business. Rolph did the same thing with his Expo. Realizing he had all these businesspeople gathered at one site for a concentrated period of time, he offered business seminars. Executives would pay a fee to listen to experts wax poetic over the great business issues and problems of the day. The synergy produced by these two endeavors was enormous. The Expo fed the seminars and the seminars, in turn, fed the Expo. The result was an even greater success for McCollister.

With the shows and seminars booming, Rolph still kept his hand on the pulse of his monthly business report. A good lesson there. No matter how well you do with the offshoots of your venture, never forget that they are offshoots. The core business is your solid base. With all his success, Rolph did not let up. If anything he was even more aggressive in marketing his paper, doing everything he could to step up the *Report*'s already highly visible profile. An annual dinner was part of this program. Hosted by the *Business Report,* it honored a different national business figure each year. The first one saluted Stephen Forbes of *Forbes* magazine. His appearance made the dinner—and of course the hosting *Baton Rouge Business Report*—front-page news throughout the state.

From a simple beginning, Rolph McCollister's empire is growing. In addition to his *Business Report,* he publishes a directory for the Louisiana Chamber of Commerce, a similar publication for the Baton Rouge Chamber of Commerce, a Louisiana visitor's guide, and—a direct offspring of his popular monthly publication—*The Real Estate Report.* Somehow, he has even found the time to launch a direct mail business. Boy, I love this. He looked at his publication mailing list—*à la* Remington once again—and realized it had an attractive demographic profile. Many of his periodicals' readers were businesspeople. They were movers and shakers looking to invest in themselves. Rolph put together a card pack that allowed sponsors to reach these people via the mails. Not only does this return a handsome profit, he is able to include his own projects in the package for no cost. He is making money and receiving free advertising to boot!

When I last spoke to Rolph, he had no intention of slowing down. He said, "Every day there's a new opportunity if you're open to it. You can't let it pass you by. Right now, the oil-based economy of Louisiana has slowed. People are holding back. Some people are scared. Not me. I'm putting the pedal to the metal. By the time things start picking up, I'll have spread the gap between me and those naysayers who are standing still."

This man can't lose. And neither can you if you adopt the same positive attitude. What I like most about Rolph is not what he has accomplished, but how he accomplished it. He did not buy a company. He did not patent some amazing technological innovation. Instead, he saw a vacuum and looked to find something to fill it. He adapted other entrepreneurial vehicles to fit his own needs. When he didn't have capital, he did not despair. He came up with a highly creative way to raise it. He saw possibility where others may have viewed liability. It's not surprising. After all, he is an entrepreneur and an entrepreneur is more than just a risk taker. He is a visionary. In the film *Butch Cassidy and the Sundance Kid,* Paul Newman's Butch says, "I see visions while the rest of the world wears bifocals." Butch probably didn't know it, but that could be a credo for the entrepreneur. Rolph McCollister can attest to that. The King of Baton Rouge has proven that opportunity is everywhere. To take advantage of it, all you have to do is be able to see it. Sharpen your eyes.

Pick out your path to excellence and you'll be polishing a crown of your own.

A Personal Turnaround

I'm often asked, "Are entrepreneurs born, or can they be made?" I might be mistaken, but I think anyone can be an entrepreneur. It doesn't matter what sort of background you come from. With the proper guidance and motivation, you can do more than just reach the stars. You can make them perform at your command.

Sean Lally is a young man living in New York City. Not too long ago, he was at one of life's junctures. He had spent four years in the restaurant business. It was a career that saw him gradually work his way up from junior waiter to apprentice chef. He had accomplished this without formal culinary schooling. Obviously this was someone to watch, a fellow of intelligence, drive, and ambition.

At some point, Sean says, he discovered that he really didn't love the restaurant business. "I think a number of things soured me on it. For one, I had hit the ceiling where I worked. The next position up was master chef and I knew I wasn't going to get that spot anytime soon. Also, I wanted to have greater control over my weekly paycheck. My earnings were limited by what my employers could afford to pay me. No amount of hard work or sweat could change my reward by very much. I wanted to find something without these limitations. Of course, maybe I also just realized that cooking was terrific as a hobby—I still enjoy doing it at home—but it just wasn't what I wanted to do with the rest of my life."

That was fine in theory, but in reality Sean had never worked in anything but the restaurant industry. He didn't have experience in any other field. When it came time to think about a new career path, he was at a loss. If I may indulge in what fellow author Norman Mailer describes as "advertisements for myself," Sean was turned on to a new option when a relative gave him a copy of my favorite book.

He explains: "*Going For It!* attracted me to entrepreneurship and selling. I knew I was willing to put in the hours to build a success. Victor's book convinced me that having that sort of attitude was half the fight. The only drawback was my confidence. I had read how Mr. Kiam said you had to have confidence in your idea, product, or service and in yourself. If I was careful about choosing the right company to represent, the first part wouldn't be a problem. It was the second part of the equation that presented the difficulty. I didn't have any confidence in myself. I must say I liked Victor's remedy for that. In his book he said 'If you don't have self-confidence, find some!' He then immediately went on to suggest a strategy for building your self-image. It revolved around drawing up a Personal Balance Sheet, reading books on positive thinking, taking courses, anything to spark your self-belief. I was willing to try that."

Without realizing it, Sean had taken an important first step toward becoming an entrepreneur. He already found the first item to jot down on the liability side of his Personal Balance Sheet. Sean recognized a major shortcoming and was going to do his best to correct it. He took out several books on positive thinking and read them religiously. They were kept on a table near his bed. Right next to a copy of *Going For It!*

His lack of confidence was so severe at first, he canceled several job interviews at the last minute. He recalls, "I just couldn't face the challenge yet. I guess I wasn't ready. But I was determined to give sales a try. One day, I saw an ad for a door-to-door food service. It sold quality steaks, shrimps, and other items to households and businesses. Perhaps it was my background in food or the positive-thinking books I had read—I like to think it was fate—but I did call for an interview with that company and I did keep the appointment.

"At that meeting, the manager asked me questions about my background and asked for references. He said, 'As long as your references hold up, I'm going to give you this job. I won't fire you. The only one who can fire you is yourself if you don't produce.' He then started to talk about the company with an almost religious fervor. He said this was the greatest job in the world. That food was a necessity and was therefore one of the easiest things to sell. The company dealt with products of only the highest quality and 87 percent of the business came from repeat customers. His last point impressed me. He said, 'It's not like selling in a shop. You get in your truck, pick out a territory, and sell for as long as you want. You are the store. You set store policy. When a shop is closed, your business is closed. In this company, you close only when you want to. Business is always open. There are no ceilings here.'

"I remembered how excited Victor was when he met his first boss at Lever Brothers, Keith Porter. Porter was apparently one ball of fire. His enthusiasm was so contagious and his ideas so innovative, Victor couldn't wait to work for him. Well, I thought, it looks like I just found my Keith Porter. He turned out to be everything I expected and the company really was a great place to work. My fellow employees couldn't be a more terrific group of guys."

Just like Remington, Sean's new employer had an incentive system. "If you sold fifty boxes of food in one week, you got a bonus. Once you hit fifty, each additional ten boxes sold earns you another bonus. That extra money was a great motivator, but I had set my own goals. First they were small. An expensive leather jacket I had eyed for some time, a new watch, that sort of thing. I got those in the first couple of weeks. Then I set my sights higher. I realized Victor was right. The entrepreneur is interested in more than just monetary gain. I wanted to make this business go as best I could. My job was a line position, something Mr. Kiam talked about. Being a salesman in a sales company, it led straight to the top. I wanted to move into management. The only way to accomplish this was to stand out and *Going For It!* gave me the ammunition to do exactly that."

The first thing Sean did was make it a point to show up at work forty-five minutes ahead of schedule. This gave him time to gear up mentally for the coming day and also let him be among the first to hit the roads with his products. In addition, it offered him an opportunity to brainstorm with his boss. This was very important. The entrepreneur understands that business is a game. You play it to win. Your sweat and toil are the keys to getting ahead of your competitors. But hard work is not enough. In order to move up, you have to get recognition for your labor. Sean's early arrival showed a strong commitment to the company and his job. The ideas he offered in these morning sessions illustrated that the company's welfare was uppermost in his mind.

Since a lack of confidence was still an issue for him, Sean attacked this problem daily. He practiced his pitch in a mirror, making sure to keep constant eye contact. He used a tape recorder to iron out the verbal wrinkles in his presentation. Sean also took pressure off himself by designating the first few selling weeks as practice runs. Getting the order was important, but it was more vital for him to learn how to communicate with people. He wanted them to share his enthusiasm for his product.

At the end of each selling day, he drew up a list. It was another version of the Balance Sheet. In one column, he recorded all his successful sales. The other side of the ledger contained his misses. He would analyze this breakdown to see what had worked for him and what had gone awry. The next day he would apply the information to all his calls.

He also learned everything he could about the products he was selling. For instance, he could tell a customer why Ecuadoran shrimp was superior to shrimp bred in the Atlantic Ocean. Sean had discovered that most chefs preferred it because it showed less shrinkage in cooking. He could explain the difference between a Black Angus steak and a piece of Grade A beef. The more Sean added to his presentation, the greater his success. The hard work was paying off and it created the most pleasant of synergies. Each sale was another boost for Sean's confidence. The rejections hardly got him down. He welcomed them as an opportunity to refine his pitch further.

This doesn't mean he didn't have his down days. Everyone does. But he was building an entrepreneurial resilience that made it impossible to keep him down. For instance, one day, he says, "I had put in nine hours on the road and I hadn't made a sale. I was so frustrated I pulled the truck over to the side of the road, got out, slammed the door shut, and took a long walk. I just had to let off steam. When I got back I found I had locked the keys in my truck. I had to walk a mile to a gas station, get a mechanic, and have him pick my lock. I had hardly any money on me so I had to pay the guy off with a box of shrimp. That capped off everything. I had worked my tail off, hadn't made a cent, and now I was out the money for the shrimp. I was operating at a loss!

"If this had happened a few weeks before, I might have chucked the whole thing. But I had learned something: *failure quits in the face of persistence.* I was tired and my persistence had been close to running empty. But that mishap jump-started my engine. I got back in the truck and called on the first house I came upon. I was resolved to get an order and it fed my enthusiasm. A housewife answered the door and I started painting my vista. I'll tell you she caught my fire. She not only bought a couple of boxes, she rang the doorbells of her neighbors and had them come out to see what I was offering. I made enough money from those sales to cover my losses and put $100 in my pocket. That episode taught me one more thing about selling. *No matter how badly things are going, take it all in your stride. There is always one more bell to ring.*"

With his confidence now in place, Sean turned his attention to marketing his company's product. He did not have an extravagant budget or the services of some Madison Avenue ad agency. If you're an entrepreneur you can get along without those things. What he had was his own creativity. Says Sean, "I remember borrowing an idea from Remington. Every now and then I would come across a fence-straddler, a first-time customer who was leaning toward buying but needed a gentle nudge. I would offer them my version of the money-back guarantee. They would post-date their check by a few days and sample the order I left them. If it wasn't up to their expectations, they could cancel the check and return the unused portion. I knew they would fall in love with this food once they tasted it and I was right. I have yet to see a single return. This offer helped me build up my customer base and created a trust between me and my customers. That's invaluable in any enterprise, especially the food business."

Sean also tried other ideas. There was one particularly wealthy neighborhood that looked like a promising territory.

However, the area had a large Jewish population and most of these people wanted only kosher food. Sean's company didn't supply that. Consequently, most of his colleagues stayed out of that neighborhood after a few unsuccessful tries. Sean followed their example. Until the Christmas season. Then he drove his truck around on a Sunday evening and jotted down the address of every house that was adorned by Christmas lights. He assumed kosher food wouldn't be an issue in those homes. The following week, he returned to those households and came away with a new crop of customers.

Thanksgiving posed another problem. Sean's company didn't sell turkeys. This made that holiday week a particularly dead period. However, Sean realized that they did sell appetizers that would make suitable accompaniments to a turkey dinner. He printed up a list of each one of these items and handed them out to his customers. He did an extraordinary business in a week that most people would have written off.

When Sean's company brought out a line of cakes, he bought several, sliced them, and handed out free samples to his customers. He was showing his appreciation for their business and introducing them to another product. He started passing out recipes showcasing his company's wares. Whenever the temperature dropped below freezing, he ignored the discomfort: "I made extra certain to put in a full day. I knew this was my time to sell. People didn't want to go out to shop so my service was that much more valuable. Also, many of them had been cooped up at home all day with no one to talk to. When they see my smiling face come through the door with this beautiful food, I invariably get a warm welcome."

This from a fellow who used to lack confidence. Boy, I'm glad he's not in the shaver business or I'd be in big trouble. I have a feeling this young man is going to surpass any goal he sets for himself. He proves that anyone can be an entrepreneur. Everything he has accomplished is the product of hard work and his powers of observation. Even his vision and creativity were talents that were honed. You don't need the right genes, a Ph.D., a pinstripe suit, or a fancy business card to live the entrepreneurial life. Take it from me, entrepreneurs are rarely extraordinarily gifted. Like the subjects in this chapter, they are merely people who are not content to watch things happen; they make things happen. Creating and building an enterprise is their main goal. The financial rewards are wonderful, but they aren't all-important. Their success comes from proving something can be done well and on their own terms. They have no time for the commonplace or second-rate. They prove that all you really need to succeed is a dream and the courage to grab it with both hands. Their lives are vivid testimonies that anyone can win as long as they keep going for it.

10

Going For It in the NFL

The wonderful thing about being an entrepreneur is that you often get to live out your wildest fantasies. When I purchased the New England Patriots football team in 1988 many members of the New England media quipped that I obviously had liked professional football so much, I had decided to buy it. In Brian De Palma's film *The Untouchables* Al Capone, brilliantly portrayed by Robert De Niro, observes, "We laugh because it's funny and yet we laugh because it's true." I'm not sure the press knew just how much truth could be found at the heart of their joke. As with any entrepreneur worthy of the name, I get involved with ventures for sheer enjoyment as much as for profit. The media probably thought I had looked at the Patriots as just another good investment. What they didn't know was that I didn't merely like pro football; I loved it.

Despite my passion for the great game, it never occurred to me that I might someday own an NFL franchise. I never thought I could afford one. Then, several years ago, I was approached by an associate of my lawyer Arthur Emil. This gentleman introduced himself and said, "Arthur was telling me that you have a keen interest in football. It might interest you to know that I'm working on a deal to acquire a franchise in the National Football League. The majority owner is being sniped at by his minority shareholders and he is sick and tired of the whole business. He is looking for a way out of this mess. If I can acquire all of his stock, would you be interested in joining me as a partner?" I asked what sort of investment would be required. He estimated that I would have to come up with between 10 and 15 million dollars. I told him I would first have to know what sort of problems the minority shareholders represented. There was no sense in buying into someone else's headache if the pain didn't cease with the purchase. If the squabble represented something trivial, say, a clash of personalities, then new ownership might be the perfect remedy. I told the fellow I could very well be interested and asked that he keep me informed. He would call me from time to time and tell me of his progress. He busted his gut trying to put a deal together but it was to no avail. Things never quite panned out. I wasn't too upset. After all, we were talking about the purchase of an NFL franchise. I had considered it a long shot from the start. Once the deal was belly-up I never gave it a second thought. Besides, with the rapid expansion of Remington the idea of buying an NFL team was probably an exercise in wishful thinking. I was too busy to seriously consider such a purchase.

My initial interest in the deal did, however, stick in the mind of Arthur Emil. In March 1988, he called me with another opportunity. Arthur had run into a man with strong ties to the New England Patriots. As most zealous football fans knew, the team had been on the block for quite some time. This gentleman had been in a position to buy the Patriots but had been unable to put together a deal. Arthur asked if I would be willing to talk to this fellow. Believe it or not, I wasn't. I told Arthur, "It sounds like a wonderful opportunity, but I am up to my neck with the Remington business. You know how things are booming. And now we're launching the Lektro Blade and Smooth and Silky. We've been spending every spare minute trying to juggle production schedules and setting up distribution. We're also looking at some other businesses. I'm thinking of petitioning Congress to have a thirty-six-hour day instituted. I'm that swamped. I don't see how I can find the time to chase after an NFL franchise. I mean, this is no small investment. I'm not even sure if I can afford one right now. Their cost has skyrocketed since I last spoke to your friend.

"Also, have you been following the Patriots and their situation? This could easily turn out to be the worst sort of wild-goose chase. It seems to me that the Patriots have been on the block since shortly after Paul Revere's ride. I think Paul and Patrick Henry had a group bidding on the team. There have been several close calls, but no one has been able to consummate a deal. All kidding aside, we're talking about some large names in that group. Donald Trump. Marvin Davis. No. It is a nice idea, Arthur, but I believe I'll pass on this one."

The receiver had barely landed in its cradle when I started to have second thoughts about my refusal. As I said before, I have a passion for pigskin. If there was any sport I would ever get involved with it was NFL football. I was mesmerized by the game's strategy and its unpredictability. For me one of the game's biggest attractions lies in the shape of the football. It isn't round. Because of this it has a tendency to take peculiar bounces. In any given game almost anything can happen. Just one or two plays or coaching decisions in a contest could have a tremendous impact on the final result. They might even sway the course of an entire season.

This lends football an excitement I find lacking in other sports. Baseball, for instance, is a great game but it seems routine compared to football. It does have a slow-building tension; that is part of its charm. However, I prefer the continual explosions that accompany the gridiron game. Basketball strikes me as being very much like baseball. I find that hockey does have some of football's excitement, but its schedule robs the game of drama. Hockey only really comes alive during the Stanley Cup playoffs. If the lords of hockey ever figure out a way to reproduce some of that Stanley Cup excitement during the regular season, their box-office proceeds will go through the stratosphere.

For me, football has it all. How much of a fan am I? Let me make a public confession. I am a 100-percent, Grade-A, dyed-in-the-wool fanatic. Let me give you two examples of my fervor for the game. My business frequently takes me abroad. Whenever I traveled overseas during the football season, I had a devil of a time trying to get NFL scores. It would sometimes take me a week to get results.

I couldn't wait that long. My hunger for football news was

too great. I taught my wife Ellen to take the scores down during the televised sports reports on Sunday nights. Once she had them she would call me and give me the results over the phone. My overseas phone bill started to resemble the United States deficit. I didn't care. I wanted those weekly scores and I wanted them as soon as possible. The system I developed with Ellen worked fairly well except sometimes the outcomes rolled over the screen too quickly. She would have a hard time keeping up with them. Ellen might get the correct score but not the participating teams. We decided to check the weekly NFL schedule in advance and write down the combatants in each contest. Then all Ellen had to do was fill in the numbers. This was a perfect solution. Getting the scores so quickly satisfied my football lust and made me a very popular guy with my fellow American travelers. They were as eager to hear the results as I had been.

The second example of my ardor for football illustrates exactly how much I was willing to sacrifice for the game. I was at home one evening watching Monday Night Football. It was a terrific contest. I was rooting for the underdog team. They scored a touchdown to come within three points of the lead and then they recovered their opponents' fumble with just 36 seconds left in the game. Suddenly they are in position to pull off a stunning upset, perhaps the upset of the season. The team I'm pulling for calls a play and the quarterback nails one of his receivers. The guy takes off and it looks as if he has a chance to go all the way. I am going bonkers. Sitting in my swivel chair, I start running along with him. I just can't believe he's going to score. I get so excited, the chair tips over. Trying to break my fall, I shoot out my hand. It is pierced by the top of a tennis trophy that had rested alongside the chair. I topple onto the floor. My head hits the ground with a dull thud. First stars and then sweet darkness. I am out cold.

I don't know how long it was before I regained consciousness, but when I woke up I was a mess. Blood oozed out of a head wound; that trophy was sticking out of my hand. I looked as if I had just crawled through an overactive demilitarized zone. You would think my first thought upon reviving would be to seek medical assistance. No chance. As soon as I recovered my wits all I wanted to know—gore and all—was "Did they win?" It was only after finding out that they had that I agreed to go to the hospital to have my injuries examined. The doctor stitched me up and told me it was a miracle I hadn't suffered any permanent ligament damage. There are probably some of you who think I had my priorities topsy-turvy when I regained my senses. But I'm sure there are millions of football fans out there who can sympathize with my actions. We zealots are a breed of diehards.

So I was gripped by football fever in its most virulent form. Though I was only a fan I had already given my body—or at least a chunk of my hand—to the game. The sport had such a compelling hold on me I decided to reexamine the Patriots situation.

The Patriots had a lot of attractions. I knew that if I were to get involved with an NFL team, my hectic schedule would dictate that it be one located near my Connecticut home. This narrowed my choices to both New York franchises and the Patriots. Even the Pittsburgh Steelers and the Philadelphia Eagles were a bit outside my geographical range. It was probably going to be a long time before either New York teams would find themselves on the open market. As a Connecticut resident I was a New Englander. The more I thought about it, the more the Patriots seemed to be the ideal opportunity. In fact, given my restrictions, they could very well be the *only* opportunity. If they were sold to someone else, the odds were I wouldn't see another chance such as this in my lifetime.

I got up and gave myself a small kick alongside the cranium. Here I was supposed to be an entrepreneur. I had spent a good deal of time espousing a gospel, urging the faithful and the faithless to seize life and the chances it offered with both hands. Then I am presented with a shot at high adventure and what did I do? I had rejected it out of hand. There was only one way to restore my entrepreneurial honor. I had to take action. I immediately phoned Arthur and told him I had changed my mind. I would be delighted to speak with this fellow.

The gentleman got on the phone and we chatted for a few minutes. Then he said, "If you're really interested in getting involved with this, let me give you the home telephone number of the Patriots' owner, Billy Sullivan. Mention our discussion and tell him you'd like time to look the operation over and put together an offer. You will have to move in a hurry. Several others have their eyes on the team. Call Billy as soon as you can."

I reached Billy Sullivan that evening. We hit it off immediately. Billy is a fascinating man whose whole life revolved around football. Within two minutes of my saying hello, Billy was recounting the entire history of the Patriots for me and giving me some idea of his own rich football background. He told me how he had worked with Frank Leahy and had started the Patriots in the old American Football League. Mr. Sullivan was both informative and entertaining. For a rabid football fan like myself, his anecdotes were a treasure. It was a great phone call. We even found some time to discuss the sale of the Patriots. Billy asked me how quickly I could move. I pointed out that I had only been approached that afternoon. It would take some time to evaluate the deal. Billy then explained that time was not an abundant commodity at the moment. The Sullivans were working under a crushing financial deadline.

The team's money worries had forced the Sullivans to put the club on the block. The Patriots had never enjoyed much financial security. They were victimized by the NFL's worst stadium lease. Their payroll was one of the highest in pro football. New England had been the league's least successful team when it came to the bottom line. In addition the family had lost a snootful on the Michael Jackson tour. The deficit had been placed at somewhere between 30 and 40 million dollars. This debacle had been well publicized and it had to have an impact on the Sullivans' ability to make a deal advantageous to the club and the family.

The corporation owning the stadium was about to go bankrupt and Patriots were being piled under an ever-growing slag heap of debt. I would soon discover that they didn't even have enough money to meet the payroll. The family was standing astride a yawning abyss. Hungry creditors with notes serving as carving utensils were beckoning from below.

The Sullivans had already borrowed 21 million dollars. Yet they still needed another million just to keep the organization intact. Aware of their dire circumstances, I promised to get cracking on the deal.

Debt payments weren't the only deadlines facing the Sullivans. Billy was an honest man. His forthrightness made it a pleasure to deal with him. Before I got off the phone with him he let me know that I was not his only prospect. He said, "Let me level with you before you go to too much trouble. We are negotiating with someone else right now. He seems to want the team, but I'm not completely sure how serious his offer is. I'm also not crazy about the initial terms of the deal. But as you can see, I have to do something before we collapse under the financial pressures. I've got to do what's best for the team and my family." I thanked Billy for his candor. I also told him we were willing to proceed with the understanding that there were other offers on the table.

The next morning I called Arthur Emil. My talk with Billy had made me that much hotter to do the deal. After giving Arthur the gist of my conversation with Sullivan, I told him to get this project moving with all haste. I had caught the fever. Only the purchase of the Patriots would bring my temperature down. Arthur had the Sullivans send all of the team's financial records to us. They arrived that afternoon. We both threw ourselves into those books.

Four days into this process we received our first jolt. Two thousand watts worth. Arthur got a telephone call informing him that the Sullivans had just signed a deal with Paul Fireman of Reebok International. This agreement appeared to represent a final sale. It granted an option to Fireman which he seemed ready and able to execute. My short adventure into the world of football looked as if it was over.

We did have some hope. Arthur and I reminded ourselves that Mr. Fireman was far from the first person to hold an option on the Patriots. Sixteen others, including such notables as Donald Trump, Marvin Davis, and Preston Tisch, had tried to buy the team at one time or another. None of them had been able to close a deal. In fact, in Boston the rumored sale of the Patriots had assumed all the newsworthiness of a "Dog Bites Man" story. New Englanders hardly paid attention to such reports. In the later stages of his directorial career, Orson Welles began work on several ambitious films. A psychological block refused to allow his finishing any of them. Try as he did, he just could never get to the last reel. To most football fans, the selling of the Patriots was beginning to look like one of Mr. Welles's unfinished epics.

Once he digested the news, Arthur said, "Well, we may be dead on this one. Everyone says Fireman is the most serious bidder yet. He is certainly capable of putting together a deal. If he executes this option, we're out. I think we should suspend the review until we see what happens." I agreed. I then wrote Billy Sullivan a note thanking him for his time and consideration. I mentioned that we had started our work but understood that it might be all moot. I also mentioned that if present circumstances were to change, we would be delighted if he would advise us. The letter closed with our sincerest best wishes. Billy Sullivan had impressed me as a fine man. If I couldn't have the team, I hoped he could make the best possible deal for himself.

I immediately put the Patriots out of my mind. I did keep abreast of Fireman's efforts whenever they were reported in the media. I have to admit I was very disappointed. However, I had to get on with my other businesses. My feelings were cushioned by my subconscious recognition that this purchase had always been something of a long shot, a sports fan's ultimate fantasy. If it would fly, great. But I wouldn't shed any tears if I couldn't get the thing airborne.

Some months after, it appeared as though the deal had died. I had received a call from Billy Sullivan's son Chuck. Mr. Fireman's option had expired. Though Fireman was still trying to put a deal together, his chances suddenly appeared slim. Chuck wanted to know if we would still like a shot if Fireman didn't succeed soon. I assured him we would. He then asked if we would be willing to put up some bridge financing on the stadium. It was sinking fast. I passed. I didn't want to get involved with it at this stage. Besides, my primary interest was in the team, not in the stadium. Chuck accepted this. Some time later, he got back to me. They felt they weren't getting anywhere with Fireman. The Patriots were up for grabs again!

Despite Fireman's option running out, our acquisition of the team was still plagued by outside influences. In addition to their financial difficulties, the Sullivans had several lawsuits pending against them. The largest one had been brought by the team's former stockholders. The Sullivan family had taken the football team private. The shareholders had started an action claiming they hadn't been paid nearly enough for their stock. The court found in their favor. The Sullivans were ordered to pay a 7.9 million dollar judgment.

That wasn't their only legal hassle. In 1986 the Sullivans had tried to get a buyer for the team through the services of an investment banker. This institution took the rather unusual step of running an ad. I liked that. It was different. It was eye-catching. It was entrepreneurial. Let's face it, it's not often you open up the Sunday paper and see "For Sale: An NFL Franchise." A Philadelphia entrepreneur, Fran Murray, was attracted by the ad. He put together a group to purchase the Patriots. They had lent the Sullivans 13.5 million dollars and received an option on the team. Not too long after this they had loaned the team an additional 5 million dollars.

When it had become time for Murray to exercise his option, he was rebuffed. One of his major partners then dropped out of his group and he was forced to scramble. He had to somehow reassemble his organization. In the meantime he tried to block the Sullivans from doing anything with the club. Mr. Murray brought an injunction against the family that made it impossible for them to borrow any more money against the team. It also prohibited the team's sale. The Sullivans were all but strapped. Murray wanted to exercise his option, Fireman was still screaming for another chance, and the New England media was having a field day with this ongoing battle royal. All these distractions made the outlook for anyone trying to make the purchase quite gloomy.

Through it all, the Sullivans pressed on. With their financial situation deteriorating daily and their cash flow dried up, the Sullivans were anxious to make a deal. Billy and I arranged to meet. We were supposed to get together for an hour. Our talks went on for four. I made it clear that any deal would have to include a peaceful settlement with Mr. Murray. We had some concerns about Mr. Fireman. Though his option had expired he was still in the background trying to put together a deal. His situation, however, was beyond our control. Mr. Murray was another story altogether.

Murray's option looked valid to Arthur Emil. He felt that if we were to purchase the team, Murray could sue us and possibly walk off with the Patriots. All our hard work would have been for naught. Billy disagreed. He explained that Murray's original group had undergone a significant change. Apparently Murray was required to notify the Sullivans of any switch in his group's makeup. He either hadn't (so they claimed) or at least he hadn't done it in a timely manner. Also, Murray had been required to pay the Sullivans $500,000 if he failed to exercise his option by the end of 1987. Murray had indeed sent them a cashier's check for that amount. The Sullivans had never cashed it. It was still sitting in their safe.

This information did not grant peace of mind to Arthur or to me. We wanted to meet with Murray to see if there was some way to either include him in the deal or at least satisfy his needs. Arthur suggested a dinner. All the principals met in a Stanford hotel and things went fairly smoothly. Murray and the Sullivans got on surprisingly well for supposed antagonists. After eating dinner, we got down to business. Arthur and I went off with Mr. Murray. We needed to know exactly what he wanted. I felt privacy would fuel his candor. Among other considerations, Murray made it clear he wanted to be part of the purchase. He was looking for a majority position (51 percent), and he wanted all his legal expenses put to rest. For his part, he would leave the 18.5 million dollar loan in the club. There were several other items on his agenda, but these were the major points.

I was quick to respond to one of the points. I let Mr. Murray know immediately that I would not settle for a minority position. I wasn't looking at the Patriots as just another financial investment. I was looking forward to the challenge of turning the club into an athletic and fiscal success. In order to do that I needed the power of a majority owner.

Murray mulled this over and said, "OK, then give me the

option of picking up an extra 2 percent of the club upon your death." Contemplating my mortality was not something I cared to do on a full stomach. It only took a few minutes for me to nix this proposal. I felt that if my family got involved with the club and wanted to stay with it, I had to be able to leave it to my heirs. Of course, I didn't want that situation to arise anytime soon. After my rejection, Murray said, "Fine. Then at least give me the opportunity to sell my share of the team back to you if I get a chance to buy my own franchise." I was amenable to that and I started to feel as if we could work something out.

After meeting with Murray, I had a similar conversation with Billy Sullivan. The Sullivans were hoping to retain positions with the club after the sale. This had apparently been another sticking point with some of the other prospective buyers. I saw no problem. I felt the Sullivan presence would be an asset to the team. Billy then said he wanted this to be a stock deal. We wanted it based on the purchase of assets. Sullivan thought this would be impossible because of the tax ramifications and the specter of those existing lawsuits. I told him I'd have to think about that one.

Our meeting finished at 1 A.M. Arthur and I then held our own private discussion in the hotel parking lot. We were there for two hours. We both agreed that this was a difficult situation. The banks were screaming for their money. We still weren't sure Murray would be satisfied as a minority shareholder. The Sullivans were reluctant to do an assets deal. Still, we felt we could work everything through if we just took it a tiny step at a time. The next day Arthur, who was pivotal in making this dream a reality, began working with the Sullivans' lawyers in an attempt to put all the obstacles into perspective.

I had to go to Europe for two weeks. Remington business. By the time I returned a lot of the snafus had been clarified. We had a complete outline of all the assets and known liabilities of the team. Since the stadium was bankrupt we took it completely out of the deal. If it was dealt with at all it would be as a separate issue. This was an easy call to make. The stadium was only as good as its lease, and that was the worst in the league. It also had only twelve years to run. In the past everyone who had tried to buy the Patriots had tried to tie the stadium in as part of the package. We felt this was a major reason for their lack of success. With all the creditors and problems attached to the stadium, it was hardly a surprise that these deals had fallen through.

Entrepreneurs must prioritize. Our focus would be on the team. A stock deal was structured to satisfy Billy Sullivan. It wasn't our first choice, but, after careful examination, we could live with it. Everything else started falling into place. By July's end, the deal seemed all but sealed. Then Chuck Sullivan came to us with a radically changed agreement. Annuities and other items had been introduced. The deal was slipping away. An entire day was spent putting the pieces back together until we finally had something that resembled our original understanding.

The papers were brought to me for my signature at midnight. They were then flown up to Boston so that they could be signed by Billy Sullivan. Billy had arranged to do this at his lawyer's office.

During all this, Mr. Fireman tried to reinsert himself into the picture. Though his option had run out, Fireman's lawyer had called the Sullivans' counsel in an attempt to reinstate the old deal. Fireman had been trying to work out the stadium situation. He viewed its resolution as critical to any agreement. Fireman felt he had reached an understanding with the creditors and wanted Fran Murray and the Sullivans to help bear the financial burden.

Fireman's attorney was told that the Sullivans were about to sign a deal. The lawyer thought this was a bluff. By the next day, however, Fireman had apparently heard that a signing was imminent.

He called the Sullivans' lawyer just as Billy was about to sign our agreement. When the attorney was told that Mr. Fireman was on the line, he told his secretary he'd call him back. Mr. Fireman said he would hold. The lawyer took the call just as Billy finished autographing our documents. Mr. Fireman had been on the phone with his attorney, Fran Murray, and Fran's lawyer. He said Billy could forget "contributing" that money to the stadium deal. Fireman would put up the money himself if Billy would agree to sell the team to him. Billy's lawyer told Mr. Fireman that it was too late. As far as the Sullivans were concerned, the Patriots had finally been sold.

Billy Sullivan couldn't wait to make an announcement, and wanted me to join him in Boston. I hesitated. Yes, we had an agreement. However, in essence, the deal was not yet concluded. We needed final word from Fran Murray. He could have held up any transaction. Billy was unconcerned. The team had been the butt of much negative publicity during the interminable negotiations. Rumors of our agreement crashing were already circulating. Billy wanted to quash the skepticism by introducing me to the media.

Unsure of what to do, I called NFL commissioner Pete Rozelle. I said, "Commissioner, we have this agreement and Billy wants to take it to the media in a full press conference. He wants to announce the sale! But I haven't completed my understanding with Mr. Murray yet and a lot of this is contingent upon that happening. We also haven't completed our due diligence. There are still some kinks to be worked out before this deal is done. I think an announcement at this time would be premature." Mr. Rozelle agreed. He offered to call Billy and share our opinion.

Billy decided to go ahead with the press conference anyway. I reluctantly joined him and we both faced a still skeptical New England media. Almost everyone wanted to know why I thought I would succeed where everyone had failed. The day after the press conference, in fact, one local paper ran a hilarious cartoon. It featured a character who looked suspiciously like my favorite CEO. Dressed in a jersey numbered 17 and bearing the name Kiam, he is seen carrying a shaver while running through a revolving door. Sixteen bodies are seen strewn outside that same door. Their jerseys bore the names of Trump, Davis, Tisch, Fireman, et al. There wasn't a flicker of life in any of them. Beneath this work the caption read, "Another lamb being led to slaughter." This summed up the general media reaction. Everyone at the press conference wanted to know why I had the audacity to succeed where so many others—heavy hitters all—had failed.

I expected and accepted their reluctance to accept our group as the Patriots' saviors. I explained that I had been party to complex negotiations throughout my business career, but had always found that differences could be settled as long as all parties remained reasonable. It was also pointed out that, unlike past deals, this agreement was not contingent upon the acquisition of Sullivan Stadium. The press was aware that the stadium question had undermined past acquisition attempts.

I also wanted to keep the record straight. This was still not a done deal. The press was told, "We expect that this will be accomplished in the near future. It is not going to be easy. There are still some key issues to be resolved. A lot of things need to be done between now and settlement. Based on the way things have gone with the Sullivans up until now, I believe this is possible." We then announced that it was our goal to complete the deal prior to New England's season opener against the Jets.

Before putting the agreement to bed, we still had to satisfy Fran Murray. An unhappy Murray could have blunted my contract with the Sullivans with his lawsuit. We had already come to an understanding with him, but it had been drawn in broad strokes. It was now necessary to get down to specifics.

We met once again with Mr. Murray. Things couldn't have been more cordial. Fran saw he had an opportunity to consummate this transaction and he couldn't have been happier. Everything seemed to be on track until Fran nearly caused us to fumble. He insisted that any deal we make be an asset deal. This was in direct contradiction to the Sullivans' wishes. Murray couldn't be dissuaded. This meant we would have to go back to the Sullivans and get them to change the deal. I was worried. If the Sullivans refused, Murray could very well pull out. Number 17's bloodied, battered body would takes its place with the rest of carcasses. It was not a pleasant thought.

Fortunately, the Sullivans' financial situation was such that they could not easily reject the proposed realignment. Gradually we pulled all the sides together. September came and went without a final agreement, but all the elements for a positive conclusion seemed to be in place. Finally, during the first week in October, we were down to the microscopic details. Minutiae such as how many Super Bowl tickets would go to X for how many years were spelled out.

On the final day of negotiations all the participants met in New York at four o'clock in the afternoon. Twenty-five lawyers worked like dogs to hammer out the final covenant. They were working against something of a deadline. The NFL owners were meeting in Dallas the following day and we intended to present our documents to them for their approval. At three o'clock in the morning, eleven hours after the meeting had begun, my representatives told me to go home and prepare for my flight to Dallas. A final agreement was at hand. I showered and changed clothes. I even found time for a quick nap. At 7:30 A.M., Billy Sullivan and his son Pat arrived in Arthur's office with the lawyers and the contracts. We signed all copies as we got into our cab. With a triumphant wave to our hardy band of supporters we took off for the airport. We were on our way to Dallas.

We just barely caught our flight. When we arrived in Dallas we were immediately whisked off to the NFL owners meeting. The league fathers gave us their conditional approval; their official nod could come only after they had a chance to go over our agreement. They couldn't very well put their imprimatur on a pact that hadn't been reviewed.

In a session before the league's finance committee, Pete Rozelle pointedly asked what we were going to do about our stadium lease. It had become something of an embarrassment to the entire league. Whenever an NFL team tried to negotiate a new lease it was odds-on that the landlord would try to use the Patriots' pact as a guiding model. The terms were that one-sided. I assured everyone that we were working our hardest to get the lease modified.

It would take almost another month and another NFL meeting before the deal was finalized. The Patriots had finally passed into my hands. A few differences between Fran Murray and the Sullivans still had to be worked out. They were, to everybody's satisfaction.

The media was called back in on October 28, 1988. By now the New England Patriots were leading the National Football League in press conferences. This time, however, we were giving the press a headline news story. We assured them that the sale of the New England Patriots had been accomplished. I was ecstatic. For an entrepreneur, the more difficult the challenge, the sweeter the triumph. What had started out as the most far-fetched of fantasies had become reality. As happy as I was, however, the full impact of the events didn't quite hit me until two days later.

I had been attending all of New England's games. The first one was the season opener against the New York Jets. Viewing the game from the Sullivans' box, I had been overwhelmed with a sense of excitement. Even though the deal hadn't been completed by then, I felt I had a personal stake in the team. Every time one of the Patriots did something good on the field, I soared. Whenever it looked as though the tide might go against New England, my heart would flip-flop into my stomach. It was such an emotional roller coaster. I was totally involved even though there was still a chance the deal might collapse.

The Patriots had won that day. I accompanied the Sullivans into the locker room after the game. I was like a little kid locked up in F.A.O. Schwarz. I congratulated a few of the players. The Sullivans had introduced me to the team when we first started serious negotiations so I wasn't a complete stranger to them. For the most part, though, I stayed in the background. This was still the Sullivans' team.

After that Jets game my wife Ellen and I rode back to New York with Chuck Sullivan. As we stopped for gas we bumped into Steve Gutman, the president of the Jets. He and his wife joined us at a diner for a cup of coffee. He told us how the weekly highs and lows were something football people accepted as a way of life. He said, "Vic, you're going home now and everyone in your car is on a high. I'm driving home from the same game and I feel beat, depressed, and a bit worn out. When you have your first loss this season you'll know what it's like. And on Monday you have to get up, forget about Sunday, and get ready for the next game. This sport is different from all others. We play so few games. In baseball you have a lot of three-game series. If you lose one game but win the other two, you're in great shape. In the football business we don't have that luxury.

Every win is a big one. Every loss could be a nail driven into your season's coffin.

"The worst thing that can happen (as it happened to the 1988 Patriots) is to fall behind in the standings early in the season. It is frustrating. It's as if you can feel the season slipping away. You start to wish you could schedule extra games so you can make up for lost ground." A few weeks later we were beaten by Green Bay and I mean we were trounced. Steve Gutman's warning that this was going to be a business of emotional extremes became very real for me.

I attended my first game as the official owner on October 30. The Patriots—my Patriots—were scheduled to play the Chicago Bears. The fearsome Monsters of the Midway. The Bears weren't long removed from a Super Bowl triumph and were still considered one of the NFL's powers. The Patriots were heavy underdogs that afternoon. Two weeks before, however, the underdog role did not prevent us from handing Cincinnati its first loss of the season. What a high that had been! Our team had seemingly found its confidence with that win. Though the oddsmakers had us in a deep hole the club wasn't about to be intimidated by the sinewy Bears from the Windy City. The team was looking forward to the confrontation. There was an electricity in the air during the week preceding the match-up. You could feel it in the practice sessions. Some of it was generated by Chicago's superstar quarterback Jim McMahon. The flamboyant McMahon, one of those rare fellows who can strut even while sitting, had called our quarterback Doug Flutie "the Mouse That Roars." I supposed Doug could have retorted that McMahon was "Mouth That Bores," but Doug was above such childish invective. The Patriots and their quarterback were going to answer Mr. McMahon on the field.

I can't say whether McMahon's gibes stirred them or not, but you never saw a more motivated football team than the Patriots that Sunday afternoon. We battered the Bears at every opportunity. Every facet of our game was working to perfection. We beat the Monsters of the Midway, 30 to 7. It was my first win as the owner of the Patriots. Five minutes before the end of the game, Billy Sullivan turned to me as we sat in the owners' box and said, "Vic, when we went to the Super Bowl we were winners. In our last few regular season games just before the end of each last quarter, we went through the crowd and around the end zone to the Patriots' bench. The fans loved it. We were celebrating our being winners. It was a way of sharing our success with them. They cheered us all the way down and everyone had a great time. This is the start of a new era for the team. This game and this win symbolizes that. Why don't you join me for a walk down to the field. Let's show them we believe we're going to be winners again!" Grabbing my coat, I followed Billy out the door and into one of the most thrilling moments of my life.

We strolled from the owners' box to an entrance at the very top of the stadium. We started to slowly wend our way down the stairs. At first we attracted little attention. Then you could feel a murmur start to snake through the crowd. Some of the fans began clapping and yelling. Their elation began to catch fire and it spread through the stadium. Reaching the field level, we felt as if the entire stadium was on its feet. When we reached the end zone we turned toward the crowd. I held Billy's hand aloft as if he had just knocked out Mike Tyson. Pandemonium. The entire stadium erupted. The football game had been magically transformed into a party. We followed our victorious team into the locker room.

As I made my entrance I was approached by Raymond Clayborn, who said, "As of today this is a new team with a brand-new owner. Mr. Kiam, we won this game for you and we'd like to give you the game ball." I was flabbergasted. I kept thinking that this wasn't really happening. I mean, short of catching or throwing the game-winning pass in the Super Bowl this was the football fanatic's ultimate dream. I thanked everybody and told them I knew that this rousing win was the start of something big.

I was right. The team was 3 for 5 when I took over. It went on to win six of its final eight games. That was as good a record as any other team in the NFL over that time. Late in the season we lost a heartbreaker to Indianapolis that all but knocked us out of the playoff picture. I flew back after that game in utter dejection. Then we came back to win our next two games and our hopes were alive again. Steve Gutman's words rang again with a new resonance.

We entered our last game of the season with a shot at a wild card playoff spot. Denver was the opposition on their home field. A win here and we were playoff bound. We didn't play well at all and the Broncos beat us. Now we needed losses by both Indianapolis and Cleveland. If both teams suffered defeats we would make the playoffs. It was not to be. Both teams won their games and Cleveland took what would have been our spot.

I was briefly but intensely disappointed. I had received my first taste of the NFL owners' life during a season and came away hungry for more. What an investment this had turned out to be. Few things can duplicate the thrills of such an intimate involvement with a football team. There is, in addition, the added joy of my family's participation. Everyone comes to the football games, home and away. Each contest has become a real family affair and has increased the quality time we have with each other.

We just can't wait until next season gets underway. There are going to be more thrills and more disappointments. More of the stuff that makes life lively. We are already hard at work preparing for that campaign. Off the field, the team's being put on a more solid financial base. On the field, we are ready to build on that marvelous record compiled during the final eight games of last season. I think the Patriots found themselves during that streak and I think it bodes well for 1989. I know this. Management and I are not in this to reap immense financial rewards. We're in it to build a winner, a champion. We're not going to rest until we bring a Super Bowl championship to New England. Let everyone be served notice now. The Patriots are going for it!

11

Glasnost on the Tennis Court

The entrepreneur must come equipped with the same spirit as those hardy souls patroling the universe in *Star Trek*'s U.S.S. *Enterprise.* They must be willing to explore uncharted territories, to go where man (or at least the competition) has never set foot. Breaking new ground is the entrepreneur's omnipresent ambition. You are an innovator. You always want to be leading the parade rather than being stuck away in some brass section playing the same tune as the rest of the followers. Knowing this, I jumped at a recent opportunity to make sports history in the USSR.

This chance came unexpectedly. In May 1988, we had held an international press conference showcasing our Remington products, particularly our new lines. Representatives of TASS, the official news service of the Soviet Union, had been invited but were not expected to attend. We had, after all, never seen them at any of our other functions. Much to our surprise they sent the highly regarded Igor Makurian to cover the conference. Mr. Makurian was the TASS bureau chief. We were delighted.

The afternoon culminated with a film highlighting our Remington International Family Tennis Tournament. The Remington Tournament has become a worldwide event. It is the only international family tennis tournament. At this time, fourteen countries actively participate and that number grows larger every year. Each member country honors us with two father-son combos and one mother-daughter pair. A national championship allows each country to choose its most skilled representatives for the world finals. As I write this, we are hard at work preparing for the 1989 finals to be held in Lugano, Switzerland.

Our tournament finds its origins back in the 1920s, when national family tennis tournaments were first organized in the United States. The Remington tennis tradition doesn't date back quite that far. I started playing the game in the 1940s. It was love at first volley. I've always felt it was the perfect recreation for the entrepreneur. Its fast pace requires participants to stretch beyond their physical and mental limits. It's so absorbing it can quickly detach you from the cares and worries of business. If those concerns do intrude while on court the game can be an excellent therapy. Just picture the face of that banker who's giving you a hard time with your financing on the incoming tennis ball. Feel the shot of pleasure that overtakes you as you mercilessly pound that baby over the net. Trust me, you will find a new definition of the term "inner peace." Whenever I'm asked what is most important in my life, I always list three things: family, business, and tennis. Tennis isn't always third. Some of my most vivid fantasies find me starring at center court at Wimbledon.

I have a special, personal interest in tennis, particularly family tennis. My son Tory and I started playing doubles in 1972. He was twelve years old. Three years later my daughter Robin and I began to play together. Tennis gave us a bond. Tournament play finds us in pursuit of a common goal. We have found this experience so rewarding we were eager to export it to the rest of the world. With that in mind, we founded the Remington International Family Tennis Tournament.

At the end of the press conference presentation, we were approached by Mr. Makurian. Our initial meeting could have gotten off to a bad start. Someone in my party (luckily not a Remington employee) looked over the bearish, obviously Russian Igor and his impressive credentials and said, "So you're here from TASS, huh? Are you a spy?" A one-minute silence that seemed to last about a decade was broken when a smiling Igor replied, "Ah, but all of us are spies in one way or another!" We all laughed and Igor said, "I liked your presentation very much. I was especially intrigued by your film at the end. Tell me, is there any chance of getting a Russian entry into your tournament?"

Tory and I said we would be pleased to have the USSR represented in next year's tournament. We were about to outline how this could be done when Igor interrupted, saying, "No. No, not next year's event. I think we'd like to play in the tournament this year." Well, that seemed to be out of the question. As Tory would explain, the Soviets would have to hold their national elimination tournament sometime within the next three months in order to choose its national representatives for the finals in 1989. This time constraint was brutal. Having hosted tournaments throughout the world, we knew how much work went into each one of them. A tennis tournament, or at least one that could meet the high standards we had already set, was not something you put together overnight. You need a publicity campaign to attract as many participants as possible. Sites must be chosen. Officials picked. You may want to print tickets or programs.

None of this seemed to faze Igor. He recognized the attraction family tennis could hold for the Soviet people. In the United States we often discuss the generation gap, that cultural and emotional abyss that often wedges itself between parents and children. As we were to find out, this is not purely a Western phenomenon. The Soviet Union had its own generation gaps. Makurian saw our tournaments as a possible bridge, one that would strengthen society by fortifying family ties. He also saw it as an opportunity for Russians to intermingle with the citizens of other countries on a friendly, international stage. In the age of Glasnost this was no small virtue. He was certain he could get TASS and his government to throw their resources behind our program. He pledged to have a tournament up and running within twelve weeks. We promised our full cooperation, but we were skeptical. I thought his promise was more innocent bravado than anything else.

I was wrong. One week after our press conference, Igor

called and said, "Everybody is very excited about this tournament. We've already started work on it. Not only that, TASS
wants to cosponsor it with Remington." We nearly fell over.
Igor assured us that many of the necessary elements were already in place. TASS had chosen a site, rounded up top-notch
officials, and already had its publicity machine grinding out
press releases. TASS also agreed to supply all the needed equipment. They were in fact able to provide everything we needed
except for one essential commodity: tennis balls. They were
apparently very expensive in the Soviet Union and were in short
supply. We agreed to bring 500 cans of tennis balls for the
tournament.

With the government news agency as a most powerful partner, we were able to slash through a lot of the usual red tape.
TASS was miraculously able to assemble a full draw in barely a
month. Throughout Moscow parents and their children rigorously prepared for the event. Officials arranged to have it shown
on national TV. We had posters prepared to call attention to the
tournament. They were somehow lost en route to Moscow.
TASS immediately had replacements printed and widely distributed. It was a first-class operation.

My wife Ellen, Tory, and I arrived in Moscow to lend our
advice and to share in the experience. The head of the Soviet
Tennis Federation was world-renowned cosmonaut Igor Volk.
In one of the opening events, he paired up with Tory to play an
exhibition match against a certain tennis-mad entrepreneur. My
partner for the match was Leo Tolstoy's nephew. We had a lot
of fun in front of a large crowd. After the exhibition we received
gifts. I asked Mr. Volk if there was anything we could give him
in return. He replied there were only two things he wished to
have: videotapes of *Top Gun* and *The Right Stuff.* We arranged to
have them sent over.

Being at this history-making event was quite a thrill. Tory
and I were given countless opportunities to share our tennis
expertise. Friendships were easily formed. The Soviet Union is
famous for its cold climate. Both Hitler and Napoleon and many
would-be conquerors had learned how treacherous that climate

could be. But we discovered early on that no drop in temperature could chill the natural warmth of the Soviet people. If we didn't know the definition of Glasnost and Perestroika before our arrival, we were quickly educated. Their true meaning could be found in something as simple as a warm smile or a heartfelt handshake.

On the opening day of tournament play, forty-two father-son teams and fourteen mother-daughter pairs worked out in the breathtaking Vista Vochnyyi Sports Center Complex. Anatoly N. Kovalev, Soviet Sports Committee chairman, and Igor Volk attended an introduction ceremony.

Play was spirited. We were especially drawn to a charming nine-year-old and her mother. The young girl was a tennis-playing Shirley Temple. This captivating duo upset several more experienced teams, besting them on sheer drive and exuberance. They lost in the semifinals but clearly won our hearts and the hearts of the crowd. Their performance represented the essence of our tournament.

The men were required to play many more matches, but this did not dampen their competitive zeal. To the contrary, it seemed to inflame it. When the last volley was struck, Vladimir and Andrei Volkov emerged as father-son champions, and Pyotor and Oleg Belgakov were the runners-up. Zoya and Anya Zhuravloya were the triumphant mother-daughter team. All three pairs will travel to Lugano. There they will face the best family combinations in the world. This will be their Wimbledon.

We had a chance to test one of these teams. Tory and I played an exhibition against the Volkovs. They were quite skilled. Both father and son gave us about all that we could handle. Our experience, however, enabled us to win, 6 to 2. The match-up was much closer than the final score would indicate. Points were hotly contested. No matter, the final score was superfluous. We all had great fun and everyone was eager to repeat the event soon. TASS and Soviet tennis officials, in fact, plan to make future tournaments national events. Because of the short preparation time this first tournament's contestants came only from Moscow. In another measure of their great enthusiasm, Moscow has bid to host the 1991 World Finals. I believe we have planted a fertile seed with this initial event. Family tennis looks as if it will flourish in the Soviet Union.

This is not puzzling because the advantages to the Soviet Union are obvious. By traveling to Lugano and other future sites, Soviet teams will interact with families from around the world. Among the competing nations are the United States, Canada, Japan, Australia, Czechoslovakia, Israel, and the People's Republic of China. This mingling has a high value. The shared interest in tennis and family life form a common thread with which relationships and mutual understanding can be sewn. The natural differences that often separate cultures will evaporate. Winning the world championship will be a secondary goal. More important will be the building of mutual trust and respect. This is Glasnost in action.

I doubt that our first family tennis tournament in the Soviet Union could have been more successful. Of course, we did more than just play a little tennis. We also found time to do some business. We were quite successful, though I did have to overcome an obstacle. No, it wasn't the language barrier. It was the clothing gap.

I left the United States for Moscow carrying two suitcases and a briefcase. The briefcase was stuffed with business paraphernalia. We hadn't had any business discussions scheduled when we embarked on our journey, but an entrepreneur is like a Boy Scout with a chestful of merit badges. He is always prepared.

One of the suitcases held my clothing: suits, shirts, socks, and ties. The usual sartorial menu. The other carried my tennis outfits. Somehow the suitcase with my clothes was misplaced. It never left our plane in Moscow. I filled out all the required forms, but it was too late. The plane had been shuttered for customs and it couldn't be searched for my suitcase. It was scheduled to fly on to Tokyo. It could be searched once it reached there. If it was found—as everyone assured me it would be—it would be flown back to Moscow. Fine. That still meant I would be without my regular clothing for at least twenty-four hours. I figured I could stand that.

The following day TASS sent a car out to the airport to pick up my well-traveled suitcase. It was never taken off the plane. Apparently, officials in Tokyo had been told to take special care of this prestigious piece of luggage. It was handled so well that it was sent directly to London without stopping in Moscow. For all I know it may have even flown first-class.

TASS officials made all the appropriate phone calls and arrangements. The airlines promised to have my things rerouted as soon as possible. I was handling the inconvenience well, but I doubt anyone who had to be in an enclosed space with me for very long was too happy. It took a total of five days to finally get my clothes to Moscow. During that time I had numerous business meetings with Soviet officials. I wore the same pants and jacket to each of them. In place of a dress shirt and tie I was forced to wear a tennis shirt. I had to have been the most informally dressed capitalist these gentlemen had ever encountered. Maybe the informality helped contribute to a relaxed, productive air. We certainly got a good deal done.

We showed the Soviet officials our product line. They were properly impressed. Surprisingly, they were especially interested in our product packaging. Each box goes through a heat fusion process called clamshell. The Soviets had never seen anything quite like it before.

Remington took part in initial discussions regarding a joint venture to produce our products in the Soviet Union. The talks were cordial and fruitful. We gauged real enthusiasm on the part of the Soviets and I think we matched it with our own. We are confident we will be doing business sometime down the road.

We had a joyous time in the USSR. TASS and the Soviet people couldn't have been friendlier or more cooperative hosts. You must give them lots of credit. To put together the tournament they did on such short notice was a mammoth accomplishment. They should be very pleased with themselves. We were proud to join with TASS in sponsoring such a success. We look forward to holding similar tournaments in the Soviet Union. Watching these families share in the fun of competition convinced us that this was a unique sporting event. Everybody won; there couldn't be any losers.

A trip to the world of Glasnost was part of an ongoing adventure. Every day I wake up to a world alive with possibility and charged with promise. You can wake up glimpsing the same paradise. It is a view of the world and an outlook on life shared by all entrepreneurs and by anyone who chooses to Live to Win!

Appendix 1

The Man in the Mirror Test

What does it take to be an entrepreneur? Do you have the go-getter's version of the right stuff? To find out, all you have to do is take the advice found in a Michael Jackson hit song. Consult your "Man in the Mirror" and ask:

1.   Do I Have Confidence in Myself: You have to believe you can move the Himalayas if that is what your ultimate success demands. In a corporation, you'll want the people working for or with you to follow your lead. You want your superiors to give you as much authority as you can handle. They have to respect your judgment.

   If you're running your own enterprise, you may want investors. Your clients have to believe you will do your very best work for them or that your products are of the highest quality. They have to catch your enthusiasm. How can you pump them up if you don't believe in yourself? As an entrepreneur, you always want to stand out. How can you hold center stage if you don't think yourself worthy of it?

2.   Do I Have Confidence in My Venture: When you make an investment in an enterprise, what are you betting on? The idea or the people behind it? The answer is always both. Your time is one of your most valuable commodities. If you become involved in a venture it must be worth your total commitment. If you start a venture plagued by doubts, you are going to run into the self-fulfilling prophecy. When the hard times hit—and, believe me, even the most successful entrepreneur encounters

some turbulence on his flight to paradise—you are going to be hard pressed to give your project the support it needs if you doubt its chances for survival.

3.   Are You Willing to Make Sacrifices: Nine to five has no real meaning for you. An entrepreneur is not a clock watcher. Business is a game. You will often need more than eight hours to score the winning touchdown.

4.   Am I a Decision Maker: You have to be. An entrepreneur wants to assume the ultimate responsibility for his or her project. The buck not only stops at the true entrepreneur's desk, it starts there also. You are often on your own. If you're running a business or a division, no one can make the tough decisions for you.

5.   Do I Recognize Opportunity: This is vital. Are you often berating yourself because you've passed by yet another chance of a lifetime? You can't allow too many of those to slip by. Get used to looking over all the nuances of every proposition. Approach each idea thinking, "How can I make this work for me?"

6.   Can I Keep My Cool: Do you feel a bit of tightness in your throat when pressure is applied to you? Do the butterflies flap up a Wagnerian opera whenever crunch time comes? That's OK, it's a typically human response. But do others around you pick up on that nervousness? If they do, you could be in trouble. The entrepreneur is a general. If his troops are about to enter the valley of death, his mere presence must say, "Our strategy is sound. This army is ready. We will fight our way through this dangerous terrain without serious casualties." Your army will be able to take a cool, reasoned approach to any obstacle. Such a stance represents the first step toward winning. On the other hand, if your troops sense you are as bewildered as they are, that the hand mapping the strategy is an unsteady one, you are in big trouble. While you might delude yourself that you are still a leader of men, you will rapidly discover there are no men left to lead.

7.   Do I Have High Levels of Energy and Stamina: Entrepreneurs shouldn't have any shortage of energy. We're much too involved; we feed off life's opportunities. If you find yourself

looking forward to your afternoon siesta or constantly thinking about the nice warm tub waiting for you at the end of the day, don't even think about getting into the entrepreneurial life. While you're napping or unwinding in the bath, some competitor is out on the prowl and picking up points at your expense. Remember, you can't always outthink, outplan, or outspend a rival. But you can outwork anyone.

8.   Am I Willing to Lead by Example: You can't ask your troops to walk on water for you if you choose to ride the *Queen Mary* over the same route. You want your team to put in fourteen-hour workdays when it is needed? Make sure you are willing to do the same. I've never asked an employee to do something I wasn't willing to do. I feel a responsibility to work harder than the people who work for me.

While we're on the subject, never, ever ask an employee to act as a gofer. When I am on the road with one of my salesmen and he tries to take my bag, he has a real fight on his hands. I just won't give it to him. I want him to know we are partners and that we are in this thing together. You want to motivate the people around you. Leading by example is one of the best methods.

Appendix 2

Your Personal Balance Sheet

Here's a valuable exercise I developed while I was a student at the Harvard Business School. It's called the Personal Balance Sheet (PBS) and it will give you an insight into your strengths and weaknesses.

Take out a notebook. Put the day's date at the top of a page. Draw a line down that page's center. On one side list your intangible assets. Anything that you perceive as a strength or a plus should go on this side of the ledger: a second language, accounting skills, love of travel, etc. Some items might appear on both sides of the page. For instance, I'm the sort of fellow who elicits strong reactions from people. That could be either a plus or a minus, so it found its way into both columns of my PBS.

Having listed your assets, you should now have the courage to list your liabilities. The end result should look something like this:

Assets	*Liabilities*
1. Willing to work long hours.	1. Too often late for appointments.
2. Creative.	2. Tendency to oversell.
3. Good physical condition.	3. Dislike detail.
4. Willing to take risks.	4. "Business wardrobe" not what it should be.
5. Fluent in French and Italian.	5. No accounting skills.

| 6. Write good business proposals. | 6. Voice lacks power. |
| 7. Etc. | 7. Etc. |

Be as objective as possible. Be especially hard on yourself when you list your liabilities. You can afford to be. You're the only one who will ever read this. Once you're finished, your work begins. Start changing those liabilities into assets. For instance, if you suffer from a weak voice, enroll in a voice class. If you're chronically late, do everything in your power to start arriving early for work or meetings.

The PBS will help you to prioritize, to make the best investment of your time. Obviously, if you have excellent writing skills you are going to keep them honed, but you're not going to give them the same attention that you would a weak voice. The PBS also gives you a sense of balance. Sure, you need to improve in certain areas, but be buoyed by the assets you already have. If you apply yourself rigorously, the PBS will be a great source of encouragement. Look over your dwindling liabilities list. You can see that there isn't anything you can't overcome if you are willing to make the effort.